T0037611

Anthem

Anthem

Rush in the '70s

Martin Popoff

Purchase the print edition and receive the ebook free. For details, go to ecwpress.com/ebook.

Copyright © Martin Popoff, 2020, 2021, 2023

Published by ECW Press
665 Gerrard Street East
Toronto, Ontario, Canada M4M 1Y2
416-694-3348 / info@ecwpress.com

All rights reserved. No part of this publication may be reproduced, stored in a retrieval system, or transmitted in any form by any process — electronic, mechanical, photocopying, recording, or otherwise — without the prior written permission of the copyright owners and ECW Press. The scanning, uploading, and distribution of this book via the Internet or via any other means without the permission of the publisher is illegal and punishable by law. Please purchase only authorized electronic editions, and do not participate in or encourage electronic piracy of copyrighted materials. Your support of the author's rights is appreciated.

Editor for the Press: Michael Holmes
Cover design: David A. Gee
Front cover photograph © Fin Costello / Redferns / Getty Images International

LIBRARY AND ARCHIVES CANADA CATALOGUING IN PUBLICATION

Title: Anthem : Rush in the '70s / Martin Popoff

Other titles: Rush in the '70s | Rush in the seventies

Names: Popoff, Martin, 1963– author.

Description: Previously published: Toronto, Ontario, Canada : ECW Press, 2020.

Identifiers: Canadiana 2020040458X

ISBN 978-1-77041-568-3 (softcover)

Subjects: LCSH: Rush (Musical group) | LCSH: Rock musicians—Canada—Biography. | LCGFT: Biographies.

Classification: LCC ML421.R95 P83 2021 | DDC 782.42166092/2—dc23

also issued as:
ISBN 978-1-77041-520-1 (hardcover)
ISBN 978-1-77305-504-6 (pdf)
ISBN 978-1-77305-503-9 (epub)

The publication of *Anthem* has been generously supported by the Canada Council for the Arts and is funded in part by the Government of Canada. *Nous remercions le Conseil des arts du Canada de son soutien. Ce livre est financé en partie par le gouvernement du Canada.* We acknowledge the support of the Ontario Arts Council (OAC), an agency of the Government of Ontario, which last year funded 1,965 individual artists and 1,152 organizations in 197 communities across Ontario for a total of $51.9 million. We also acknowledge the contribution of the Government of Ontario through the Ontario Book Publishing Tax Credit, and through Ontario Creates for the marketing of this book.

PRINTED AND BOUND IN CANADA

PRINTING: FRIESENS   5   4   3   2

MIX
Paper from responsible sources
FSC   www.fsc.org   FSC® C016245

Table of Contents

Introduction

The comparison is a lark — but it's funny, so I'll give it anyway. Under the black country skies of Trail, British Columbia, in the mid-'70s, heavy metal ruled. It was as big a deal in my hometown as in the dual cradles of metal civilization — Detroit and Birmingham. Where they had steel and car parts, we had a lead and zinc smelter, an employer of thousands in our small town and a satanic mill that sat on the hill, looming over the city center. In fact, that's where you went after high school if you weren't going to university; you went to work "up the hill."

Okay, comparing Trail to the towns where Sabbath, Priest, the Stooges and MC5 were created is laughable. Plus my dad was a teacher, my mom was a nurse and I grew up wanting for nothing in a spacious house built in 1970 by the family in the idyllic suburb of Glenmerry. But me and my buddies were still all angry young metalheads, and I'm pretty damn sure we were listening to Rutsey 'n' roll Rush at eleven going on twelve before 1975.

So "Working Man" indeed, if not exactly for me and my immediate circle. That song really connected in Cleveland, and it made a hell of a lot of sense for the busted-up hard partiers working at Cominco. In my late teens, running the record department and selling stereos at a couple different stores, I got to know quite a few of those people (from a wary distance). They were scary and cool, and more than occasionally they would drop ten grand on a pair of Klipschs, JBLs, Bose 901s or carpet-covered Cerwin Vegas, usually powered by a new Yamaha 3020, much to the delight of my boss Gordon Lee, who still runs Rock Island Tape Centre forty-something years later.

Of course, all these guys were Rush fans too, cranking "Bastille Day" in their Camaros and Mustangs (yes, Gord threw me in the deep end as an installer) and pontificating over *2112* while they nurtured their private pot stashes growing in the cupboard. They knew about Rush because I sold them their friggin' Rush records but also because we had the quintessential rock radio station in KREM-FM, broadcast over the border in glorious high fidelity from Spokane, Washington, where they worshiped these wise Canadian swamis of sound. In fact — fond memory — they played the entirety of *2112* when it came out, and of course we were all ready with two fingers to hit play and record as the sun set.

But there was another bed-headed gathering of beer buddies poring over the seven Rush albums we will be celebrating in this book, and that was the aspiring players. I was one of those. The day I jumped in my purple '77 "baby Mustang" (a Toyota Celica) and drove seventy miles to Nelson to pick up my nine-piece set of black Pearls, inspired equally by Neil Peart and Peter Criss, was magic. (Forty years later, I got to show Peter the receipt as he signed some records for me at my book table at Rock'N'Con in London, Ontario.)

Indeed, this is why it was such a joy writing this book,

remembering the camaraderie in bands, however short-lived, talking over Neil Peart fills with Darrell and Marc, Geddy bass lines with Pete and Sammy and Alex licks with Mark and Garth — and yes, he looked exactly like Garth from *Wayne's World*, and I wasn't too far off Wayne. Rush was our rarefied, mystical music textbook, Neil and his wordsmithing challenging our brains at the same time. (I'm sure for a long time, we thought Geddy was scribbling all these fortune cookies.) Rush made you want to excel on a bunch of levels at once, and I swear that was their *purpose* for high school kids worried about what comes next.

Geez, man, they were perfect. Prog rock proper was too creepy. *Tales from Topographic Oceans* may have well been the Moonies coming to get you. At the other end, all our metal bands — Sabbath, Purple, Nazareth, Rainbow, UFO, Thin Lizzy, Kiss, Aerosmith, the Nuge and at the obscure end, Legs Diamond, Riot, Angel, Starz, Moxy and Teaze — were friggin' all right with us. But Rush made you try harder. They politely asked to pour your energies into something more positive. Eat right, use those weights in the basement.

Neil was pushing the philosophy and literature at one end, and as players, man, what they did for kids' self-esteem is immeasurable. We had a purpose, a hobby that was a never-ending hard nut to crack. And yet I gotta say something about Rush: they made it just this side of attainable. I think if we'd got the slide rules out and did the math on *Close to the Edge*, *The Inner Mounting Flame*, *Aja*, *Red*, Brand X or Buddy Rich, we'd have all hung it up. But Neil with his regular rolls down those tuned toms? More often than not, building his beats with only one of his two bass drums? Much of what Rush did . . . well, you could get there as a kid. *I* could get there as a kid.

That's a personal reminiscence of Rush in the '70s, to be sure. But from what I've gathered from friends all over the world (admittedly, most of them white men in their mid-fifties), it's a near-universal experience.

I want to tell you a bit about the history of this book. As you may be aware, this is my fourth Rush book, following *Contents Under Pressure: 30 Years of Rush at Home and Away*, *Rush: The Illustrated History* and *Rush: Album by Album*. And since those, there have been a number of interesting developments that made me want to write this one. To start, only one of those three books, *Contents*, was a traditional biography — an authorized one at that — but it was quite short, and given that it came out in 2004 before Rush was officially retired, it was in need of an update. I thought about it, but I wasn't feeling it, not without some vigorous additions.

That, fortunately, took care of itself. In the early 2010s, I found myself working with Sam Dunn and Scot McFadyen at Banger Films on the award-winning documentary *Rush: Beyond the Lighted Stage*. Anybody who works in docs will tell you that between the different speakers and non-talk footage that has to get into what might end up a ninety-minute film, only a tiny percentage of the interview footage ever gets used, the rest just sits in archive, rarely seen or heard by anyone. Long and short of it, I arranged to use that archive, along with more interviews I'd done over the years, plus the odd quote from the available press, to get this book to the point where I felt it was bringing something new and significant to the table of Rush books.

So there you have it, thanks in large part to those guys — as well as the kind consent of Pegi Cecconi at the Rush office — the book you hold in your hands more than ably supplants *Contents Under Pressure* and stands as the most strident and detailed analysis of the early Rush catalogue in existence.

MARTIN POPOFF

chapter 1

Early Years

"We didn't have a mic stand so we used a lamp."

No question that the Beatles were and still remain the patron saints of rock 'n' roll. And February 9, 1964, the first of the band's three consecutive appearances on *The Ed Sullivan Show*, would provide the nexus of that sainthood: that night, the Beatles inspired myriad adolescents to take up the rock 'n' roll cause, including the heroes of our story.

But if you wanted to drill down, get more hardcore and find out who might be patron saints of *playing*, it wouldn't be out of line to bestow that title upon those heroes — Geddy Lee, Alex Lifeson and Neil Peart and their Canuck collective called Rush.

Of course, Neil, "the Professor," chuckling through his Canadian modesty, would deem that premise absurd, citing the likes of his personal saints of playing, perhaps folks like The Who and Cream, maybe Jimi and his band, Led Zeppelin or maybe "underground" origami rockers like Yes, Genesis and King Crimson. But pushing back at Neil, one might point out to the drum titan that time moves on. Over generations, waves of bands and rock 'n' roll movements ebb and flow. Film stars from the '30s and '40s are forgotten, big band orchestras are forgotten, doo-wop bands are forgotten, '60s and even '70s radio playlists are ruthlessly pared down to what can fit on the back of an envelope — no one cares what you think anymore.

And so, as time passes and the '60s greats are forgotten, the members of Rush seem poised to become the new "patron saints of playing." And maybe they'll stay there. In the mid- to late 2000s, the world turned to pop and hip hop with more and more music made by machines. If indeed rock died further through the parallel precipitous contraction of the music industry, marked by recorded music being made essentially free, then we might be able to pick those patron saints once and for all.

As drummers are wont to point out, no parents ever had to force their kid to practice their drums, and by side glance, this is why the patron saints of playing are not some sensible choice like Mahavishnu Orchestra, Gentle Giant, Kansas or Brand X. It takes some fire in the belly, some excitement, some fuzz pedal, to light up a teen and their dreams. And that is why Rush is the band that wrote the manual for more of our rock heroes from the '80s and '90s than anybody else. They inspired those who have made all the rock music before the genre's miniaturization a few years into the 2000s. Debatable as it might be — and these abstracts, of course, are — if the widest, most productive and beloved flowing Steven Tyler scarf of rock history until the end of guitar, bass and drums runs from, say, 1977 until 2007, then Rush songs are the ones woodshedded most by the players who populate that time span, the songs that advanced the capabilities of hundreds of your favorite rock stars, making them good enough to be heard.

But before all that, the Beatles shot like a bottle rocket emitting white heat around the world, and that included Canada, where Geddy Lee and Alex Lifeson (we'll hear about "the new guy" later) were politely taking notes in Willowdale, Ontario, a vague suburb northwest of Toronto. The class chums were barely teenagers when rock changed conceptually from individuals to bands. And already there was set in place a maturity and focus built of the duo's Canadian experience, with which to deal with the cultural sea-change rifling through school lockers worldwide.

Gary "Geddy" Lee Weinrib was born July 29, 1953, in Willowdale, so he was the perfect age to understand the get out of jail free card slipped to him, one imagines, by Ringo. He also had a brother and a sister in a family headed by two Holocaust survivors, Morris Weinrib and Manya Rubenstein, now Morris and Mary Weinrib of North Toronto.

"They both worked originally in what they called the 'schmatta' business," explains Geddy, concerning his parents, "which was on an assembly line, sewing clothes and things like that. But they worked their way up to a lower middle-class kind of income and raised me in the suburbs. So I was a product of suburban life. Listen to the song 'Subdivisions'; that's where I grew up. It was a bland, treeless neighborhood. A new subdivision."

Geddy says that being one of the few Jewish kids around made him stand out. "They bused us to a school when we first moved to that kind of neighborhood, and, as a young kid, it was pretty terrifying. It was a tough neighborhood. That part of Toronto was just on the border of being transformed from farmland to subdivisions, so it was in transition. You had the leftover mix of different kinds of social backgrounds, so there were a lot of pretty tough kids — what we called greasers back then — with not much to do except beat up the new kids. So, it was an exciting time. I hated living in the suburbs, and my first opportunity, I got out. And I think a lot of kids that I hung out with felt the same way. Everything was going on downtown. We wanted to go downtown — we spent our time going downtown."

"My husband had a sister in Canada, and we didn't have anywhere to go," begins Geddy's mother, Mary. "And she made papers for us and we came here in 1948. My husband and I stayed with her for a while; we didn't have any trade or a profession, so it was very hard in the beginning. My husband had a friend from years before, when they were just children in school, and he volunteered to teach us — and he was going to be a pressman, and I was going to be a finisher, for clothes. So in about two weeks, he gave us some lessons, and we learned every day. And then another cousin got us into a factory. Garments. My husband was making a dollar an hour, and I was making fifty cents an hour. And after a while, I was so fast that they gave me samples to work on, on piecework, so I was making more money.

"So we finally moved and had our own place, and two and a half years later, my daughter was born. I remember when we would look for places to live, the first thing we would say was 'We have a child.' If you had a child, it was the hardest — couldn't rent anything. And after we moved, Geddy was coming, and when we had two children, the landlord, this blond lady, would not accept us. We didn't have money for a down payment, but my husband went to this society that helps people and they lent us the money, and we bought a house, and we waited for Geddy to arrive. I remember every room in that house; I had rented every room just to make up for the five thousand dollars we owed. And Geddy was born, and my husband was so excited because he was a boy, and we already had a girl.

"And it was a nice neighborhood," continues Mary, "on Charles Street. It was a really nice neighborhood, easy. It was a mixture of young and old people. Afterwards, we moved to Willowdale. Actually, first it was Downsview, and then to Willowdale. Allan was born in Downsview. My husband sold the house overnight: we went to a wedding, and his cousin was there, and he said, 'You know, Morris, I have a customer for your house.' It was a bungalow. So my husband gave him an enormous price and said, 'If she'll pay it, I'll give her the bungalow.' We came home from that wedding, two o'clock in the morning, and his cousin is sitting in the driveway and said, 'Sign here.' So the next day we had to go look for a home, and then we went to Willowdale.

"Everybody knew everybody, and it was nice — nice neighbors, great place to be because all the kids were the same age, with a lot of friends all over. It was a nice neighborhood: shopping was easy, everything was easy. I remember when we bought a store in Newmarket and we used to drive to Newmarket, and it was treacherous. There were no roads, there was nothing, everything was muddy, and if it was raining, you could hardly get through. So my husband used to say, 'You'll see, in a few years all of this will be built up.' And sure enough, a few years later everything was built up." Typical of her sunny disposition, Mary Weinrib remembers Willowdale more positively than Geddy.

"Pretty boring," says Geddy. "Not much to do. So that's why music became so important to us because we would go to each other's basements and listen to music, and everybody had different favorite bands. That was the social life. There was nothing much else. The occasional concert, drop-in center, that kind of thing. When I was twelve, my father passed away. And we were kind of a religious family, a Jewish religious family, and in that kind of household, when a father dies, the son, the firstborn son, is supposed to . . . has a lot of responsibilities in terms of the grieving process."

Morris had never fully recovered from injuries he sustained in a Nazi concentration camp. As part of Geddy's grieving duties, he says that he attended synagogue twice a day, morning and evening, for eleven months and a day, and he had to abstain from rock 'n' roll, even removing himself from music in school.

"There are still songs that were popular that year that people talk about and everyone should know it and I go, 'What?'" continues Lee. "There's just a gap in my learning. Anyway, when that year was over, I kind of dove headfirst to try to catch up to being a normal kid, to play with other guys in the neighborhood. And I often wonder if that's what really made me hungry to be a musician, the fact that it was kind of kept from me for a year."

His mother called Geddy a "great kid, quiet; he really had a good sense of humor, and he was a happy child. And he was actually very respectful since he was a child, good in school, had lots of friends; he was very good. Until his father died. It was hard. We moved, and two years later, my husband died. And Geddy was, I think, about twelve. He was really a big help to me because after my husband died, I was in shock. And then we had a store, and two weeks after, I was thinking I can't go to that store. I can't go. They used to give me all kinds of pills and this and that. Once when I was really, really crying and Geddy heard me, he came in and sat on my bed and he said, 'Mommy, I know why you're crying. You don't know what to do at the store, right? Daddy would really want you to open the store and try, and if you can't make it, you know you tried.' And the rest is history. He left, took all those pills, called the girl who helps at the store, because she had a key in Newmarket, and he said, 'I'm coming out.' I just want to give you what kind of help this child was. Even later the same year. It was December, Christmastime, I needed somebody to come and help in the store. I had a couple of girls, and Geddy volunteered. And all day long, he was at the cash. He didn't even want a lunch."

Driving home on Christmas Eve, Mary decided that Geddy deserved a present for working so hard. Geddy said that Terry next door had a guitar for sale for fifty dollars. Once his mother was over the shock, and as they arrived home from the store, she had given him the money.

"We're telling him he's now the man of the house," continues Mary. "You're now the man that is the head of the house. So this kid, after about two or three months that I was at work, he said, 'I'm so glad, I'm so happy, Mommy, that you are working and I can go to school because I thought I had to go to work instead of school.' You see, his father was actually a musician when he was young. In those years, there was no thing where you could become a big star. If somebody needed a drummer, he was a drummer at a wedding. If someone needed a guitarist, he was a guitarist. When we were in Germany, we lived with an old German lady and we had one room. And she had a mandolin, and he always used to talk about music and this lady says, 'Here, have the mandolin. Play!' So he used to, every morning, go under my window and make up all kinds of songs with a mandolin. And when we were coming to Canada, I said, 'You're not taking that big thing with you?' And now I wish I had it. So he takes after his father, really."

On Geddy's religious duties after his father's death, Mary explains, "All year, he used to go to say prayers to his father, twice a day, morning and evening. I had a friend who used to take him, take him to school, take him at night, bring him home. Yeah, he was really young. Actually, he taught himself his Torah, and taught himself to say the prayer. A week before his bar mitzvah, I called the rabbi and said, 'Here, we're having that bar mitzvah, I don't know if this kid knows anything, because we didn't have a teacher to teach him.' But of course, the rabbi was sitting beside me. I was crying for a big reason, here my heart went, and the rabbi put his hand on my shoulder, and he said, 'Mrs. Weinrib, I wish I had your son's gift. Your son has a gift from God.' Who would believe that? You know what I mean? I just thought [he said this] because I'm crying.

"Even before, when my husband was alive, the first thing he brought to the house was a piano. We didn't have a stitch, nothing, no tables, no nothing, and we were teaching Susan piano lessons. One day, on a Sunday, the teacher came and she taught them something new. And I invited her for tea, and all of a sudden, we hear playing, and the teacher says, 'You know, I have to go and congratulate Suzie. She really did a good job.' And we walked in, and it was Geddy. And the teacher said to me, 'You can't let this go. This child has a very good ear for music. You have to give him lessons.' And he was like ten years old. But at the time, we could just afford it for Suzie.

"All teachers told me this, actually, so I knew. His father had the same ear for music. This man, in the morning, woke up with radio, went to sleep with radio, and in the store, the music was blasting. And you know what? He used to make fun of the Beatles. My husband used to say, '"Yeah, yeah, yeah" — with this he's going to sell records?' Always when I hear the Beatles, I remember what he used to say to me."

Soon Geddy would be listening to the Beatles again, but in the meantime, it was hard for him to miss out.

"Yeah, it was; it was very hard. He couldn't have any. Maybe, in my presence, he never listened to music on the radio. He was really doing his thing because he had to go and say prayers. And after the year, he really came out. He was himself. After a year, you can start. Especially when he already had his guitar. Because his father died in October, and I got him the guitar in December, the twenty-fourth actually. And then I remember, he had to do a year in enrichment class to catch up, which was in a different district. And then the next year, he went to Fisherville Junior High School, and sometimes he knew more than the teacher did.

Because he had this background already. And that's where he met Alex. He used to bring him home. I used to love Alex. He's such a nice, cute guy, very polite, very nice and a very good relationship."

Indeed, comic relief for Geddy came from this new partner Alexandar "Lifeson" Živojinović, born August 27, 1953 in Fernie, British Columbia. "First time I ever became aware of Alex was at R.J. Lang Junior High School; he was easily noticeable back then because he was a bit of a teacher's pet," chides Lee. "I also had a friend, Steve Shutt, who became a well-known hockey player, and we went to school together, and he was one of the few guys that I met in high school that actually was much hipper than he looked. Steve was funny because he used to grow his hair every summer when he wasn't playing hockey, and as soon as he had to go back to hockey, he used to cut his hair, so he was like this hidden freak. We got along pretty well back then, and he was the first guy who made me notice Alex.

"Because I was playing and looking for other people to play with, he said, 'Well that guy there is a good guitar player. You should hook up with him.' Steve would talk to me because he knew I liked music, and I was playing an instrument, and he would talk to me about this guy, Alex Zavonovich — that's what he called him; he mispronounced his name — and he said, 'You should call this guy up; you guys could jam together.' So that was the first time I became aware of him. But I didn't actually make contact with him until we were in the same class next year in Fisherville Junior High. He was a funny kind of kid, a yuck-it-up guy, and he got me laughing. So we hit it off in school. Plus we liked the same kind of bands, and there was the fact that he was a guitar player. I was playing bass, so it was kind of a natural fit for the two of us. We would all sit at the back of the class. I think he was the first friend I had in that area where we kind of got irreverent together.

"Anyway, so it was actually Steve's suggestion that I hook up with Alex. And then, I'll never forget, the next year we were in the same class, and he always wore this paisley shirt and had his hair combed and always sucked up to the teacher, I remember very clearly. But that's how we met, and then we found out that we were both musicians and eventually it led to us playing together. He was very likable. He was very funny. He's still to this day the funniest human being I've ever known. He's got a charm about him, you know. When you meet him, you just like him. So I liked him, and we became good friends."

Alex's parents, Nenad and Melanija "Milla" Živojinović, also arrived in Canada after World War II; they first met in Yugoslavia. "My father was kind of sent out to B.C. to work in the mines, as a lot of Eastern Europeans were at that time," begins Lifeson. "My mother's side of the family . . . my uncles wanted to look for better work, so they ended up out in Fernie as well, and we left when we were very young. I think I was eighteen months old or two years old when we left — I really have no memory of our time there. And then we moved to downtown Toronto and I grew up there and in the north part of the city.

"I became really interested in music at around twelve and got my first guitar. My parents bought me a cheap Kent Japanese acoustic guitar. I think it was ten or twelve dollars. You know, it had the guitar strings two inches above the neck, and they were the thickness of telephone cords. But it was really exciting. I was just so overwhelmed by music and the sound of the guitar. I listened to the Beach Boys, the Rolling Stones, the Beatles and all of that stuff in that era. And the following year, I got an electric guitar, again a cheap Japanese electric guitar, from my parents at Christmas."

Alex had negotiated to get this guitar — his first electric — in return for turning in a good report card. His parents, pleased with his grades, kept their end of the bargain, although they had to borrow the money to buy the instrument. Says Milla, "He wanted to have a group with this next-door neighbor we had, but nothing happened there. So we got the electric guitar. He played constantly, in the morning, in the evening, after school, all the time."

Like Geddy's, Alex's upbringing was quite ethnic, not out of step in a city and country built by immigrants.

"We ate very ethnic foods, all my parents' friends were other Yugoslavians, Serbs, Croats, a real mix. Typical for a working-class Eastern European family in Toronto, we couldn't afford a cottage or have that whole cottage lifestyle, which a lot of my friends grew up with. It was very normal in Toronto to have a place up north or east or west. The thing that we used to do was go to Lake Simcoe, to Sibbald Point, and all the guys would play soccer and all the moms would cook and unpack food, put out the blankets. There was a museum up at Sibbald Point, and we'd go to the museum and swim. And every weekend in the summer was spent up there because it was free and you could drive up there and there was plenty of room. I remember always stopping for Dairy Queen on the way home. Very Ontario, absolutely.

"It was typically working middle-class," continues Alex. "The summers were spent playing with friends and running around. There was school and hockey and winter sports, just like anybody else. I'd say it was a very normal upbringing. My parents were very hard workers: don't complain about it, go do something. I really respected my dad for that. And my mom was a nurse for most of her life and worked at Branson Hospital for twenty years or something and still does volunteer work. She still tries to be very active. Yeah, it was a really great upbringing. I certainly don't have any bad memories of growing up.

"When I moved up to Willowdale from a central part of the city, I was ten or eleven years old and John Rutsey was a neighbor.

He lived across the street, and we both had a great love for music, and we played baseball and football. He had a couple older brothers. We used to have great times doing sport-related stuff, but we fell in love with music at around the same time, and he sort of gravitated to drums and I did the guitar. In fact, we started a band then called the Projection, which I still think is a great name. It was a few neighborhood friends, and we all knew the same six or seven songs, mostly Yardbirds, and we would play these parties in basements. You didn't get paid for it or anything, but we would set up. We had small amps and basically no equipment, but we would play these seven or eight songs over and over and over again. It was really, really cool and I can still see it . . . We did one gig — if I can call it that — in my parents' basement and it was dark and we had a black light and the whole deal. We continued to do things like that and we kind of put a band together with different people, but he and I were the core of it. At the same time, I met Geddy that year in junior high school, in grade nine."

Alex's mother, Milla, fills in some of the backstory with respect to how the family wound up in the East Kootenays of British Columbia.

"I came to Canada in 1951, June 18, with my parents and my two brothers," explains Alex's mother. "I was sixteen and my brothers were fifteen and seventeen. My dad was of Russian descent, and in 1949, Tito, the president in Yugoslavia gave the ultimatum to people coming in from different countries to take citizenship. And if they didn't wish to take citizenship, they had to move out. And my dad had a sister in New York he hadn't seen for twenty-odd years, and he decided he didn't want to take the citizenship; he wanted to move out. So we had to go to Trieste in Italy, and we were there for six months, in Provogo camp.

"We waited to hear the quotas for immigrants, and they were offering us either Australia, New Zealand or Canada. We couldn't go to the United States, even though we applied because of my aunt. So then we decided to come to Canada instead of Australia, which was too far, and my dad wouldn't be able to see his sister as much. And so we came and worked on the farm. To be able to come to Canada, you had to come and work on the farm. And we stayed on that farm for, I think, a little over a month. We were actually very lucky that we didn't have to finish picking the sugar beets because that was hard. We'd just started, and the owner of the land, he said, 'I see you can't work on the farm,' so he was kind enough to let us go.

"And then we met a Serbian friend and moved to a small mining town. My older brother worked in the coal mine and my younger brother worked in the sawmill and I worked in a restaurant. I was washing dishes for twelve hours. And my dad was an older man, and he was injured in the First World War. He had one artificial eye, and he wasn't that well, so he didn't work at all. But after a few months . . . there is a religion called the Doukhobors. They're Ukrainian, Russian actually, and my dad being Russian, they asked my dad to teach Russian to their children in school, and that was the only job he had for a few months. And then I met my husband Mac, Alex's father. He came to work there in the coal mine after his wife passed away, and after a year or so of dating him, we got married.

"And then a year later, Alex was born," continues Milla. "And then we stayed until Alex was about twenty months. I got pregnant with my daughter Sally, and we came to Toronto. My parents and my brothers were here. We moved in April 1955, and it was beautiful, actually. We moved near Harbord and Bathurst. And Sally was born after a month or so, and my husband was looking for a job. And then after he found a job — he worked in O'Keefe, you know, beer — we moved a few places. It was difficult having children, and we moved when my parents bought a house. We moved upstairs with them, and we stayed about two years. Then we bought a little house on Glencairn, close to Bathurst, and we lived there until Alex went to school there, grade one and two, and then we moved to Pleasant Avenue.

"When he was in grade one or two, Alex was a little worrier. When we bought the house, my husband got injured and he was in the hospital having surgery. And he overheard me saying that we didn't have money to pay the mortgage. And he went to school and his teacher, she asked him, 'Alex, you're so sad. What's happening?' And he said, 'My mom doesn't have money to pay the mortgage.' And she wrote me a letter and he brought the letter home and I was self-conscious when I was talking to people on the phone, for him not to hear. Because he was a worrier."

Despite financial hardship, Milla, like Mary, has happy memories of the neighborhood. "It was nice; it was mixed. When we lived on Pleasant, we had Jewish people. I think we were the only Christians on that street. But where we moved, a street called Greyhound, there were Italians, Chinese people, Canadians, Greek people, so it was mixed nationalities. I can tell you one thing — that I'm Canadian, I love Canada, and as soon as I came to Toronto, I really enjoyed life. Being in Fernie, that small mining town, I didn't really; I was quite depressed there. Because there was nothing to do. It was a coal mine, so everything was dirty, and there was one theater, one bank and one restaurant. But when we came to Toronto, it was so different. Especially *when* we came. We came in May, from a town just on the border of Alberta and British Columbia, and in May it was beautiful weather and the flowers were coming out and it was just lovely."

As for Alex, Milla says, "He was a very, very good child. I was bringing them up to respect people, to love people, to not have any hatred to any other nationalities. I come from a country where there were Croatians and Serbians, but I never had any of that either. I had a lot of Croatian friends. Alex was always friends with different nationalities — I remember a Hungarian little boy, when we lived down on Brunswick Avenue, near Bloor. Alex was a good child. The teachers used to send a very nice report about him. He was very calm, but when he was a teenager, well, this was his dream: to become a rock star. My dream was for him to go to school — and then he quit grade twelve. And then he said, 'Well, I'm going to go and finish the following year.' He went, and he was a counselor, the president there. He did very well, and the teachers were really liking Alex, and they came over once to our place and they talked very highly about him."

Both Milla and Mary were against their two angels going rock 'n' roll. But who was to blame for the boys catching the bug? Fortunately for familial relations, Mary didn't blame Alex and Milla didn't blame Geddy.

"I liked Geddy," laughs Milla. "To tell you about Geddy, I remember talking to his mom. And his grandmother was a sweet lady; she used to call me and say, 'Is my Geddy there? Well, you know what? He's going with shiksa now.' He was dating a shiksa, a Christian girl. Nancy was a shiksa. She would get so upset. And I would say to Geddy, 'Your grandma is calling you to go home.' So we had fun with them. And then we started going to concerts that they had in Toronto together."

"Geddy brought Alex home one day," recalls Mary. "And he seemed to me like a nice, intelligent boy. Quiet, not like a wild animal. And I liked him right away. And I still like him. Good sense of humor, like Geddy, and they got along very well. The rest is history. I remember one day I was going to tell something to Geddy, early morning, and I walk into his room, and I see blond hair on the floor, somebody covered up with blond hair. And I'm thinking — a girl? And I close the door carefully, and I think, wow, Geddy let this girl sleep on the floor. And I'm going to work, and an hour later, I call Geddy — he's up — and I said, 'Geddy, how can you let this girl sleep on the floor in your bedroom?' 'Mum, it's not a girl. If it was a girl, she wouldn't be sleeping on the floor.' It was Alex! You see, Geddy loved his bed. He could never go to a sleepover. His bed was his everything."

Milla didn't blame Geddy for sending Alex down the risky rock 'n' roll path. "I realized that this was what Alex wanted. I mean, he was a self-learner. He never took any music in school, any teaching from anybody. He just went on his own. And that was another thing that I was very proud of. I knew there was something he inherited from someone because he just did so well by himself. The lyrics and all that, and the notes — he could read well.

"But it was me more than my husband," says Milla, on attempts to steer Alex right. "His father, everything was okay with him, very positive. I was a little bit worried about his future. If he doesn't finish high school, what's going to happen? And if the group doesn't succeed, what's going to happen with his future? Because I tell you, I worked nights, I worked factories, I went to nursing school in 1970 to finish nursing and worked hard, worked in electronics and everywhere. And his father worked two jobs; he was a plumber and an electrician, and he worked for Massey Ferguson as a stationary engineer, second class, for twenty-five to twenty-six years. Plus he went on his day off and worked. So I think that's why Alex always, always respected hardworking people. And today, that's why sometimes I say to him, 'I'm fine.' He will always ask, financially, to help me. I would say, 'I'm fine.' He would say, 'Mom, you worked so hard; I just want you to be so, so comfortable.' His father passed away five years ago [this interview took place February of 2009], and he respected him so much because of that, of that hardworking. He loved him so much too. And that hard work. And that's how, you know, myself as a child, as a teenager before I came [to Canada], I went to school and I had to work too. We wanted him to be something, to have education, and well, he chose something else, and he did very well."

Alex knew the value of non–rock 'n' roll work as well. Like Geddy helping out his mom in the store, Alex did the kind of work teenagers resent but then later look back at and realize was character-building.

"Yeah, I worked at Dominion for a while, in the meat department; that was in grade ten, just exactly the time we started the band. And then I also worked with my dad. He worked many jobs. He was an engineer at Massey Ferguson, and he had his own plumbing business, like a one-man plumbing business. But he would take me out. In fact, later on, when I still worked with him, and we were playing the Gasworks and all those clubs in the early '70s, I would go out and help him from time to time. He would pick me up in front of the Gasworks at one thirty in the morning when we finished playing, and I would go with him and we would work all night on some plumbing job, and he would take me home at eight o'clock in the morning and I would completely collapse until five o'clock in the afternoon and then head down to the gig later that evening. And then he would do the same thing.

"And I tried my best to get out of that whenever I could because it was always hard. Yeah, those two were the main little jobs that I had. There were always things around the house that I got volunteered for. But you know what? It was a source of a little bit of money and it paid for the rent of the Marshall amp and gas for the van and things like that, so we all pitched in. Because those early days, we really didn't make any money. Maybe a hundred dollars, one fifty, and even earlier than that, fifty dollars — the first gig we played was ten dollars. Although ten went a long way in 1968. Well, not that long.

"But my parents came from war-torn Europe," says Alex, explaining their mindset. "They lived through six years of war. Geddy's parents — they were in concentration camps. My father was in work camps in Austria, but Ged's parents were in the most notorious of camps — and they survived, barely. In fact, Geddy lost his father at a young age because of his experience in those camps and the toll that it took on him physically. I remember my father . . . I don't think we ever had a single meal where he started eating before we did. It was just the thing that he had about looking after his children and making sure that they were going to be okay. And that is the root of that whole thing. I want to make sure my kids are okay. Any parent is like that, really, but there is something about Eastern European parents who had gone through that nightmare. It's in their genes. They're looking at centuries of warfare and difficulty and losing children in horrible ways. So I think it's really ingrained in their psyche to be that way. My parents wanted me to be a dentist because it was a good-paying job. People will always need to have their teeth fixed, and it's a profession."

Seconds Geddy, "My mom wanted me to be anything — but a professional. It wasn't always a doctor, but doctor/lawyer, like a run-on sentence. You know, she wanted us to be successful. She was a Holocaust survivor — their education got cut off. They never got to fulfill their dreams, whatever they were. In fact, they were probably cut off before they knew what their dreams were. My mom was twelve, I think, at the beginning of the war. This was a natural thing with immigrants coming. I don't think there's any difference between a Jewish family to an Italian family — they want their kids to do what they never had the opportunity to do. So my mom was just like that. And after my dad died, I started hanging out with that juvenile delinquent Alex Živojinović, and I was getting more and more into music, and she got worried about me. Because my hair was growing, and I was staying up later and I wasn't coming home. I was such a nice and quiet good boy at home, and suddenly my habits were changing. So of course she tried to stop that, as any parent would, but it was unstoppable. I mean, she probably wouldn't admit it now, because everything is rosy, but I think at the time she probably thought Alex was a bad influence on me. And he was."

Adding a bit of detail to what he did at his mother's store, Geddy says, "[I] used to go in on Saturdays, and in the summertime, I would go fairly often. But it was strange for me because it was a little town, the town of Newmarket, a very different environment from what I was living in. It was this little main street mall, a hub of activity. It was kind of cool, in a way, because it was so foreign. And my mom was running the store and I was basically a stock boy running up and down the stairs and putting stuff on the shelves and opening boxes downstairs. And there were a couple of kids in Newmarket that also worked from time to time in the store, so I got to know them a bit. It was really quite a different environment, but I have a lot of fond memories of it.

"People were pretty nice to me and they liked my mom. My dad had passed away but he was quite a well-liked guy, and they really felt for my mom, and a lot of people helped her continue the business after he passed away. I remember there were a few people who worked in that area. They used to carpool and they used to pick up my dad. And there was one guy who was a barber, maybe an Italian, and before he passed away, I would go with my dad and they would pick him up early in the morning. And on the way they would stop at a coffee shop and have breakfast and order a toasted western, and I thought that was just so exciting. Because as a kid in my family, we never went out for dinner. We ate at home. Most kids did. Mom cooked, and to go to a restaurant was like a big deal. So it was like a road trip, driving from the suburbs of Toronto, a forty-five-minute drive to Newmarket, and I loved it. And, of course, as I got older, it was harder and harder to want to spend your Saturdays working at the store."

The generation gap was starting to show, and in Geddy's family, it was complex.

"Oh yeah, we used to have a lot of conflicts in my house, because my grandmother lived with us. She was an incredible woman; she kept my mom and aunt alive in two different major death camps. And so here she was, all these years later, having survived just the most horrendous thing anyone can imagine, living in a new world. And my father had just passed away, and so the family was seriously mourning, and here one of their kids was suddenly behaving in a way that they had no reference point for. I was growing my hair, listening to this music, playing with these guys. And so, years later, I look back on it and I understand what they were freaked out about. And my grandmother would scream at us in Yiddish, in Polish, and throw things, and she was very upset and of course we thought it was all a big joke. But we were probably torturing her, the poor woman.

"But I was guilted out, because my dad had died, and here I was not doing what my mom wanted me to do. At that age, your head is in the clouds a bit. I mean, looking back years later, I understood what I was really going through. I felt, when I was thirteen, fourteen, I had so much experience with death and dying and death-like things, I turned myself off to a lot of realities. I think I just said, I have to do this, I want to do this, and I'm not going to pay too much attention to my conscience or my guilt over the pain it was giving my mom. And I was giving her a lot of pain. She was very unhappy that I was leaving school and picking this as a job. She saw nothing but bad things in my future, so that was hard for her to witness. And my sister was pretty wild at that time too. Single immigrant mother trying to keep three kids together, it was a hard life for her, and she worked really hard.

"But I know that Alex and I never shied away from doing the work," continues Geddy, "especially if it was music work. We were lazy, like most kids. But I think it's human nature — if it's something you really like to do, you're not lazy about it at all. And I think that still holds true. When I'm off, and I don't have enough going on, I can be really lazy, but when it comes to doing something I love to do, there's no question about it. Fortunately, I still like to play, so it's never become a thing to be lazy about. Alex was like that too. We just enjoyed what we could. You can call it selfishness, youthful hedonism, I don't know, just being completely irresponsible and playing in a rock band. It took a bit of success to prove that I would a) survive, and b) there would be something that she would not be embarrassed about. And maybe she would actually be proud of something I did."

"We just sort of gravitated to each other," adds Alex. "We have similar backgrounds. We were outsiders in class, but I think we were outsiders more by choice than anything. And we really enjoyed each other's company. We started to get into music. Music was already a part of our lives, but the connection between the two of us started when we were learning to play our instruments. I think Ged's background in music came similar to mine, through a lot of the pop music from the '60s, the British invasion, all those bands like the Searchers and the Rolling Stones and the Beatles of course. And for me, and with John Rutsey, our original drummer, we gravitated toward the West Coast, the bands that were coming out of California at that time. Not just the psychedelic stuff, but the Beach Boys, and then we listened to Jimi Hendrix, and I think for both Geddy and myself, that turned everything around and we started to explore other areas of music. The Who were a new band at that time. And that had a major impact on how we wanted to play. Very strong bass players, as well as obviously great guitarists. It gave us a starting point for what we wanted to achieve eventually and a standard that was set for us."

Laughs Mrs. Weinrib, "He was listening to a different kind of music than I used to listen to, you know? But it was him — he was young, and why not? But it was very loud. And my mother used to be in the basement, and they would be in that business, and my mother used to cook in the bedroom, had a little kitchen, used to always say to me, 'You know, it's hard for me to hear, but they are really getting there.' And the neighbors were really good about it too. I remember they would ask the band to stop at eight o'clock. And so they did. They'd complain, 'Why did you have to have the music here? And why is it so loud?' But one of my neighbors, Mr. Sniderman, he talked to Geddy and said, 'Geddy, we love you, we're not going to say nothing if you stop at eight o'clock.' And they did. They'd stop at eight o'clock."

It sounds like the neighbors had a point. "One day we had like a credenza there with glass," continues Mary, "I'm telling you, the impact of the volume, the whole glass came out. I remember my mother calling me from home, calling the store, 'You should see — the whole glass fell out from the credenza! They're playing here! It's so loud!' It was just because of the music. It was so loud, and everything was vibrating, and it brought the whole glass out of the credenza. Many, many things happened. I can't even remember, so many things happened. But my mother was very good about it. She was very good with him. And after a while, I figured the louder the better for me. I was so used to the music, it was unbelievable. Some of them used to say, 'How can you listen to that music so loud?' And I said, 'The louder the better.'"

Mary admits that she and her mother used to argue about the noise. Mary would sometimes stick up for Geddy. For her, it was easy, perhaps because she was at the store and removed from the drama. Still, it sounds like Geddy's grandmother was a softie at heart and that the relationship was more complicated than it seems at first blush.

"Yeah, my mother really didn't like the music," clarifies Mary. "When Allan was still a very young child, people were coming and going. There were so many people, and she was usually cooking in the basement, and they were all gathered around there with the music and all this, and she was really heartbroken. She used to call me ten times a day. Geddy had a very hard time with my mother, how she wanted him to stop and he wanted to play. But she used to feed them and all that stuff, in spite of it. My mother used to say, 'You have to buy this kind of meat because this one likes this and this one likes this.' She used to make them dinners and lunches and everything while being upset and fighting with Geddy! Why does he bring all those people to the house? But she used to cook for them. She couldn't get out. Friday night was his big night to go play. And my mother wouldn't let him out of the house until he makes the prayers for her. Because Friday night, you have prayer. And so he made prayers and then he could go. She let him get out."

When Geddy wasn't creating music himself, he was studying the greats, which soon would include more provocative fare than the Beatles, namely The Who, the Kinks, the Yardbirds, Cream and Jimi Hendrix. Like many rockers his age, Geddy wistfully relates that he was the exact right age to witness what was arguably the greatest leap forward for rock 'n' roll: from the Beatles through to 1969.

"Yes, he was always listening to music," says Mary. "Writing music, even when they used to go to school. Used to go to school and come home, go to the gig, whatever they had to do, and come home and write songs at night and then went to school.

And at school, he was sleeping most of the time. One day, I get a phone call from the principal. 'We have to have a meeting. I want to see you.' And I thought to myself, 'What did this kid do?' And we had this meeting, and it was the principal and his guidance teacher, and they were talking to me, 'Geddy has to quit school.' And Geddy didn't want to quit school because of me. He didn't want to hurt me. So then he decided to talk to me, the principal and the guidance teacher, and they explained to me that Geddy is a good kid and he wants to pursue his dream and I should allow him to quit. He doesn't need your permission, but it shows you what a good child he is. He wants your permission."

The principal said that because Geddy was playing gigs at night and coming to school the next day, he'd constantly be falling asleep and be unable to function. As Lee recalls, "It was a bit of a blur when I look back at high school because I was in the full throes of trying to be a musician. So we were doing gigs at night at high schools in Magnetawan, you know, exotic destinations in Ontario, and I was sleeping in a lot and missing classes a lot. I had the single greatest guidance counselor that any student could have, and he tried to keep me in school for many years and rearranged my schedule around my playing schedule so that I could still stay in school. But eventually I had to make a decision, so I didn't get much past grade eleven."

Adds Mary, "The guidance teacher says to me, 'I bet my last dollar that Geddy is going to make it big.' I thought he was just trying. I just wanted him to finish school and have a profession. Because he has no father, who is going to advise him what to do? And anyway, I looked at him and said okay, I get it, and then he started working at home, and trying to play little clubs and had millions of different bands there, and that's the way it went, all the way because somebody said something good about him. Even my neighbors . . . when he had the long hair, 'How do you let your son run around with his long hair?' And I said, 'Geddy, everybody's talking about your long hair; why don't you cut your hair?' And he said, 'Mom, your neighbor doesn't know me. I have to have my hair because of my profession.' And if I used to talk about drugs or something — that's what I was scared of — he used to say, 'Mom, nobody can make me do anything, and I promise you, I'll never let you down.' And he never did."

As for that long hair, Mary says, "I really didn't like it, but after a while I got used to it. Every day, I used to say, 'Please cut your hair, please cut your hair.' And he would say, 'I need the hair. This is my music — you have to have the hair.' One night I got up, and I decided I'm going to cut his hair myself. So I took the scissors, and I went into his room and he was sleeping and I was going to cut his hair. And as I was holding the scissors, he turned his head, and I said to myself, I might hurt him. Am I crazy, standing here to cut his hair? And I never cut his hair.

"But I was very worried. Because especially in rock, the people, Ged used to say to me, 'Mom, you know groups like us only last five years. If we're done after five years, I'll go back to school.' And I knew he would, you know? And this was after he released his first album, his first single. I used to buy every single I could and I'd sell them at Newmarket, and I would have kids helping me, and I would give it to them to play at recess, and I had all kinds of posters in the window, and really, really advertised and talked about him.

"Of course I wanted him to be a doctor or a lawyer," laughs Mary. "Because it was a profession that was solid. As I said before, being a single parent, in a way it was very hard for me because my husband could be a strict father and a loving father at the same time. When my husband was alive and something happened, the kids used to come to Mother and I would make everything nice. But when I was a single mother, I couldn't do that. And that was very hard. And after, when he went in for his business, I wanted to help him, I really did, however I could, and I took pride in him. My proudest moment was actually when he got his first Juno as upcoming group. I remember I was on the sofa and I jumped so high, and they had to slap me to calm me down because I could not believe it because they were actually going to get it. Because everybody was so against Rush, it was unbelievable, from the beginning."

"I was not an insider, put it like that," adds Geddy, assessing his last years of formal education. "My high school was Newtonbrook and it was in Willowdale and there were a few people that I was friendly with there that I still know, but for the most part I felt pretty much an outsider and didn't really fit into cliques. And I was finding myself as part of this group of musicians and that really was the first thing that I could identify with that, really, I thought I was pretty good at. So I think that was the buzz for me, and it was kind of a way to be cool on my own and a way to escape my nebbishy past, I think. I think that's the classic Psych 101 story. Yeah, I didn't have much affinity for education at that time, and I was a so-so student. I think if you looked at the classes I was taking my last year at school, I took all subjects that ended in the word arts — graphic arts, screen arts, theater arts — with the exception of history and English. I dropped all practical subjects, and then of course was told by my teachers that I would never get into any higher education. But I really didn't care at that time because I think in the back of my mind I knew I was going to be in the arts somehow."

The same drama was going on over at Alex's house, and it seems like the only reason it didn't reach a breaking point was because Alex had moved a large portion of his own family strife over to the Weinrib home.

"His mother always complained about him, to me anyway," says Mary, of Geddy's charming blond friend. "We used to talk on the phone constantly. We were both in big trouble. But she always says she likes Geddy, he's so quiet, he's always nice. Alex behaved when he came to my house. Whenever I saw Alex, so polite and nice, so I couldn't understand what she was telling me. In my opinion, he was okay. Sometimes he used to sleep over and sometimes Geddy used to give him food. I really don't know where he used to sleep. But they stuck it out, the two of them; they made it. And my mother used to talk. She would have a conversation with Alex's mother, and she was saying the whole house is just falling apart here, from the booming noise. She was complaining. Because Alex's mother used to tell me, 'Mom called me,' because she had her number, you know?

"Yeah, Alex's mom and I used to talk always on the phone, at each other's shoulder, because she wanted her son to be a dentist. I wanted my son to be a doctor. So we had another big conversation, crying, and I couldn't even talk because my basement was jumping back and forth. The music was so loud, it was unbelievable even to just have a conversation. It was like loud explosions. And I was worried. I was worried about Alex too, fighting with his mother. It was a very difficult time for me — being a single mother was very difficult, and I had other children too. Plus my neighbors were criticizing about the hair, what kind of mother I am, letting my son wear long hair and make noise all over the neighborhood."

Mary is reticent to talk about how things were going in Alex's house, but she implied it was a bit more desperate than the almost comical situation going on at the Weinrib rehearsal hall.

Alex's mom, Milla, also recalls this tense period in the band's history. She says, "And all this noise that we had in the house. The kids from the street would come close to listen, and then my husband worked night shift, and I used to come down in the basement, and I used to say, 'Enough is enough,

Alex, please!' And Ged of course, he was there already, when we moved on Greyhound. And Ged was on Pleasant Avenue too, but on Greyhound we had a smaller house, and you could hear everything. On Pleasant we had a big house, and it was quite roomy. And I used to come down and I used to chase them out. But they started playing in schools, they started playing in clubs, and Alex couldn't study, and he would go to sleep late, couldn't get up, and we were very upset when he quit school. But he said he's going to go next year, and he did. But I wasn't very supportive to say, 'Yes, son, you're going to do well.' I probably should have. But I said to him, 'Just go to school — this is not for you' and all this. Because I tell you, he used to go out, and I would sit in the living room and wait for Alex until two, three o'clock in the morning. And he would say to me, 'What are you doing, Ma? You wanna see my eyes?' Because I wanted to see if he was taking drugs. And so it was tough. He knows that we were very worried about him."

Fortunately, the band was progressing rapidly and becoming increasingly business-like. But there were humble beginnings, including Geddy's first jams with Alex.

"I remember them really clearly," says Ged. "I don't remember much in between but I remember the early days very clearly. He used to call me all the time to borrow my equipment 'cause I was one of the few guys that had an amplifier. My mother was working at the variety store all the time, so I would work there with her on the weekends and summers and she would pay me, and with the money I saved from working for her, I bought myself an amplifier. I remember the day I first bought it — it was fantastic. I went to Long & McQuade and I bought this Traynor. I had no way of getting it home, so a friend of mine and myself we schlepped this thing home on the bus from downtown Toronto all the way to Willowdale. And it was a freezing cold winter day and we actually pushed the thing on the ice; that's the only way we could get it to my house."

Alex adds, "We used to go to music stores all the time and pull a Gibson off the wall and play that instead of the crappy Canoras that we owned. And dream about having that kind of equipment and that amp. We would do that stuff together as kids. Like so many thousands or millions of other budding musicians do. It's great; it's a part of a particular slice of life, and it's something that all musicians share. If you talk to any musician that's had a successful career, that's done something, they came from the same place. They weren't automatically famous and great and fantastic. They were kids, at one time, that drooled over a piece of equipment they couldn't afford or have. Or wanted to play like that guy or this girl. We're all from that same little pool, that same family, where music gets right inside of us and takes over."

"So Alex knew I had this amp," continues Geddy, "and so he used to always call me to borrow the amp. And then one day he called me, and I thought he was calling to borrow my amp again, and he said no, our bass player hasn't shown up or can't make the gig tonight at this local coffee house, can you fill in for him? So I said sure, I came down. We were playing this drop-in center in Willowdale called the Coff-In, I think. And we jammed and we sort of loosely learned the songs; we only knew so many. And then we just played at this coffee kind of drop-in center. And it was fun, and I think we each got six or seven bucks for doing the gig and then we went to the local delicatessen and we had chips with gravy — I remember that day very clearly."

Corroborating the tale, Alex says, "He had an amp, so, yeah, it was a very big asset. He was one of the few people who had an amp. Because of his great job at Times Square Discount, his mom's store. And I would borrow his amp from time to time; he was very generous that way. So we got this gig when John Rutsey was in the band. Jeff Jones was someone that I had met. He was a bass player who went on to play with Red Rider. I jammed with him through mutual friends a couple of times and then he came out to do this gig.

"So we did this one gig and we played the half dozen or dozen songs that we knew over a couple of times. It was quite fun and there was an offer to do it again the following week. He had other commitments. He couldn't make it, and I don't know if he was that interested. He wasn't really a close friend; he was more of a jamming guy. But Jeff said, 'You know what? I have another band and I can't make it.'"

Alex says this all went down in September of 1968. Coff-In was in the basement of a local church, and with no Jeff Jones, Alex asked Geddy to do the gig, which, he says, was performed for a crowd of about thirty-five. They were paid ten bucks.

"I remember we didn't have a mic stand so we used a lamp," says Alex. "We just taped the mic on the side of the lamp. And I think we used one amp for the two of us. We rented a Bogen fifty-watt amplifier. And two columns — they were six-inch speakers or something — sounded terrible. And a Bogen vocal amp. So everything was in the simplest form. Vintage gear now, yeah; it would be thousands of dollars for that stuff now. But we played the gig and it was really exciting.

"The songs were basically the same that we had done with Jeff. And they were the songs that all us fifteen-year-olds were playing at the time. You know, 'Sunshine of Your Love' and maybe 'Spoonful' and 'Fire,' those sort of things. It wasn't a big repertoire of maybe a dozen songs that we all knew. We probably played there, oh, a dozen times. For a while it seemed like we were there every Friday night. We went from ten bucks to thirty-five bucks in the end. It was big money, actually, you know? Because I remember working in the gas station, in the summer of 1971, and I was making fifty-nine bucks a week, working the gas station five days a week. And we made thirty-five bucks for a one-night gig. So that was big money, thirty-five bucks.

"We managed to spend the whole ten bucks quite easily over fries and Cokes," continues Alex. "We talked about how we were gonna conquer the world. And we really believed that, sitting there. And I was good friends with Geddy for a year at least before that, and we'd been jamming at least a few times a week. So we had already been pretty comfortable with our musical relationship as well as our personal relationship. But thinking back, I would have to say that little after-gig moment . . . I can remember the way the restaurant looked and us sitting around the table and how excited we were. It was really — I can't believe I'm gonna say this — a big rush for us to have experienced this thing, this gig. It was our first gig as a band, and we became a band that night. And we stuck with it, he and I."

Alex clarifies that this summit didn't take place at the famous, long-standing Pancer's Original Delicatessen, which adds the tagline, "since 1957." Despite there being Rush pictures on the wall, Alex says, "There is Moe Pancer's, which is south of Sheppard on Bathurst, but then there's Red Pancer's, which is the one we went to. I think Red Pancer's is long gone. They were relatives, but I think they were estranged from each other. They were in business together, but they separated. And Red might have died years ago, I don't know. But we never went to Moe's. I've been to Moe's, but we never went there. First of all, it would've been too far to walk. From the gig at the Coff-In, it was only an eight-block walk through the suburbs to go to Red's. And it was open late, and that's why we went there that night after that first gig together.

"But yeah, I can still remember it; I can remember what it was like in the restaurant and sitting in the booth. I think they had red vinyl on the seats. How exciting it was. It was like a dream coming true. Although we were nothing; we didn't even have a repertoire of songs. But it was the starting point and from that point on we continued to do, I think, one or two shows a month at that same venue, at that drop-in center. And we started writing our own material, and we got a little more serious."

Part of getting serious was Alex adopting a sort of stage name. "My name starts with a zed and it has all those vowels and it's twelve letters long," explains Lifeson. "And my whole life my name has been mispronounced. And I couldn't imagine going on the road and going through the rest of my life with my name being torn apart. Lifeson is just a literal translation of Živojinović. And my father at one time thought of changing our name, basically for the same reasons, and then decided against it. So really for my professional stuff, I use Lifeson, and for my personal, private stuff, I use my real surname. So it's just the convenience, the convenience of not hearing my name butchered all the time. As it is, with Lifeson, I get Leafson, Lifeberg, all kinds of different names, but it seemed to be a convenient way to have this stage name. But I didn't expect that, forty years later, I would still be using it."

Alex confirms that he and Geddy didn't change their names at the same time. "With Geddy, Lee is his middle name, so he just sort of dropped his last name."

Another step was the penning of original music. Recalls Alex, "The first song we wrote together — and this was probably two weeks after we decided that this was gonna be the band; it was in early October — and it was called 'Losing Again.' And it was just kind of an upbeat bluesy, riffy thing. I still remember the song; it was very, very basic, so I think I could probably play it again. I do recall that being the first song we played. We were so excited about it because we'd only been together for a few weeks as an official band, and we were already writing our own material. And that was a really exciting concept for us. We don't have to be typical of a lot of the bands that were around at the time that were just bar bands, or not bar bands, but just high school dance bands that knew a bunch of material from the pop list of the day. We had our own material that people could grow to hate when we played these gigs."

"That was certainly part of our drive," continues Alex. "It was a risky thing because a lot of people didn't wanna hear that stuff. They want to hear all the classic songs that they know. Particularly if you're playing a high school dance. They want to be able to dance to things they're familiar with, not some eight-minute bluesy jam that, you know, they have no idea of what it is. But if we hadn't done that, we wouldn't be who we are. There were lots of bands that played that circuit that knew all the hits, and they were the ones that made the three hundred bucks, at the dances. Whereas we would get the hundred-and-fifty-dollar gigs, but two-thirds of our set would be original material. It was a good training ground for us."

"The high school circuit was the only way for a lot of Toronto bands to stay alive," adds Geddy. "Ontario bands, not just Toronto. And it wasn't just in Toronto. In fact, most of them were outside of Toronto and as far afield as you could go. And there was this position in a high school called social convener, and it was very big for high schools to have dances and those dances needed entertainment. So a lot of us got hired to play these various dances, you know, Halloween, Sadie Hawkins Day. And that was the way you stayed alive, especially if you weren't old enough to play in a bar. But they always shouted requests for songs they could recognize, and we were bound and determined just to play our own songs regardless of how crappy they were at the time."

"Generally it was a small group of high school students or junior high school students lined up against the back wall, standing as far away from the stage as they could," laughs Alex. "Because we always played our own music. We started writing our music right from the very beginning, as simple as it was. By the time we were actually doing those gigs, after the first couple of years of just learning how to play and practicing all the time, we weren't really a dance kind of band. Two-thirds or three-quarters of our music was our own original music, and some of it was really long, ten-, fifteen-, twenty-minute long songs, and we were sort of jamming, went through all kinds of things, and it was very difficult for people to get locked into, a beat, and to dance to. So those gigs were pretty bizarre. There were some that were very, very bizarre, that's for sure. I remember one case, our PA blew up, literally. Flames and sparks came flying out of the speakers, and we did the gig without any PA, so no vocals. That was in Cochrane, Ontario, or something."

Also part of building and becoming the band were the pilgrimages the guys would make down to Toronto's very hip Yorkville district. Rush rued the stigma of being a band from the burbs.

"Yeah, we would go downtown," remembers Geddy. "A friend of mine, his father had a little restaurant downtown, in Yorkville actually, called the Cabbage Roll. And we sometimes would wash dishes there. In fact there was a club in Yorkville called the Flick, I believe. Anyway, it was upstairs and this restaurant was in the back. And I remember on break going up and looking at the band. And there was a well-known band in Toronto called the Stitch in Tyme, and they just did covers. They didn't write their own songs, but they were really good. And so their gear was always set up there, and I remember on a dishwashing break, sneaking back and you can see all their gear set up on the stage, really cool, and I would go out and have a smoke with all the hippies on Yorkville thinking this is really cool. But of course they were real hippies and I was this little pisher. And so I started hanging around there with Alex and John and that whole gang. But the hippies, of course, these were real people living their lives, and we were just kids. We thought we were cool, but what kid doesn't think they're cool? Every kid thinks they're cool, and every kid thinks they're funny, but that can't be true. That's what keeps you sane, I think, as a teenager."

"We were both kind of outcasts in our class," adds Alex, "and I suppose it was because we thought we were a lot cooler than everybody else. So we kind of stuck to ourselves and didn't really hang out with anybody else in our class, and of course John was in a different class. There were some other people that we had mutual friends with, so we were part of what we considered that elite group of people at Fisherville Junior High. Yeah, so we had a lot in common, and we would jam at his place or we'd go to my place, sort of back and forth. But there were a lot of other things outside of that, that we shared interests in. We really, really grew up together. We went through the whole experience of first girlfriend and all that other stuff that you go through as a teenager, and we've really shared a long life together he and I, very much so."

Part of Geddy's and Alex's advancement toward being a serious band was their study of the greats, those bands, usually British, who were showing teenagers the world over how much noise they could make and looking cool doing it.

Notes Alex of Geddy, "As a bass player, he had great models. John Entwistle, Noel Redding . . . they were amazing bass players for that period. And Jack Bruce, of course; Cream was a huge influence on us in those early days. That kind of set the standard for the way he wanted to play — to be a very active player. He played guitar a little bit earlier on, so the transition was pretty easy, I think. And then of course as a vocalist, that had an impact as well. There were a lot of great singers around that he, I guess, tried to emulate, or at least draw from. I think once we got into Led Zeppelin, the way that Robert Plant sang, had a huge influence on him. Had a big influence on all of us. They really were the model band, I think, for that period where we started to come together as a band and as musicians."

Like Geezer Butler in Black Sabbath, Geddy indeed began on guitar. Alex, however, missed this part of Lee's evolution.

"I didn't know Ged when he played guitar," Alex says. "So the transition was already completed by the time we started jamming together and playing. Because that's what we did after school. We'd plug into his amp and play. There was one guitar and one bass. So I'm not really sure about that transition. I'm sure he was interested in guitar like everybody was interested in guitar. But once we actually started playing and learning instruments, that was his chosen one. It was just like John Rutsey in the early days — the drums became his thing, but I don't know if in his heart he wanted to be a drummer. I think he wanted to be a guitarist as well. But everybody had their job that they sort of gravitated to."

Says Geddy, "I was nominated to be the bass player when, in the first band I was in, the bass player couldn't be in our band. I think his parents prohibited him or something, and we had no bass player, so they said, 'You play bass,' and I said okay. And that was how simple it was. That happens to a lot of bass players. Everyone wants to be a guitar player, but I was happy to be bass player. Bass player is like being a major league catcher. It's the quickest way to the majors. Nobody wants to be a bass player. It's a great instrument, it really is, awesome way to spend your time. I had teachers you know; I'm just carrying on the tradition of Jack Bruce, Jack Casady, Chris Squire, a fine tradition of noisy bass players that refuse to stay in the background. So I feel that's my sacred duty, to carry on what they started."

"His sense of melody and activity are very unique," agrees Alex. "And I think he's influenced a lot of bass players because of that. One of the challenging things for me as a guitarist playing with him — and with Neil for that matter — is how active they've always been. I think, more recently, it's shifted a little bit, and it's a little more simplified. But if you listen to Ged's bass playing internally, and how he plays, the little nuances that require a really strong detailed focus, it's amazing, the little melodies that he incorporates and the little things that he's doing, that a lot of other bass players perhaps don't do. Or some do that I would say emulate him.

"He came from that school, Jack Bruce and John Entwistle. And Chris Squire was a big influence on him in the early days. But he's developed his own style and he plays a lot of chordal things that a lot of bass players don't. Which forces me to sort of play an opposite role. And it's great because it gives me somewhere to go that's different and challenging. Later he became a little more basic in his rooted playing. Again, because he senses that this is what the song requires. You know, it's always about the song and providing for the best arrangement for the song. I think all of us look at it that way. A lot of times bass players can be one or the other, but he manages to really bring it all together. I think also because he sings — that adds to that."

Geddy charts his evolution toward his reverence for these masters of big, buzzy bass, starting with Roy Orbison and when rock took hold of his consciousness more generally.

"What were the songs that got me playing?" he asks. "The first thing that comes to mind is 'Pretty Woman' — such a great classic riff. I'm sure a lot of musicians will quote that as an influence, but it cut through, right? Why did it cut through? It's the riff that cut through, and riffs are a big part of rock and progressive rock, right? And metal. And then I think of 'For Your Love' by the

Yardbirds and that chord progression where the chords ring out. Kerrang — that sound is in that song. And I heard those songs and those are songs that made me want to play. I wanted to play that. So there's something visceral in that early music.

"The early Kinks, for sure, early metal, for lack of a better term. Of course nobody even heard of the phrase then. They really grabbed your ear. And the great thing was there was only one kind of radio. So if one of those songs made it on the radio, in amongst a gazillion Motown songs and Mantovani and all that crap that they used to program. And then in all of that you hear 'You Really Got Me,' one of these riffs, it's just like the music suddenly came alive. And for me and all my friends, we reacted to it, and that's what made us want to start bugging our parents to let us buy a guitar.

"But it was not just the guitar sound; it was the way it was structured using the guitar as the theme. I guess you could go back even further to some of the instrumental bands that used to come on radio. Like there was Booker T. & the M.G.'s that used to do 'Green Onions' and all that stuff, and then there was that band that played all the Mosrite guitars. The Ventures, was it? 'Pipeline,' those songs. And then the Yardbirds had taken that attitude with the guitar and started using guitar themes; that was really fresh and really featured the guitar player."

Beyond the abstract inspirations came the building blocks, forces of nature like The Who. The Ox was Geddy before Geddy, and Keith Moon was the Professor before the Professor. Even if Cream, another blueprint for what became Rush, represented most forcefully the concept of the power trio, it was The Who that proposed the progressive, as it would manifest in progressive rock and then in the progressive metal of Rush. And as Alex has alluded to, there's an obscure, precious, almost warped role for the guitarist atop a rhythm section like this. That's why both Townshend and Lifeson spend a lot of time providing color commentary, texturizing, darting in and out.

"There were two things about The Who that stood out," continues Geddy, "two aspects that made you completely fascinated. One was Keith Moon. There had never been such an explosive, complex drummer as Keith Moon before. His drum patterns were shocking. And they were in pop songs on AM radio. And the songwriting. Those guitar chords. And yet they were a strange band because you listen to 'Happy Jack' and it's such a weird song. It's almost like a jingle, and yet underneath it's a bit of fury. But I think Townshend's broad guitar strokes and Keith Moon's explosive complex drumming were the two aspects that separated The Who from everybody else.

"Plus there's their whole image, right? The fact that they smashed their guitars; that was something you talked about. Keith Moon kicking his drums over. One of the early bands I played in, the drummer was a huge Who fan. And I remember we auditioned at this local junior high school to play the Sadie Hawkins dance. This was pre-Rush, right? And at the end of his audition, he kicked all his drums over. And we were just in a classroom, okay? We're auditioning for three teachers in a classroom. And at the end of it, he kicks his drums over, and drums are flying and cymbals are flying, and of course these teachers are completely appalled by that idea. And the guitar player and myself are just looking at him, like, you just blew this gig for us, dude. What are you thinking? They don't care about The Who — they're teachers. But that was a big part of their image. And they looked really cool, and their album covers were highly creative, and they were one of the first bands, I think, to take that to an extreme. The whole concept of an album cover. Their ideas. They were cutting edge."

As for Cream, says Geddy, "Personally they were hugely important. Before Zeppelin. They did these long, breakout jams.

They were one of the first bands to jam on record. Guitar, bass, drums, just going at it. Nobody was doing that. You consider them a blues band, really, yet they weren't behaving like a blues band. They were behaving a bit like a jazz band, like something no one had ever done before. 'Spoonful,' that great version that they used to do . . . of course when we first became Rush we played 'Spoonful' for ten, fifteen minutes. We were jamming. We didn't have the chops to jam it properly, but we mimicked them. So that was huge. Their willingness to do a song and just to go out there every night and jam it and just play. Three-piece playing. So they were the prototype for Rush in many, many ways. We loved what they were all about. Clapton's playing, but not just Clapton — Jack Bruce took the bass out of the background and dared to have an aggressive bass sound that was distorted. He was such a great player. And Ginger Baker was a god to drummers — he would do a drum solo for twenty minutes. Nobody was doing that then. So we're still carrying that tradition of Cream on. There's a lot of things we learned from Cream that we still do. They kind of set the stage for power trios, I guess."

Connective tissue — or more like tough leather or horse hide — between Cream and Led Zeppelin were San Francisco outcasts Blue Cheer, Cream to the extreme.

"For me, Blue Cheer, in many ways, they were the first metal band," reflects Geddy, using that word that wouldn't become fully codified until about 1975 and then, somewhat accurately, applied to Rush. "But they didn't think in terms of metal. Those terms didn't exist, right? What they were after was volume; part of their shtick was to be the loudest band ever. Wherever they would play, whenever they would play, they had amps for days. It's interesting how volume eventually kind of evolved into metal crunch, and bands learned from that whole evolution that you could get a heavy sound without it being super loud. The taming of metal in that regard.

"But it was volume and fury that they were all about. And as a young player, of course, that blew us away. Their version of 'Summertime Blues' and some of their early songs were . . . you just had to try to play them. You had to learn them. It had that tone because recording a band at that volume ended up being distorted on tape. And so there's this new sound, kind of take the Kinks but make them really, really loud. The other thing was — and I guess it was their downfall — they were not songwriters, really. They never really had that ability to move beyond that one moment. So they had this image, Paul Whaley with his really long, blond hair, the three-piece thing, really super loud, super cool, but songs didn't come, you know? So there was nothing really to keep them going, to sustain them. They were an idea that was like a flash.

"The Who used to play 'Summertime Blues' as well," continues Geddy — Rush famously covered the Eddie Cochran classic on their 2004 EP, *Feedback*.

"There's something about that song. Well, of course, what it's all about is bored kids in the summertime. Just perfect for rock, right? So I don't know how they fell upon that. Whether they had heard The Who play that song and decided to do their own version of it, which seems likely to me. But yeah, Eddie Cochran, and there was the old blues guys too. We got introduced to the blues guys through the English guys imitating the blues guys. Through Led Zeppelin, through John Mayall & the Bluesbreakers, through these other bands that we liked. We learned who Buddy Guy was, Willie Mason, all these guys, learned those names through them. And then you'd listen to the original and it didn't quite turn you on in the same way the electrified versions did. You'd go see them and you'd appreciate them, and you'd have respect for them, but when you went home you didn't put on those records. You put on the British, louder versions of those records. That's what you wanted to groove to.

"But John Mayall always had the best guitar players. Some of the best British guitar players came through his stable. I guess in Canada we have Ronnie Hawkins; in Britain they had John Mayall. He hired the best musicians. And so if you picked up one of his records and you heard great playing — it was all about the playing at that stage of my life. So yeah, Beck and Page and even Mick Taylor — killer guitar stuff. We all followed the guitarists back then — they were the magic men of my teenage years."

And so into the set list some of these classic stepping-stones went. Recalls Geddy, "We did a version of 'For What It's Worth.' We used to do this old Motown song called 'Roadrunner,' but it didn't sound anything like 'Roadrunner.' I don't know why we called it 'Roadrunner.' We made it into this long extended jammy thing; Alex used to play a really long solo, but of course they were all like that. We used to play 'Crossroads,' 'Suffragette City' by David Bowie. I don't know if we ever played Zeppelin in the bars. I know when we were just a high school band we used to play 'Living Loving Maid.' In the early, early days, we used to play Jeff Beck's 'Let Me Love You,' from *Truth*. Also 'Morning Dew,' some Yardbirds songs like 'Shapes of Things.'"

Larry Williams's "Bad Boy" (made popular by the Beatles) got airtime right up until December of '74. From the basement band days through the break of the new decade, other acts Rush (and pre-Rush) covered included the Stones, Eric Clapton, Ten Years After and Traffic. Original compositions, such as "Keep in Line," "Morning Star," "Child Reborn," "Love Light," "Slaughterhouse" and "Feel So Good" also emerged.

From the source DNA provided by The Who, Pink Floyd and the Moody Blues, as well as conceptual gestures from the

Beach Boys, Pretty Things, the Mothers of Invention and the Beatles, a new genre known as progressive rock was born, and this new genre would live on in what Rush continued to do. For all intents and purposes, this music — at its nexus point in 1969 and 1970 — became the adopted genre of Rush, certainly once Neil Peart joined the band.

"When I go back to the progressive period," begins Geddy, "the bands that affected me — and I think the other guys in the band were equally affected by these guys — it began with Jethro Tull, Yes and Genesis. The first time I heard them, I was knocked out by them and challenged by the music they were making. And that led to a myriad of other bands like the Strawbs, who kind of grew out of English folk music, yet developed to be quite a melodic progressive band. And bands like Van der Graaf Generator, who were very popular in Canada, maybe not so much in parts of the United States. Van der Graaf, in particular, had a much darker sound, a little akin to ELP but almost like ELP's darker twin. Less flashy in terms of instrumentation and virtuosity, but great mood and interesting stuff.

"The first time I listened to Yes I was a teenager, and a buddy of mine turned me onto them. Here was a band that had an aggressive sound in certain ways. Like Chris Squire's bass tone was really aggressive, and Bill Bruford played really powerful drums, yet there were these complex melodies and these time changes. I think the first thing that grabbed me were the time changes. They were unpredictable, they were hard to count through, and as a young musician, of course, I was challenged by that, and I loved that.

"And the sound of Jon Anderson's voice, the nature of the lyrics, open to interpretation. There's still many Yes songs that I don't know really what they're about, but I *think* I know what they were about. At least they were about something to me, and I think that's a part of aggressive music that gets overlooked, the fact that you're allowed to imagine what the song is about and how the song speaks to you in an individual way. So the lyrics are cryptic, and that's enticing to a young teenager, right? 'What does it mean?' It was challenging as a young musician to even attempt to imitate, and kind of threw me into a flight of fancy in terms of what was the song about. It's almost like there's a puzzle here and it's up to me to try to figure out, musically, lyrically and conceptually. Now whether that was the case or not doesn't really matter, but that's the way it appealed to me, and that sent me on this kind of journey looking for more progressive music and trying to emulate that as a young musician."

Incongruous perhaps, but progressive rockers tended to have a strange affinity for classical music. "Yes, and those are the kind of things that made critics hate progressive rock," agrees Geddy, "because they didn't like what they considered a bastardization of the classics. In general, critics seem to prefer pure music, not fused music. And progressive rock is nothing if not fusion. It's the ultimate fusion for rockers, right? So yeah, and I think to kids, suburban kids like myself that didn't listen to a lot of classical music growing up, this was, in a way, our first introduction to it through an electronic means, and that kind of legitimized it.

"So yeah," Geddy continues, "you can look at somebody who's more educated about music listening to those bands at the same time as a fourteen-year-old and getting very different reactions. The more educated listener is going to think they've just ripped off the classics, but the young kid's going wow, this is a new sound. This is kind of challenging to me. I don't know the background of this, so then you start researching it. The first time I heard of Erik Satie was through Yes. So names start tumbling forth that, to us uneducated suburbanites, were intriguing. And we started then buying classical records, listening to classical music. So I don't think it was a bad influence. It was a great influence, in fact.

I have a lot of friends who also got turned onto classical music. It's interesting because with other bands, like John Mayall & the Bluesbreakers and even Zeppelin, you started getting introduced to old blues guys, like the original versions of songs that Cream would do. And it's really not that much different than getting introduced to Beethoven or Bach or Tchaikovsky through Yes, Genesis and what have you. Or Mussorgsky through ELP."

This is where Rush would get their own sense of drama, that epic sweep that was there as early as their first record in songs like "Finding My Way" and "Working Man." By *Fly by Night*, they'd mastered the art of drama, even more so come *Caress of Steel*.

"A lot of the progressive bands wanted to add drama to their sounds," explains Geddy. "Not just texture, not just melody, but drama. That was the kind of pompous, bombastic thing of prog rock at that period. A little more pomp. So yeah, they were drawn to the dramatic pieces. A lot of prog rockers — I know we did at the time — preferred to look at our pieces as kind of vignettes. Like we were doing soundtracks for movies that didn't exist. Storytellers, in a way, through music. And of course, the dark titles and the dark concepts were fun. They gave you lots of different colors on your palette because it really wasn't cool to make music that was too boppy, too poppy, too happy. It was much cooler to be dark and brooding, especially when you're a teenager."

But the full-on art rock version of Rush would have to wait. In the early days, the band was an amalgamation of barroom rock 'n' roll, post British blues boom riff rock (i.e., nascent hard rock, bands like Cactus and Mountain), Midwest rock (whatever that means) and finally U.K. glam rock. And all of this is personified by the band's drummer, John Rutsey, who is usually spoken of as a symbol of the old Rush. John, born July 23, 1952, was a year older than Alex and Geddy and, like Geddy, was growing up fatherless. The Rutsey patriarch, *Toronto Telegram* crime reporter Howard, had died from a heart attack, and so John was living with his brothers and his mother, Eva. John himself later suffered a heart attack, caused by complications from his lifelong battle with diabetes, and died in his sleep on May 11, 2008.

"I met John in '64, I believe," recalls Alex. "We moved into the area and I met him in junior high school, in grade five. He lived across the street from me. He was just this other kid on the street, and we became friends soon after I moved into the area. He had two older brothers who were really great, Bill and Mike, and they would play football and baseball with us and stuff like that. They were very cool. And John and I both had a great love of and interest in music, and we would listen to Bill's and Mike's albums all the time. And I remember when The Who's *My Generation* came out, and the first Hendrix album, and all that happened through his brothers, which was a great introduction for us, listening on a little record player in their basement.

"We wanted to learn how to play and we wanted to have a band, and we had a band together. I think it was the summer of 1967, the Projection, which was a couple of other guys, another neighbor, Gary Cooper, and Alan Grandy, Ian's brother — Ian was our soundman for many years, one of our roadies. And we would play just basement parties that would happen amongst our friends, for no money, obviously. But you could have as many chips as you want and a couple of Cokes. You can imagine what we must've sounded like because we were fourteen years old. But we were very enthusiastic, and that led right up to Rush. In the meantime, when I started school in junior high and met Ged, we would play together, but separately. I don't think we ever played together with John at any time until the actual band started."

Ian Grandy, who became Rush's top road crew guy from the basement days clear through to the early '80s, adds, "Rutsey was the genesis of that band. My younger brother was in a band with

John and Alex called the Projection — that's well known. And they were playing 'Heart Full of Soul.' I saw a thing the other day, of Geddy and Alex playing 'Heart Full of Soul,' so, just like back when the guys were playing the Coff-In. But my brother was in a band with them, and Rutsey and my brother were in grade four together, I think. So that's how all that happened. At one point they rehearsed in my basement, and my parents parked outside in the snow while their equipment was in our garage."

Hence the special thanks on the back of the first album to "Mr. and Mrs. G. Grandy."

"Right, it was either the summer of '71 or '72," Ian continues. "It's one of the reasons they're thanked on the first album. My mom and dad, they'd go to work and the band would come over about ten thirty, eleven and hack around 'til two. And it's kinda loud, so we'd put the dog out in the backyard and the cat would go outside. The playing would go on in the basement; we just stored the stuff in the garage. But Geddy's mom would tell him, 'Go to school, get a job, get good marks, don't play music, get new friends.' He'd go, 'That's all, huh?'"

"John was one of the funniest guys I knew," continues Alex. "He had an amazing dry sense of humor. But John was also very, very moody, and he could turn on you out of the blue. And I remember it was very painful, because you'd be ostracized, and for a month he wouldn't talk to you — he wouldn't call, he wouldn't accept your calls. He would turn people against you or threaten them with ostracization, threaten them with not being his friend, things like that. Very juvenile. And then one day, you would get a call from him; it would be like nothing happened. And this would happen every eight or ten months or so. It would happen to one person and then another person and then another person. You wouldn't be in the circle anymore for a month or six weeks or something like that. And then suddenly he would call and say,

'What's going on?' It was the weirdest thing. And it happened to all of us; it happened to me, Geddy. It was just some weird mood thing. It made it very difficult to be with him sometimes. I don't know what it was with John that made him do that. But I think later on he recognized that was a problem or issue that he had, and he regretted it."

Rutsey was essentially the leader of the band. Unearthed footage of the band playing Laura Secord Secondary School, in which John does the talking from the authority of the drum throne, makes this clear.

"Well, yeah, he was the actual leader on our union contracts. John was the one who did all the talking, and he had a mic and I just remember, some of these gigs, particularly when we were out in the middle of nowhere playing these bars in Northern Ontario, he would lay into the audience in such a dry way, it would go above everybody's heads. It was hilarious, and he had control of that mic the whole night, and there were some really stellar comments that he would make. I mean, he was very, very funny and very quick. I think it was part of his character, his personality. He was more of a leader, less of a follower, and maybe that's why he had those issues about control over people, and his friends and things like that."

"John could be the funniest guy in the room," explains Geddy, "and he could be the most bad-mood dude in the room. His moods swung wildly. I think he was kind of a troubled guy, and he lost his dad early, like I did. I don't know if that's a contributing factor. He was quite an independent guy, very hard to feel buddy-buddy with. Alex and he had a much closer bond because they kind of grew up together, across the street from each other. I was always a bit of the outsider with him, so our relationship was up and down at times. He was a really smart guy, stylish guy, snappy dresser, and he had a really quick wit. But he could cut you down quickly and make you feel really small. He could knock you off your pedestal pretty fast. Very funny guy though, and when he was warm, he was great. So kind of a mercurial personality."

As for his musicianship, Geddy says, "I don't know if he was so unique as a player. He was kind of like a stay-at-home defenseman, a solid backbeat drummer. Very opposite to Neil. A Simon Kirke or Bonham kind of drummer. Those were the guys that really hold down the beat, don't shout 'Look at me' — that was the kind of drummer he was. He was good at it, but I don't know if that made him unique in any way as a player. He was a good solid drummer in a traditional sense. But in a lot of ways the band leader. He was the funniest guy in the band. And that was before Alex became the funniest person in the world. I think he learned his comedy chops a little bit from John. Because John was a super funny guy."

Give Rutsey a microphone at a gig, Alex says, and "he would say some ridiculous things. And you've got to remember, we were playing a lot of bars, and sometimes there were matinees where there are sleeping guys in the back of the room burping. You had a lot of latitude. And just to see if people were paying attention, he would command the mic and say the most ridiculous things, and the three of us would be cracking up, of course. Unfortunately, he had the shitty job of being with us through the toughest part of our career, when you're slogging it out in the bars and playing high schools and you're driving in a van three hours a night and you're making no money. But you're young too, so you're resilient as hell. And the fact that he was a diabetic and had some physical restrictions, I think, weighed on his mind. You know, he had to give himself injections, do that whole thing, and so that set him apart as well."

John took his role as band leader seriously, says Geddy, introducing the guys to things they hadn't heard before. John "was just very opinionated about the music we played. He was the first guy on to any new thing. First guy into Zeppelin. He was a big Grateful Dead fan. He would bring a lot of music to Alex and I and say, 'Hey, check this out.' He had his ear to the ground, and you couldn't make a decision without him giving his opinion. And he was the lyricist of the band in the early days too. So what I sang, he wrote. Until he started rebelling against that in his own way, but that was more a reflection of his own internal war. He was kind of at war with himself; that's how I would describe John. A guy who could be so great and so funny, and so opposite to that, without too much warning. He kept to himself a lot, had a real secretive side. Alex and I knew exactly what we were always doing with each other. With John, you never really knew. He would disappear after gigs, or he wouldn't show up at rehearsal. And I think that was his kind of internal war."

Famously, it was John's brother Bill that came up with the name Rush. "We were trying to come up with a name for our band, and he suggested Rush," says Alex. "It's the hip connotation with the drug scene, the hippie scene at the time. And the definition of the word, because we were very fast players and it was a nice short, snappy name. So we thought yeah, okay."

Along the way, the band had been called Hadrian, and Geddy had been in bands called Ogilvie and Judd and even one called Lactic Acid's Jeff Jones.

"We continued doing that for the most part until '71, I guess, when they lowered the drinking age to eighteen," says Alex, referring to high school dances. "And then all of a sudden there were all these bars you could play. We went through some difficult periods. John had some health issues, so there were a few times when things kind of just went into limbo. We had some changes in the lineup a couple of times. Joe Perna was the bass player for a little while; Geddy was gone for a bit and then he came back. Geddy's brother-in-law played in the band in the spring of '69 for a few months, playing piano and guitar. We were still playing a lot of bluesy stuff. Mitch Bossi came later [lasting February to May of '71]. Lindy Young was in the band for a little while, and then he quit [Young was in from January to July '69]. Mitch came in, I think, just as we were doing the bar gigs; he might have done a few of the bar gigs."

"John Rutsey was a sick young man," adds Alex's mom, Milla. "He had diabetes and he was on insulin, and his mom used to call me often and ask me if he was there. Because he had to have a certain amount of food at a certain time. And I remember John Rutsey just left home once and stayed with us, and they were practicing and practicing, and I said to Alex, 'You know, John has to go home now. His mom is worried about him.' But I think Alex was worried about John himself. Because he wasn't eating on time and all that."

"I remember doing a gig at the Thunderbird Motor Inn in Thunder Bay, in October of '73," says Alex, telling a tour tale from the club days. "It was freezing cold. They had us at the far end of the motel. There was no heat down there; the rooms were around fifty degrees. Every night you would hear 'zzzzzzz' as we would turn the hair dryers on under the sheets to keep warm. And the guy wouldn't pay us after the first week. And we didn't have any money, so we had to eat and drink in his restaurant. And one night, I remember, he sat us down and said, 'Come on, boys, we're going to have some drinks.' We had all these drinks and had a great time, and we got the bill for it! He actually gave us the bill for it. But we had a real fun time up there back then.

"I also remember doing a gig at the Meet Market. It was the old Colonial Tavern on Yonge, right across from the Eaton Centre. It was a jazz club, but downstairs they had a rock club. And you can imagine, being in that location, what kind of crowd they brought in. And I remember I had surgery — I had my wisdom teeth taken out — and we were there doing the gig; I was eighteen, nineteen. And I was sitting on a chair onstage because I was on Percodan, and my mouth was killing me and I had smoked some hash. And this fight breaks out. Every person in the place is in this fight, and it's all happening right in front of me, while I'm sitting in a chair playing. And I just remember looking at Geddy and him looking at me, like, 'What is going on?!' And we're playing a song called 'You Can't Fight It' on top of it all."

The next important development in Rush's evolution was acquiring a manager. Ray Danniels was the band's first — and only — manager, an incredible rarity in the music industry. Ray steered the ship until the end, mostly from the band's house-styled offices at 189 Carlton Street, just east of Toronto's downtown core in what was a fairly rough part of town.

"Well, he was a kid," says Alex, with respect to first meeting Ray, who had approached the band with a proposition at one of their high school gigs, having been familiar with them from their packed shows at the Coff-In. "I mean, we were fifteen years old, and Ray was sixteen years old. He left home about a year earlier. He moved to Toronto, moved into Yorkville when it was a hippie hangout, hooked up with some people. There was a band called Sherman & Peabody. Greg Godovitz was in the band then, and Ray used to live in their basement; he would sleep on the mattress in their band house in Willowdale. And I don't remember how we met, some common friend. After a while, Ray said, 'Listen, do you guys want a manager? I'd like to manage the band.' And of course he had no skill or experience, but he was a hustler. So he started managing us and set up some gigs and got posters and drove around on a friend's motorcycle putting posters up on telephone poles across the city, all that stuff. And eventually Ray became more of a promoter; he started promoting other bands, and then he started an agency, Universal Sounds, and then that agency grew. So he was set very early on, in terms of where he wanted to go, in a business sense, musically. And our relationship has existed since then."

"I think I probably met John Rutsey first, and then I met the guys, through the area I was living in," begins Danniels. "Their personalities have not changed that much over the years. Geddy always had a serious side to him, although he was a lot of fun. Alex was always a comedian first and a guitar player second — that's how he was as a kid and that's how he is to this day. We were all into the same bands, whether it was Cream, Buffalo Springfield, the first Led Zeppelin record, all of those, not the most mainstream bands at that time. We were all Who fans. At that point, the Rolling Stones were massive, and it was the tail end of the Beatles being big. Creedence Clearwater was a bigger mainstream band, but we were all into these more progressive bands. There was a whole hippie element out there that we were into, but I don't think any of us were into the Grateful Dead as some people were. It was more acts that leaned toward the British bands, as well as Buffalo Springfield."

It's hard to imagine in this day and age, but Ray was doing all this at sixteen years old — living on his own, promoting and managing bands and also serving as a roadie for the local hippie act Sherman & Peabody.

"Yeah, for about three weeks or something, I lived in the same house with these guys; it was kind of a band house. And I did some roadie work with them, and that's how I actually got a chance to see how their manager worked and what he was capable of and not capable of. And, actually, some of the guys were going to law school and became attorneys. One of them is a music business attorney. So it was a fascinating way to pick up on what they were doing. And part of me watched them and thought, 'Gee, I could do that, and I could do it better.' So it was an attraction and I just kind of fell into it. I started a little booking agency at that point, and I started to book bands and they were one of the early bands that I was booking, and they of course were still in school. They were still living at home, and I was on my own. So it was a very different lifestyle, and I was trying to pay the phone bill and make something out of this and turn it into a business, and they were very much a part-time band playing high schools on weekends, and later on it became clubs.

"I want to be successful with this and I wanted them to become successful," continues Ray. "We had become friends fairly early on. Yeah, it was a huge desire to see them successful. I was on my own from the time I was sixteen. Toronto and Yorkville, San Francisco and Haight-Ashbury, New York and the Village — it was the whole attraction of being in that '60s era, to be part of that. I was living it. What's now the only five-star hotel in Toronto is where I lived. It's funny how things go full circle. It was a lot of fun. There was an innocence there. That moment of time in the '60s, there was a real innocence. There was an innocence, but there was also the reality of the Vietnam War, so you had draft dodgers coming to Toronto. And people were smoking an awful lot of pot. The birth control pill had become mainstream in that decade, and that totally changed the relationship between men and women. It was a very fun time. It was a time where you couldn't really get anything that penicillin wouldn't cure, unlike later on, when suddenly, I have kids, I have four kids, and their generation has to contend with diseases that kill you and that penicillin doesn't fix. So there was an innocence there."

But Ray didn't mind leaving the hippie hub of Yorkville to go to the soul-crushing burbs to look after his new charges.

"No, my life with them was more up in North York, where

they were practicing. There was a fourth member of the band at one time, Lindy. It was at his house, which was Geddy's wife's house. Geddy married Lindy's sister Nancy. And then we were at Alex's house, Alex's parents' house. So our world was more up there, in North York. But yeah, I was booking some bands and I thought they were really good. And we were close in age. So it was a combination of liking the same music and closeness in age, and they were so young that they couldn't play the bar circuit. The drinking age in Ontario at that time was twenty-one, so they couldn't play there, nor could I book bands there. I wasn't old enough to go into the bars. So it limited me, as a young guy starting a career, to events that had no liquor license: high schools, churches, whatever."

But before the drinking age changed, the high school dances were the big-deal shows. "Yes, because often they would call them dances," Ray says, "but in reality a lot of them were closer to concerts. And it depended on which band was there, whether it was a dance or a concert. But it was usually a gym that had a permanent stage. Often schools would allow three or four other schools to attend, and some of these would be three or four hundred kids, and some of them would hold a thousand kids. And some of them would run it twice a year and others would run it every three or four weeks. And it was throughout Ontario. You would go all the way to Northern Ontario on down. But these weren't really dances. I mean, they were billed as that to some degree, and I'm sure there were some students that bought a ticket thinking that this was going to be a band they could dance to . . . but as Rush became known, and known within that, they had fans even that certainly knew what they were, what kind of music they were going to hear."

Mirroring the tales of the flyer wars of hair metal–era Hollywood, Ray was out there promoting Rush on telephone poles.

"Well, that was your means of advertising at that time," laughs Ray. "The staple gun was your best friend. You know, rule number one was tear down the other guy's posters first, then put yours up. And I would get fined all the time. There was a bylaw that you couldn't put anything on a telephone pole. So we would do it anyways and every now and again they would fine us. We would get a fifty dollar fine and you would pay it and it was just the cost of doing business. But you couldn't really afford advertising in the traditional sense, or very little of it, so that's how you got the word out. Plus it was word of mouth. The high schools would promote from within, but there were other places that were predominately church auditoriums that you could rent. You would rent it and you would put on your own event there, or there would be a couple promoters that would do very small-scale things, three, four, five, six hundred people. But yeah, the means of it was advertising in the local community newspaper. You couldn't afford the *Toronto Star* or a big paper. But mostly it was the reliable staple gun and away you went."

As Alex alluded to, shows were a mix of originals and covers, the band adjusting the mix as circumstances demanded.

"It was a combination," says Ray. "The material on their first record was material they had written when they were very young, that they were working on. And they were doing covers that they liked, and some of them phenomenally well, and some of them ended up on the *Feedback* record. There were things I wish were on that, that I could remember them doing, like David Bowie's 'Suffragette City.' Some of the stuff they did back then was just killer."

Ian Grandy agrees. "'Suffragette City' was big. They would open the night with that. By the third or fourth set, everybody's totally getting drunk and they'd rock. But they just rarely covered things straight. They put their own little twist to it."

And then 1971, the drinking age was dropped, and the live music scene exploded.

"Huge — overnight. There wasn't a lot of discussion about it, I remember. It was something that happened very quickly — the Ontario government decided that the drinking age would go down to eighteen. So all of a sudden the clubs that perhaps weren't doing as well as some of the other clubs saw a huge market. They could be going after the eighteen plus. And you're talking about the baby boom generation, so it was a massive number of kids that age at the time, and it meant that suddenly I was a successful agent. A lot of the bands that had been playing high schools could suddenly get into these clubs and perform there, and for an audience that was more than willing to go see them. Of course, the side effect of that was the high school business started to suffer. There was probably a three-year transition between the clubs taking off . . . well, the clubs took off very quickly, but the high school business started to erode after that.

"So there were two or three rooms in Toronto that we started playing on a regular basis," continues Danniels. "Sometimes we would go on for a full week, which was the way these clubs booked bands. And then I started to change it up and we would only go in for three days at a time, or one or two nights at a time, and it became more of an event when we played these places. And then it went from playing for no cover charge to suddenly selling tickets and it was a small concert. It was a blueprint for what we see today when an act goes on tour."

Ray says that the guys were run ragged, playing within a three-hundred-mile radius of Toronto, with London, Ontario, being a particularly strong market. But if they were exhausted, they never took it up with Ray. "No, I think that would've been with their parents and their family," Ray says. "The band always came first. Unless Yes was playing at Massey Hall — they wouldn't play because they were going to the show. But Geddy's mom has always been incredibly supportive of him, and his brother and sister, so I know she would've been so concerned. She's the kind woman she is. She loves her kids and she lives for her kids. But when she saw success and saw that he was good at this, I think support went from school to the band just as quickly."

chapter 2

Rush

"He was kind of a wizard character to us."

Around the turn of the decade, lo and behold, Alex's girl-friend, Charlene McNichol, became pregnant. Charlene gave birth to their son, Justin, in March of 1971.

"I was always hoping that Alex would get married to Charlene," reflects Alex's mother, Milla, "and that they would have Justin with them. And he came home one day — he was twenty-one — and he said, 'You know what, Mom and Dad?' We were sitting watching TV, and he said, 'I'm going to move Charlene. She's moving from one apartment to another.' And he said, 'I'm going to take her out for dinner too.' It was her birthday or something. And I was very happy. I saw a maturity then in Alex too, because before that he wasn't around much. He did pay for the child, but he didn't see Justin that much, because he was always away on a tour. But then I saw that he became more mature about every-thing, and then they lived together for a while and then they had a little backyard wedding after a couple years.

"I remember, when he was sixteen, he took our car," adds Milla, recalling another example of Alex's responsible behavior at a young age. "We had an old Chev, Pontiac, whatever, and he went with some teachers to play for kids; it was like a cottage or something. And he smashed the car. There was some kind of fight. He opened his window and got attacked and he went right into a big pole. But when he did that, he came home and said, 'You know, Mom and Dad, I did this. I'm sorry.' He said, 'You know what? I'm going to pay you for the car, first check I get from my concert.' And you know what? He did that. The first check he got, he came and says, 'Here, two thousand dollars.' He was very responsible that way. Even for his son Justin. He would work in the garage, filling gas and make money and pay on time for Charlene and Justin."

To recap, the late '60s and early '70s were a time of flux for Rush — the paying of dues, as it were. This period marked several milestones for the band. September 18, 1968, might be called Rush's first professional gig ever, and September 25 was the first gig with Geddy — both of these were at the Coff-In. In the spring, Alex and John played as Hadrian, with Joe Perna on bass.

Here's how Geddy recalls the Hadrian debacle. "This is how Ray came into the band. Ray was kind of a hustler, this young guy living wherever. He'd run away from home and was living in Yorkville village at the time, and he was kind of a hippie, trying to make a buck any way he could. He approached the guys for management and didn't really talk to me much. And then suddenly I was told the band was dissolving. He'll hate that I'm telling you this story, but I'm going to tell you this story. I remember I was going to rehearsal one day, and that's when we were a four-piece band. My wife's brother Lindy Young was a keyboard player for us. So I ran into him on the way to rehearsal, and I said, 'I thought we had rehearsal,' and he said, 'No, the band broke up.' Apparently they had decided that I wasn't suitable to be in the band anymore. And I think this was at Ray's urging. They reformed with another bass player and they changed their name. I went off and started another band and played in another band for a few months."

At this point, Geddy joined a band called Ogilvie with Sammy Rohr and Xavier "Sam" Dangler, followed by a stint in the band Judd, same lineup but adding Lindy Young. At one point, Hadrian included among their ranks Bob Volpi.

"So anyway, I get tossed from the band, they started another band, doesn't work out, the next thing I know I'm getting a phone call from John Rutsey, 'Please come back in the band.' So I came back in the band. By that time, the keyboard player was gone and we reformed as a three-piece and that was my first introduction to Ray Danniels. He had to live that down for a really long time. But he was just a hustler basically and had the smarts to know he could make a buck as an agent, and so he was our agent. And he was an agent for a lot of bands, and then he decided there was more money to be made at the management level. So he kind of crossed into that. His early days were not shining examples, but he kind of turned himself into a pretty darned good deal-maker."

Geddy says that Ray, in the beginning, "was there to get gigs and make the money. And after years of arguments and us being pigheaded, stubborn, we eventually worked it out . . . it was a kind of a perfect marriage in a way because we didn't want to be handled. We wanted to do our own thing and he wasn't really interested in handling. He was interested in getting gigs and booking tours. And of course all that changed as we evolved as people and as our relationship evolved and now he's a good, trusted friend and a great advisor.

"But the reason that our relationship worked so well was because he leaves us alone. I mean I think there is only one time in our whole history that he's actually heard one of our records before it was finished. That's an incredible amount of trust for a manager. It shows a lot of respect that we trust him to do his end and he trusts us to do our end. And if there is a problem, we'll discuss it, but until there's a problem let's not assume there's a problem. And I think that's where a lot of management people fail their artists. By getting so hands-on and so manipulative that they, the band, lose sense of who they are themselves and where they're going. You have to let a band make mistakes and learn from them and then you figure out who you want to be. Not much different from parenting. You gotta be there, but you can't be too controlling. But anyway, it was an unlikely team, having him aboard, and we certainly didn't get off on the right foot. But over the years I've forgiven him, and it works pretty well now."

Following Geddy's touchy return to the ranks of Rush, they played scattered high school gigs until the band's first show under the new drinking age: their gig at the storied Gasworks pub on Yonge Street in Toronto in the spring of 1971. A mix of high school and bar gigs ensued, including, in July 1972, a six-night stand at the Abbey Road Pub, followed by a residency twice as long back at the Gasworks in August.

Liam Birt, who ended his days with Rush forty years later along with Geddy, Alex and Neil, joined the crew in 1972. Working as a guitar tech and with lighting, Liam rose to the all-important role of tour manager, the guy who has to solve all the problems on the road.

"I had actually just left high school," begins Birt, "and I had been working the last couple of years of high school with friends of mine who had a high school band. Being a little unsure as to what I was going to do with myself after leaving school, I was hanging around the local music store, and I think one of the Toronto icons of that era was in the rental department speaking with a friend of mine that worked there. He was the one that told me that the guys in Rush were looking for a technician, roadie, and he asked if I knew who they were. And I said yes, they played at my high school the year before, and he recommended that I go down to one of the local Toronto clubs, the Abbey Road, where they were performing because one of their roadies had disappeared.

"So later that same evening, I went down to the Abbey Road and met with John, who was, I guess, the leader of the band at that point, and the other roadie, Ian. And we had a quick conversation, and it was pretty basic; it all came down to 'Can you work for seventy-five dollars per week?' At that point in my life that was just fine, and it was 'Fine, can you show up on Saturday night and help us load out?' That was really the beginning of it all for me. I was a bit awestruck. I was seventeen years old, they had a name for themselves, although it was mostly in bars and high schools. But they looked the part. They had platform shoes, they had sequined jackets, they looked like rock stars. I felt like a kid coming in from the suburbs with a very limited knowledge of what I was doing. But they seemed willing to take me on, and over the course of many decades, we learned together.

"It's funny, the legal drinking age was eighteen, so I spent the first nine months working for them sneaking in and out of bars wearing what I can only refer to as my older-looking clothes. And making sure you walked in with the band so you didn't get harassed. So I was living on the edge, trying to make sure I could actually get in to work every night. We'd work six nights a week, five sets a night usually, starting around eight o'clock, finishing around one. It was pretty tedious, long hours, a totally opposite schedule from what I had been used to going to school prior to that. And you either grew up fast and got used to it or you were going to flounder."

Further on Rutsey running things for the band, Liam says, "Someone always had to sign off on the contracts, and I guess that was John's position at that time. He seemed to make sure the band got paid at the end of the night, you know, prior to the days of wire transfers and everything happening magically behind the scenes electronically. It was either cash payments or checks and it was up to John to make sure that they actually got paid, and he was listed as the leader of the band on the contracts, I believe, at that point."

Liam says that Geddy and Alex were "very close friends, and still are to this day. They're really, very different people that are truly two peas in a pod. They play off each other beautifully. Alex is probably the funniest person you'll ever meet in your life; he just has a natural talent. If he wasn't a musician, he could've been a comedian. He can make anyone laugh; make anyone feel at ease. They're both superb people to be around. And very hardworking. I mean, it's the one thing that actually made them. They seldom had much radio support; they did everything themselves. They worked six days a week. They worked as many shows as they possibly could. Even in the early days of touring, we would be gone literally for months on end, never really knowing when we were going home again. The only thing that kept them alive was just getting out there and putting forth their music, be it to a handful of people or a few hundred people. That's the perseverance that finally paid off for them in the long run.

"I actually took the job thinking it would buy me a little time to figure out what I wanted to do with my life," says Liam. "But it was interesting and exciting. I had just become very interested in music a few years prior to that, and I was buying some time, I think, trying to find a purpose for myself. As far as getting a sense of greatness out of them in the early days? No. I think we were, initially, all along for a ride. I certainly didn't expect to still be there four decades later. So, no, I didn't foresee it coming, and if anything, as years went on, it looked less and less likely that anything really serious would come out of all this."

Rush were regulars at the Abbey Road through 1973, with a highlight of that year being a historic pair of shows supporting the New York Dolls at the long-gone Victory Burlesque Theatre at Queen and Spadina in Toronto at the end of October. "Around that time, we started getting those type of gigs, opening slots," says Geddy. "Our manager started a promotion company to promote other bands as well, and they used to run shows at the Victory Burlesque Theatre in Toronto, which was a great old strip club, venerable old strip club from the days of vaudeville. The New York Dolls, that was really quite a trip. Just being a fly on the wall while these guys stumbled in was something I'll never forget. Not exactly a lot in common musically, but we opened that show, which I think brought our first review ever, which of course was bad. It was the first of many bad reviews to come."

Explains Ray, "I had become a concert promoter at that point, and I had taken over the Victory Theatre, which was an old burlesque house. It had eight hundred seats on the floor and another four hundred in the balcony. And it hadn't been used for years, but we opened the balcony and started doing shows there."

Also at the end of the October, clear into mid-November of '73, was the residency at the Thunderbird Motor Inn in Thunder Bay, Ontario.

By this point, reinforcements for Ray had arrived in the form of Vic Wilson. Wilson, like the band's "new guy" to arrive soon, Neil Peart, was native to Ontario but had made the pilgrimage to England to try his hand at rock stardom where it mattered. He was back home by 1971 and was trying his hand at the business end of things.

"I was the president of Concept 376 in Toronto, which was a booking agency, and Ray was one of the owners of Music Shoppe," explains Wilson. "And we butted heads all the time. If you didn't work with Ray or myself, you didn't play in a rock 'n' roll club in Toronto. So, one night I was out with the manager of the Piccadilly Tube; we had dinner, and he invited me back, and he said, 'Your opposition will be there tonight, Ray Danniels.' And I said, 'Never met him before.' So I went down there; we were just sitting around talking and drinking, like we did on most days, and Ray said, 'Let's have lunch tomorrow.' So he came and picked me up, and we went to Julie's, a pretty fancy restaurant in a mansion, for lunch. And that's where SRO Productions started. We figured there was a management company needed. There were lots of agents managing bands at the same time, but there was no management representation. So we decided we would start a management company. And then in December of '72, we opened offices, along Eglinton Avenue, and that was the start.

"Ray was young," continues Wilson. "I was twenty-seven, seven years older. And I'd been in business since 1960. I don't know how long he'd been in the business at that time. I met Rush when we opened the office, and that was probably just before Christmas. It may have been January 1, who knows? They were working with Ray at Music Shoppe, and he was the manager and agent at the same time. They walked in the door and they walked right past my office into Ray's office, and I guess it was 'Who was that?' We actually got to know each other very well. It was three young guys, and there were two roadies too. Liam Birt was the roadie in those days and Ian Grandy. So there were five who you dealt with, like a team. But no, they were good to work with, and they did what we asked them to do. They took direction well. All they had to do was produce onstage and leave the rest of it to us. And that's what we did. We took care of business.

"They had it in mind what they wanted to do," reflects Wilson, making note of the guys' work ethic. "If you've got your mind set, you either agree with it or you don't. So we let them go. They had free rein of what they wrote and what they recorded, and we didn't interfere in that at all. Rutsey was fine; he was talkative. Geddy, he wasn't that talkative. I mean, he talked to Ray a lot. And Alex used to bring me soup at lunchtime. His mother used to make soup, and he would bring the soup in. It was a happy family, SRO. Most of the leadership was done by Rutsey. But no, there were three guys, they got along well, playing music. And they wanted to record and were looking toward the big time, eventually."

On the subject of witnessing Rush live for the first time, Vic is pretty sure it would have been at the Abbey Road in early '73. "I saw some huge boots, some tight pants and long hair and a little bit of makeup. You know, I come from a different school, so it wasn't a shock, because I was in the industry, but yes, they looked the part and played the part. You could see the resemblance between Geddy and Led Zeppelin. They got branded like that because of Geddy's voice, and that's basically what I figured happened. Geddy's voice definitely made it unique for Canada, for sure. And they had ambition. They wanted to make it and we saw that in them. So if somebody wants to just get out Saturday night and play, that's one thing. But if you want to make it your life, you have to dedicate yourself to it, which they all did. They were like three brothers, like a family. Worked together, always together, and worked hard at their trade.

"The first big show they did with us was New Year's Eve," adds Vic. "Ray and I went into the promoting business, and we started doing rock shows at the Victory Theatre, which was a striptease club down at Dundas and Spadina. And our first show was the New York Dolls, and Rush opened that show. So all the old trenchcoaters saw New York Dolls and thought it would be great. Well, when they got in there, they got the shock of their life. So they all peeled out and left and we gave them their money back. But they were doing the circuit everyone was doing in those days. The Coal Bin, Abbey Road, the Generator, the one Roel Bramer owned, the Gasworks, Piccadilly Tube. We started to get some action out of the Colonial Tavern in those days, but that was just kind of Mike Elias throwing stuff against the wall, see if it worked. I know Mike very well and we still talk about it today."

Liam remembers Yonge Street as the hub of rock 'n' roll activity back then. "Very much so, although Abbey Road was more off of Queen Street, Queen and University area. Most of the bars probably held at best one fifty to two hundred people, if that. But there were all the Yonge Street establishments. At the Gasworks, they almost felt like the house band after several years of being there. Piccadilly Tube was another establishment a little farther down Yonge. The Meet Market — I won't take the name any further than that — which was kind of around the back of the Brass Rail, which I think we played once. But there was a multitude of clubs up and down Yonge Street where you could go see Rush — or even their competitors, like Triumph — all playing for the same dollar and hoping to attract a crowd every night and get booked again next week. The Victory Burlesque — that was a different vibe. They opened up for the New York Dolls in there one time, but it wasn't really a club vibe.

"More exciting were the high school and university shows, going to the University of Windsor, where you'd be gone for a weekend. You'd be staying at the 'fill in the blank name' motor hotel for a couple of nights, and that in itself was exciting because it wasn't the drive home at two in the morning anymore. We'd go to the wilds of Northern Ontario and think that we were about to fall off the face of the earth. You couldn't possibly drive any farther north. We'd regularly go through bouts of frostbite up there."

Back in the relative cozy warmth of the office, "I was more the administrator," explains Vic. "I handled publishing, the accounting, for the first year or so. And in later years, I did everything outside of North America, and Ray did North America. Arranging tours, record companies, I dealt with them all. Creative, they carried that. I thought they had their own direction and we let them go in that direction. We always said, 'Write us a Top 40 hit' but they refused to do that, so we lived with it. Bob Seger once called Rush the most popular band in America without airplay."

The next milestone for Rush was the release of a single, although neither of the songs on Moon Records MN-001, not the A, not the B, represented the band's best foot forward. The A-side is a cover of "Not Fade Away," credited to Petty/Hardin, made famous by Buddy Holly. The B-side is "You Can't Fight It," credited to Geddy and John. The Rush original is non-LP, and it kind of deserves to be.

"We wanted to record something, so they said let us do 'Not Fade Away' and a B-side, which was written by John Rutsey," remembers Wilson. "So they went into the studio and recorded it. And Moon Records began, and it was distributed by London Records, Alice Currie out of Montreal. And the only reason we went there is they were willing to do our distribution. Not our promotions, but they would pay for the pressings and then collect it out of sales. So, great deal — that's what we went with. We went and did 'Not Fade Away' as a single, the old Buddy Holly hit, also done by the Rolling Stones.

"We were about to release it, and the day before we released the single, somebody said to me, 'Do you have a mechanical license?' And I said, 'What's a mechanical license?' And that's through publishing. You have to have permission to record it. It was mandatory licensing in those days, so we were okay. But I needed to connect with the publisher, and it was Pure Southern, Matt Heft of Montreal who ran Pure Southern in Canada. So I chased him all over Canada, phoning here, phoning there. And finally, he called me back and he said, 'Yes, Vic, what can I do for you?' I said, 'I'm in a predicament. I'm going to release this thing tomorrow. I need a mechanical license right away.' And he says, 'Yeah, release it. I'll call you when I get home.' And Matt Heft and I were friends until he passed away a couple years ago. He was ninety-three, at that point."

"You can ask my wife," laughs Vic when asked how the company financed the recording session. "For six months after the company opened, she said, 'Could you bring some money home?' Because we had a mortgage to pay. So everything we made went back into the company. Every penny, Ray and I. There was no budget. We just went in and paid, I think, two hundred dollars a night, from midnight or one o'clock until the next session coming in in the morning. We cut a deal with Eastern Sound. I knew someone who worked at Eastern Sound, John Stewart, who we asked to actually produce the first Rush album. He turned us down. And Dave Stock was the engineer there, and we went in, and Dave Stock turned the dials and we recorded it and 'Not Fade Away' was born."

"Initially I was trying to get them a record deal, and no one was going to sign them," says Ray, also on the subject of financing the record. "I couldn't get arrested. And so it became obvious it was going to take whatever it took. I think I had a mortgage on my house at the time, and my business was doing well enough that I was doing okay. I certainly wasn't wealthy, but I was doing okay. So I was able to find the money, and it was done on a bit of a shoestring budget and away we went. And then we tried to place the record, once it was done, and still there were no takers, so I ended up being a record company. Which in hindsight was a wonderful way for it to have happened. Started Moon Records, which then became Anthem."

Danniels is pretty sure that coming up with the cash didn't involve borrowing from Geddy's mom, and he is relieved that she confirms that she was not involved. "Thank God, because if I did, I never paid her back. Although, interestingly enough, she owned a variety store at the time, and she was very supportive of sticking the record and the first single in the store. And I think she arm-twisted kids to buy it, so she was our first retailer. She put stickers in the window. She's wonderful, and she's always been incredibly supportive. And about her concerns with him in school as a kid, I know Alex's mom fairly well and I knew Alex's dad, and you couldn't find more supportive parents — normal, middle-class, in both cases, immigrant parents who came here to see their kids do well, to do better. So it doesn't get any better than that. The number of times these guys would've put up with three-hour rehearsals in basements is beyond me, as an adult. At the time, I didn't think about it as much as I would now — very supportive."

"Well, it wasn't really Buddy Holly so much as it was the Rolling Stones," qualifies Geddy, when asked why the band thought "Not Fade Away" was cool enough to do, if it even was way up into 1973. "And John was a big Stones fan. When we made the decision that we wanted to work and actually get some jobs in bars, we had to play some songs by other people, because you would have to submit a list of songs that you played to get hired in some of these bars. So we had this amongst our own material. We had to kind of scatter some names of bands, so we would look for obscure songs by other bands that we could do our own version of and make it possible for us to get paid some money.

"And I don't remember who brought that song up — good chance it was John — but it became a very popular one when we played it live, and so of course we didn't know about what songs we should do on the record when it came time to make that first single. The people around us, Ray and the guy who was going to produce it, said, 'Well, you should do that song because you should always do a cover song.' So we did. But, yeah, it wasn't Buddy Holly. No connection with the early days of rock 'n' roll. We had liked rock 'n' roll after it had been to Britain and come back again."

"We were playing that song in our set when we were in the clubs," confirms Alex. "And our version of it was quite heavy and powerful. And, of course, the powers that be at the time thought that would be the most likely song as an inroad to getting played on radio. A cover of an established song gave us a greater chance. We recorded that . . . we were playing at the Gasworks. And we would tear down after the show at one o'clock and move into the studio, Eastern Sound, which is gone now, and record in the after-hours because it was cheaper to record from two o'clock in the morning until nine o'clock in the morning. And we recorded over a couple of days, and that's when we did that, and the first version of the first album.

"The engineer/producer at the time, David Stock, was English and was working in our office, and he came from a more poppy, English background. So when we went in to record, that's kind of what the record sounded like. It was very light and there were problems with the way the record was recorded and we were very dissatisfied with it. The drums were out of phase, and I think they were recorded on just two tracks. Things were missing, the sounds were awful, and it was just a real mess. And that's where we sought out Terry Brown, and we recorded a bunch of songs, dropped songs done originally, re-recorded a bunch and did the record, basically, with him in a few days."

Alex keys in on the mix as a big part of the problem with the original recordings. They weren't happy that Stock mixed it himself and that they couldn't be around for the mix. They felt disconnected from the process.

"That was basically financed by Ray and his partner Vic, at the time," continues Alex. "I think it cost us about ten thousand dollars to make that record. I wish we were spending that kind of money now making records. But at the time, they had to scrape it together and it was all a big chance."

Wilson's earlier framing of "Not Fade Away" as a deliberate stand-alone single is a little off. The two songs comprising the single were part of the recording process that resulted in the eventual self-titled full-length debut record.

"Yes, that song was on the original album," confirms Alex. "That was on the first album, but when we re-recorded the record, we dropped all that stuff. And then we put on, I think, 'Finding My Way,' a couple of other songs. But that was originally on the first record. We didn't do that as a separate item. It was all done at the same time. We dropped a couple, we put in more of our own songs, and we recorded a few songs, and then repaired the songs that were poorly recorded and then mixed it. And that was all, I think, with Terry, in five days. That's what I recall. We didn't go into the studio just to do a single. We went in and we recorded over two days, the whole record. And we were quite dissatisfied with it."

"Garden Road" and "Fancy Dancer," also recorded at this time, didn't make the debut record either. "Yeah, they were sort of riffy songs," says Alex of these, "very repetitive, mostly twelve-bar sorts of things. They wouldn't have survived the test of time, I don't think."

Fortunately, Rush didn't have to go with these recordings for their first record. The guys met up with English producer Terry Brown, who greatly improved the band's existing tapes while also adding substantially to them.

"We were playing a circuit of bars, and that's about the time that our manager, Ray Danniels, was trying to start his own record label," begins Geddy, confirming Alex's story. "He figured the best way to promote us would be to have a record label, so he started this label pretty well for us called Moon Records, and we scratched together enough dough to record in the evenings, in the wee hours of the morning, actually, after our bar gigs. So as Alex says, we would play the Gasworks bar downtown. We'd do five sets a night, load out after one o'clock, load into Eastern Sound down on Yorkville. It was kind of an eight-track studio, a small studio, and we would record all night long and load the gear back into the bar, catch a few hours sleep, go do the gig and come back.

"But we were kids. We didn't care, you know; we were very resilient back then. We were so excited to be in an actual recording studio. But that's how the first album got put together. And I remember going back to listen to the mixes. This guy we were working with was English and he had been an engineer in England before, and he mixed the whole record in three hours. So we came to listen to it and we were so disappointed because it was so wimpy. At that time, it was about big power chords and all that, so it was disheartening.

"But our manager had a partner, Vic Wilson, who knew Terry Brown, a pretty successful local producer and engineer who had his own studio, Toronto Sound. And he took the tapes to him and said, 'Can we fix these?' They came to see us at the Gasworks or some place like that and said, 'Oh yeah, this doesn't sound like the band.' We went in the studio with him for three days and we re-recorded a bunch of guitars and we dropped a couple of songs and recorded a few newer songs we had written since then. And that was really exciting 'cause it kinda sounded like us. And that was really how that first album got put together. Done in very short order on a very low budget."

"My recollection of that whole time frame," says Liam, "is we'd work at the Gasworks, do the five sets, six sets a night, finish at one, load out of the Gasworks, be out of there by two, three o'clock in the morning, and the cheapest studio time we could get was from three o'clock in the morning 'til six a.m. So, we'd go in for three or four hours at a time, up to Yorkville, and they'd work for a few hours. We'd leave at daybreak and repeat that cycle for a couple of weeks until our stint at the Gasworks ends, and the studio time was done. It was brutal — it really was. As time went on, it actually got down to me negotiating with the studios, setting up the time, putting the budgets forward to our office and, you know, hence all of a sudden, I became known as the President. I seemed to have my finger in every little pie, and I was just looking out for them in as many ways as I could."

"I think that the circumstances under which we met Terry set the tone of our relationship with him," reflects Geddy. "The fact we'd done this record with another gentleman and it was such an unmitigated disaster in our eyes, it sounded so bad, it was so uncool, we were so heartbroken, our management said, 'Well, why don't you go meet with Terry Brown at his studio, Toronto Sound, play the songs, talk to him?' He just had this air of 'I know what's wrong with it, and I know which songs are lousy, which you should drop, and do you have any other songs?' And we threw some songs together and played them, and he picked A, B and C, and we thought this guy is really cool, this guy knows what he's doing.

"And then we went into his studio and started re-recording some parts, and recording the new songs, and they sounded how we wanted them to sound. And we were just so blown away by that, he became the father figure right away. He turned a terrible disaster into something we were proud of — he knew exactly what to do. He was kind of a wizard character to us. We thought he was amazing. And he was so nice and so considerate and got the best out of us, and we immediately had this warm feeling about the guy. He became our mentor for a lot of reasons like that. He was always very decisive with us. And he was always so 'This is the right thing to do; this is not the right thing.' He had a very responsible attitude toward work, and he would work all hours. And he was just a good guy, you know?"

Geddy continues, "There was no question that his accent legitimized him to us, and we didn't have to go to England to find him. He was right here in Toronto. And him coming from that scene, you gotta remember how green we were at that time. When we met Terry, we had one real recording session in our lives, and it had gone terribly. So he was the savior. He was from the country where all our heroes were from. All the bands that we listened to at that time, all the great guitarists, rock artists — they were all Brits. So he was the embodiment of that whole culture, which we yearned to be part of. We really wanted to learn from that world that he came from. Now, he wasn't schooled in prog rock or even that much hard rock. His background wasn't that involved, but he certainly was a lot more experienced than we were at the time, so it was pretty intriguing for us. And besides the fact that he had a great ear and he could give us the sound that we heard in our heads. Our previous experiences with engineers were not so successful in that regard.

"He represented but he also delivered," continues Ged. "He couldn't just talk about it. He could make you sound like that.

He helped us give birth to the sound that we heard up here [points to his head] and we hadn't figured that out yet. We didn't know how to take our sound — the one that we imagined we should sound like — and put it on tape. And yet he did. And he happened to be British. He was legitimized on all fronts, from an imaginary point of view and also from a reality point of view. He had the goods."

"We didn't like the final outcome," confirms Vic, referring to the David Stock recordings. "It really just didn't work, and it was a bad mix. So I went to Terry Brown, who I'd been working with before. He had recorded with Downchild Blues Band who I'd been working with, and Greaseball Boogie Band, so many of us who recorded at Toronto Sound. So I took it to Terry and said, 'Can you do anything with this?' And he said, 'Yes, we can do a remix.' He had experience in those days, and he is still doing it for a living. But he had that experience of mixing. He had worked with Dr. Music, Doug Riley and all those people. So he knew what was going on and he did his tweaking and it worked. And that was the album that got the deal at Mercury Records."

Terry Brown had cut his teeth on roles ancillary to production for all sorts of big British acts, working at Olympic and Morgan. But Canada proved to be an opportunity to move up the ladder.

"I was born in England, in Watford . . . meager beginnings," says Terry. "I stayed there 'til my late teens. Then I worked in London, at two or three of the really top studios, so I had a chance to work with a lot of professional musicians, including Jimmy Page. He was doing working sessions and playing on a lot of people's records, like Dusty Springfield and P.J. Proby and a lot of people who we knew as kids and who had all the hits. And then I started working with a lot of pop bands as well and got to work with The Who. And met John Entwistle, who was very instrumental in putting the Rotosound strings together for the bass players. Which, of course, became Ged's choice of string and that became like a signature sound for the Rush band. And it's kinda stuck with me ever since — if I'm working with someone who uses flat-wound strings and plays with a pick, I have to go the bathroom and throw up.

"So this sort of went on until my late twenties. In '69, I went to Toronto and I met Doug Riley, who became my business partner. He's unfortunately passed away. He and I became very good friends. We started a studio together in Toronto that took the technology of London, which was way ahead of the game at that point. We took that technology to Toronto and opened a big multi-track studio in November of '69. That was my main reason for being here, to build the studio. I hadn't done a lot of production. I was just starting to get into it. I had done a solo artist, Dave Nichol, here in town — engineered quite a lot of stuff and was sort of involved in the production — but not really officially. So at that point, it was time to start wearing a production hat and getting more involved. I didn't really have a lot of credentials in production back then.

"Rush first came to my attention through the management company, Vic Wilson and Ray Danniels, and Vic called me up and said he had a band, three guys who are trying to put something together. They had been working on the graveyard shift, making a record, and they needed some help putting it all together now. They had sort of finished most of the recording, and I said, 'Could you bring them over to the studio?' He did, and we started working on it. But yeah, Vic Wilson basically had a connection, a British connection, and he said, 'I know this teabag over on Overlea Boulevard, he's got a new studio, I'll give him a shout.' So that was the first time we met; they showed up and we did three days together," says Terry. Suggesting a slightly different story, Geddy says Brown "came down to see the band at the Gasworks a couple times."

"We didn't really do that 'getting to know you' thing," explains Terry. "It was like they came in and we started work. It was really quick, a really short window. But it was a lot of fun and we had a lot of things in common, just in terms of getting along and recording. I had a fair amount of experience at that point. So they were very comfortable that they were going to get what they wanted. And also they played very well. So that was a great combination, really — their playing and my experience. We put the two things together and came up with a great sounding record in three days.

"I shouldn't say they weren't happy," says Terry, with respect to what they had from the David Stock sessions. "They just got to a point where they didn't know what to do with it. They had recorded all this stuff, and I don't think they really knew how to get the best results with what they had at that point. So they came to me. They had recorded, I think, seven or eight tunes, and we listened to them and sorted them out and just prepared little bits and pieces that we needed to do and mixed them. Basically, it was a mix situation. But we recorded three new tunes as well, 'Finding My Way,' 'Here Again' and one other — 'Need Some Love,' I think. I remember it coming out and sounding good, when it was finished. So there was obviously some good stuff there."

Says Terry of his new business, "We had a lot of bands coming through Toronto Sound. We were one of the top studios at the time. We were the first multi-track studio in the country, so we had a lot of bands coming through our doors. Rush was just another band at that point. And after my three days, I remember being extremely enthusiastic, just by virtue of how well Geddy sang and how well Alex played guitar. And John Rutsey too was very competent at playing drums. Geddy's vocals were something out of this world at that point, just astonishing.

"And Alex's guitar playing was amazing," continues Brown. "He would double things, he would double the guitar track, and you would swear that there was only one guitar playing. He was that good — one take. I'll never forget to this day, I put the original guitar on the left speaker, and we put the new guitar on the right speaker, and he doubled it from top to bottom, flawlessly, in one take. And it sounded like one huge guitar, it was so accurate. And I had this huge grin on my face, and that's just stuck with me forever, how good he was at that. I remember the guitar sounding like it was in mono because he doubled so accurately. It was quite a thrill, actually. Because at times I would try and do that in different scenarios, and it would be a real struggle and take hours.

"Plus it was the writing. The writing was good, and there was an intangible energy that was coming from the band. That is what struck me as really good. I mean, the whole thing went together really well. I enjoyed working with them so much. The stuff sounded great, I thought, and had tremendous potential. Funny enough, people I was working with at the time were saying to me, 'What do you see in that band?' And I'd say, 'Well, I see a lot of success here.' So when people said, 'What do you see in this band? It's just a loud noise and you really don't hear anything,' I'd say, 'Well, I think you're wrong. I hear strong melodies, some great playing, unique vocal sounds, great guitar playing, and I think they're going to do very well.'"

The maturity and the responsibility of the guys that likely developed because they had to grow up so fast came across in the studio. "They were great guys," says Terry. "They loved what they did and were totally into the music and being rock stars. Which was so cool, you know? A really great experience all around. They certainly struck me at the time as rock stars. I mean, I'd worked with quite a lot of rock stars prior to that and they didn't seem any different. These guys are destined for stardom, I thought. No one agreed with me at the time. Well, not no one, but my peers were frowning."

Terry tries to describe exactly what he did for the *Rush* record, saying, "Well, it needed mixing badly. I mean, it was just raw tracks. We had to come up with something that sounded contemporary. So that was my job, really, at that point. And I was the studio engineer, like the main engineer at the studio. And I was hired to put it together. I wasn't hired as producer. It was just 'Fix this up for us. We need some help.' So that's what we did. We also cut three tracks, so in that respect I guess I was in the producer's chair. But it was never discussed that way at the time."

The gestation period for *Rush*, issued on Moon Records in late March of 1974, was long. The original Eastern Sound recordings had been done back in April of '73, with the "Not Fade Away" single emerging in the summer. After the band recorded with Terry in mid-November, the album was ready to be issued by December of '73 but had to be delayed due to an industry-wide vinyl shortage. Also, Ray and the guys were still holding out for a proper record deal.

"We were offered a record deal by Daffodil Records," notes Vic Wilson, "which was run by Frank Davies. All we wanted to do was recoup our costs, but he couldn't come up with the money, so we thought, 'What should we do?' And the great idea comes: 'Why don't we open our own record company?' And so we did. Which led us to Alice Currie of London Records in Montreal. Alice paid to press everything, and that was the release of the first Rush album. It was huge excitement. We hadn't reached a pinnacle by that time, but to us, we met our goal, which was to get Rush out on the street, on an album. That was the whole idea behind everything, to give them a record. And then shop it in America. Everybody thought that was best, anyway, in SRO. But, hey, you pays your money, you takes your chances. We put up the money and they recorded, and we had the faith we could do it and be successful. But it was a tough sell."

"Moon Records was a really smart move," reflects Terry. "You know, there are always so many different ways to do something, so if he wasn't getting results in the traditional sense, the label was a good way to start."

Ultimately, 3,500 copies were cooked up as an initial run on the band's own two-tone blue Moon label, as MN-100, with the front cover proclaiming "Rush" in red, as opposed to the more widely distributed pink from the band's eventual Mercury deal. More supply was needed though, with the indie release ultimately selling upward of 5,000 copies in Canada and another 7,000 in the U.S. on import, mostly around Ohio due to radio play on WMMS in Cleveland.

Rush, issued in late March 1974 in Canada only, opened in dramatic fashion. "Finding My Way" was a song written and recorded fresh for the Terry Brown sessions. First we hear Alex unadorned and electric. A classic Geddy scream sets the listener at attention, simultaneous with bass and drums. Before forty-five seconds have gone by, Geddy peels off two high and powerful "ooh yeahs" — the most Led Zeppelin–esque thing Rush would do throughout their years of playing. This likely caused some of the criticism that the band was too derivative, but it was helpful as well — in 1974, who didn't want more Zeppelin in their lives?

To be sure, Led Zeppelin was still definitely on everybody's minds. The band was still huge, having issued five records by this point, the most recent being 1973's *Houses of the Holy*. But there was a sense that a new guard was needed. Deep Purple was splintering, and Black Sabbath was getting tired. Odd man out of the big British institutions and soon to be forgotten, Uriah Heep were at their modest peak, having just issued *Sweet Freedom* and a well-regarded double live album, *Heep*. They would figure prominently in the early history of Rush.

In the prog world, the big bands — Tull, ELP, Yes, Genesis, less so King Crimson — were all a clutch of records into their careers and doing good business. Over in North America, the likes of Mountain and Cactus were delegated to Nowheresville. The New York Dolls were about to fizzle, despite a second record in May of '74. Kiss issued their debut in February of '74. Aerosmith issued their second album, the well-regarded *Get Your Wings*, the same month *Rush* came out, albeit as a Canuck indie. Bad Company would debut in June, playing the kind of hard blues rock Rush was about to put aside.

Up in Canada, April Wine had just issued their third album, *Electric Jewels*, but more pertinently, Bachman–Turner Overdrive was garnering some success with their first couple of albums. BTO being Canadian and selling records south of the border factored favorably in Rush getting their major label deal with Mercury Records out of Chicago. In fact, in the ensuing press materials for the U.S. release of Rush, the label boasted, "With the release of the third Bachman–Turner Overdrive album and the *Rush* album on the same day, we'd like to make one thing perfectly clear: Mercury has *two* Canadian bands."

Back to the opening track on the *Rush* album, there was also something Zeppelin-esque about Alex's exciting guitar intro. His style, to be sure, but even the very idea of solo electric guitar chords taking center stage. Also to be fair to the comparison, the guys in Rush loved Zeppelin.

"One of the records that really stands out was the first Led Zeppelin album," says Alex when asked to name key inspirations. "Because it was only available as an import when we — or when

I — ordered it. I went down, and there were only six or eight copies that came in. And I remember picking it up at night, at eight o'clock or something, and racing back and getting together with Ged. And we looked at it, oh my God, it's a piece of gold. Put it on and we listened to it together and it was a life experience for the two of us."

"Everything was right about that band," agrees Geddy, while also differing on a key detail. "God, what wasn't? From the minute . . . I remember the first time John Rutsey brought that record over to my house, I was sitting there with Alex, and the three of us . . . he put that first riff on and it just had magic. The guitar sounds were amazing, and nobody had heard Robert Plant before. Nobody had heard a singer with that audacity, control, energy. The sound of John Bonham's drums, all anchored by John Paul Jones's rooted, super-cool bass licks. I mean they were just the perfect band. When I first heard them, the three of us looked at each other, like this is the kind of stuff we dreamed of creating, and here's a band that created it and had the chops to pull it off.

"And they were progressive, you know? They were rooted in blues, they had that jam-ability of the long solos, but they started bringing other influences in, and their influences weren't so much different instruments, but they brought different cultural influences in. Different modes, different tonalities, and Jimmy Page was the kind of guitar player that had so much confidence in his writing, he wasn't afraid to put in a guitar solo that wasn't heavy. That had a dinky sound. Of course, we would be shocked. So he had diversity and confidence within their own writing abilities, right? They threw all these different flavors into that kind of rock thing, and that was a progressive idea. A fresh idea."

That's a key point. Though Rush didn't act particularly Zeppelin-esque from moment to moment, the spirit of a record like *Caress of Steel* or *2112* upholds that sense of surprise, the peaks and valleys, the light and shade, as Jimmy so famously frames it, that Zeppelin had.

"Oh, it was Mighty Monday, they called it," continues Ged, on getting to witness the mighty Zep live. "It was right around the corner at the Masonic Temple. And we'd gotten tickets and we waited. John, Alex and myself, the three of us went together. It may be one of the few times we went to a concert together. But we lined up for hours out front. John had seen Zeppelin already — that was their second appearance in Toronto. They had come through, I think, six months earlier, before the record was released in Canada. And I think they were playing with the Faces, opening for them or something. And John used to go to a club called the Rock Pile, which is now the Masonic Temple. You could be a member. I think I still have my Rock Pile membership card somewhere. It was all a very Haight-Ashbury vibe."

Led Zeppelin's first appearance in Toronto, at this venue on Yonge Street just north of Bloor, was on February 2, 1969. Their second, the one Alex, Geddy and John all attended, was on August 18 of the same year.

"So John said if this band comes back, you have to come see them. But by then, of course, they were now breaking in America hugely. And we lined up and we waited, and we were in basically the second row, sitting on the floor at the Masonic Temple. And I think they opened the show with 'Train Kept A-Rollin',' and you'd never heard a sound like that. And it was just like Page didn't walk out onto the stage, he floated out onto the stage. We were in complete awe of these guys. And it was so hot. There was a heat wave going on in Toronto at the time and we were just melting. Didn't care. Plaster was falling off the ceiling as they played on and on. It was just an amazing show. We were completely blown away by them. Dedicated fans forever after that. But everybody loved that record. It didn't matter what they did afterwards. And that song 'Communication Breakdown' was the song. At least for us, in our group of friends, that just killed it. And we were like, whew, 'We're not worthy.'"

Ian Grandy says that after John had seen Zep the first time, the band got the album and were poring over it within a few days, learning three or four songs from it to put into their set, with Alex even adopting Jimmy's violin bow idea. Once Alex got to see the band, he recalls leaping up and Jimmy noticing him and giving him a head nod.

Despite the persistent comparisons in the press, Terry Brown somewhat dismisses the idea that Rush was Canada's Led Zeppelin. "I'm not so sure. They sounded like Led Zeppelin, so the press said. I didn't hear that myself; I must've missed it, but I didn't feel that. And certainly working with them, that wasn't the band that came to mind. But there was a lot of talk about that. So there was a lot of negative press. And, in fact, when the record came out, it was a hard sell. As far as the English scene goes, I don't know if they would have had an easier time in England. No, I don't think they would have, frankly. From what I know working in England, there were some pretty hot bands coming through the studio every day of the week. So maybe they would have been a small fish in a bigger pond. There was more of a unique writing thing going on that I didn't hear from Led Zeppelin, which was more blues-based. So I think for me, I never drew that comparison. It was the furthest thing from my mind."

Next on *Rush* comes "Need Some Love," another fresh recording from the Terry Brown sessions. At 2:19, this is a quick and energetic rocker, tight and almost rigid against a half-time chorus that grooves nicely. The half-time vibe sticks around for Alex's reverb-drenched solo, which is very professionally integrated into what's going on, basically multiple tracks of guitar. In fact, the guys seem to be enjoying John riding his ride cymbal so much that the last half of the song is all conducted at this pace, with Alex taking us out with Gibson/Marshall-textured divebomb chords that are Jimmy Page all day.

"Take a Friend" is mostly drawn from the funky barroom hard rock of the day, nothing special, very 1974, save for the dramatic prog rock intro sequence, which reprises briefly at the end. For this one, the band used the original Eastern Sound recordings and there's really no significant difference between those and the newer recordings — the sound is fine, but the songwriting is dated and relatively unremarkable. Still, "Take a Friend" is pretty heavy for a Canadian band in 1974. It's drenched in guitars, and then there's that singer, who we get to hear belt it out solo after a stark stop, Geddy further shocking the listener with echo applied to his voice. Much of the rest of the time, he's singing harmony with himself. Back behind the drums, John keeps admirably busy.

Side one of the original vinyl closes with "Here Again," at 7:34, a long dirge that evokes images not only of future soft Rush passages from the prog era but also similar marriages of blues boom and doom we hear from the likes of the U.K. big four, namely Sabbath, Purple, Zeppelin and Uriah Heep. This one comes from the Toronto Sound sessions and features multiple guitar textures from Alex, including acoustic. Geddy is singing high and extreme, and again, to be fair to the comparisons, his blues phrasings evoke those of Robert Plant. Interesting though, if heavy metal is a form of post-boom British blues music, so are these sort of morose, hard-hitting ballads.

"I wrote the lyrics on 'Here Again,' but everything else was just sort of thrown together," recalls Alex. "The funny thing is John was the lyricist in the band at the time, and he wouldn't submit the lyrics for any of these songs. So Geddy had to quickly put some lyrics together for it. And I think John probably regretted that his whole life. There were the lyrics we were using for these songs live, but he didn't want them to be on the songs. It was just like, 'Well, why?' 'I just don't.' 'Well, all right.' So they were a rush job, and it shows."

Geddy recalls this slightly differently. "We used to write the songs, and John would write lyrics. And sometimes he would say to us, 'I don't have them ready yet,' so I'd say, 'Well, I'll just make some stuff up. I'll just sing some off-the-cuff lyrics until you're ready with it,' when we were doing bars and stuff. So when it came time to record those songs that I'd been bluffing, I said, 'Okay, where are the lyrics?' And he said, 'Well, I didn't like them, so I tore them all up.' And I was supposed to start recording that day. So I just sat down in the studio and started scribbling off lyrics and wrote as many as I could. And they ended up being the lyrics for those songs on the first album. It was all done over a period of two days because we didn't have any lyrics. I don't know what was going on in John's head. All I knew is that I kept asking for lyrics and he kept saying they were coming and one day he said, 'I tore them up. They're not happening.' He was not . . . he had moments that were not strictly logical."

And so from day one, on the original Moon issue to this day, the credit for all the material reads "Lee & Lifeson," with the exception of "In the Mood," which goes to Geddy alone. The production credit on the record goes to RUSH (all caps), with a pointless executive production credit going to SRO. David Stock is not mentioned at all, and Terry is called a remix engineer.

As for how the album fits into the blues boom, side one opens with "What You're Doing," which demonstrates how some considerably heavy metal can still harbor pronounced connections to the blues. Indeed, the entire structure of this song is that of a blues song, and yet it's the heaviest song on the record. Compare it with "Wicked World" by Black Sabbath — both are doomy, both dovetail in modern heavy metal riffing, but both sit on sturdy blues frames. "What You're Doing" is one of the songs on *Rush* that makes use of the bed tracks from the David Stock sessions but was then worked on a fair bit by Terry as well as the band, who did some overdubs.

Next on *Rush* is the insanely catchy "In the Mood," opened in fine '70s style with a little cowbell. Geddy says this one, besides being the first song he and Alex wrote together that he "kind of liked," is also the first Rush song he ever heard on the radio — though he and Alex have also been known to say that "Finding My Way" was the first Rush song they had heard on the radio, courtesy of Dave Marsden and CFNY. Again, "In the Mood" hails from the original Eastern Sound sessions, and it sounds fine.

"Before and After" is a languid instrumental ballad for its front half, suddenly turning aggressive rocker for its back half — the band throwing both Led Zeppelin and Black Sabbath shapes. John Rutsey had to be fairly active here, closer to what an early Neil Peart might do. Like "What You're Doing," this is another song that was worked on both "before and after," across both recording sessions.

The closing track on *Rush* is "Working Man," which has gone on to be one of the most famed and beloved of the band's anthems. "Finding My Way" and to a lesser extent "In the Mood" and "What You're Doing" live on too with some modicum of stature, but it is "Working Man" that was the band's first classic.

"The songs were written over a long period of time, as most bands' first albums are," notes Geddy. "For a lot of bands, their first album is their best album because it's a collection of material they've been working on for their entire childhood, for the whole prehistory of the band. People consider a band not to exist until they record. So on our first album, those songs had been hanging around quite a while. We'd been playing them in bars and so the recording was quick, but the songs had been around. It is a bit weird to consider that history is still hanging around us, is still kind of following us. I guess there are some songs like 'Working Man' and 'Finding My Way' that have become just identifiable as our songs, so they're there to stay."

"We were playing those songs for three years when we recorded them," seconds Alex. "Really, we went in and we hit record and played them and that was it. I wish it could have been like that all the time; it was so simple. We knew those songs inside out, so it was quite easy to do that. Those records hold up and those songs hold up, and we were recording on eight or sixteen tracks. Now you have an unlimited number of tracks and it gets so involved, and I think you miss the point sometimes. If you got those great results in such a limited environment, why not continue doing that instead of making things overly complicated and expensive?"

The architecture of Alex's riff in "Working Man" is interesting; it's Sabbath-like and sludgy, remembered in the brain as slow, and yet technically the song is fairly up-tempo. Also adding to the slow vibe is the track's seven-minute length, its huge descending note sequences, its massive concert-ending wind-up, as well as the fact that a lot of it is jammy. (Of note, if, after so many years, you've gotten bored with the jammy bits, in 2008, Rush unearthed a version with a completely different guitar solo, designated a "vault version." This allows the long-time Rush fan to love "Working Man" all over again.) But, yes, it's easy to compare "Working Man" to "Dazed and Confused" or Ted Nugent's "Stranglehold" or, philosophically speaking as well as musically, Lynyrd Skynyrd's "Simple Man." But again, it moves at a brisk clip. All told, a lot happens in the song, and on top of that, there's Geddy's lyric, which captured the plight of working men everywhere and especially notable to our story, Cleveland.

"There were a few of those moments, I think, and one of them was when our record got sent to the U.S.," explains Geddy. "A friend of ours who worked for a record company here who was not associated with us but just a friend liked the record and he sent the record to a woman named Donna Halper at WMMS in Cleveland. She started playing the record as an import, which gosh, I mean radio stations used to do that stuff back then. And she got a lot of calls, phones lit up, and really that was a pivotal moment for us."

Adds Alex, "Donna was a program director at WMMS in Cleveland, and she got a copy of the record from Bob Roper, a friend of ours who was working at Warner Brothers at the time. 'Here's this local Toronto band that you might be really interested in; here's a copy of the record — check it out.' She played it and got really great phone response, late night kind of thing."

"That very first Moon record, the record that Bob Roper sent me, I put on the turntable and played 'Working Man,'" recalls Halper. "And to this day, when I look at it, I can still see myself saying, 'This isn't on A&M. Why is he sending me this?' And just dropping the needle on 'Working Man' and going, 'Oh my God, this is a Cleveland record.' I had no idea at the time that it was going to take off the way it did, but boy did I know that was going to be a record for us. And this is it — this is the record!"

Chuckling at the memory of how the cover looked, Donna notes that it was in fact slightly better than the eventual issue on Mercury, where the logo went from the original red to pink. "Oh God, moments of pain. Moments of suffering. What they did was they just changed the color to probably the most ugly shade of fuchsia that I've ever seen in my life. And I must tell you, I don't like the pictures on the back of the record album — I really don't. To me it looked kind of like a 'loving hands at home' production. It's like quick, get the Polaroid. Here's a picture of you and a picture of you and a picture of you. And I don't really think that these pictures reflect who the guys are. I remember looking at it and thinking it really did look like somebody down in somebody's basement put it all together. But again, back in those days, you got stuff like that sometimes."

Filling in the details of how a radio station in Cleveland pretty much broke Rush in the States, Donna explains, "Once upon a time in a kingdom far away, I was the music director at WMMS in Cleveland. And that was a big deal. And in those days, Cleveland was known for being a rock 'n' roll town, and WMMS had just taken over as the number one rock station in Cleveland, back in the days when a music director and a program director could get songs added without going through some committee in another city and didn't have to listen to anyone. We basically made decisions.

"So I was up in my office, and I was listening to the new music . . . We actually did that, we actually listened to new music! And we were deciding what we wanted to play that week, and that's not the royal we. It was a committee of people on the staff. I was the go-to person as the music director, and John Gorman was the program director, and he had the final say, but we saw eye-to-eye on a lot of stuff. We knew what was right for Cleveland. So I was going through all the normal records, and suddenly I get this thing from Canada — and it comes from A&M of Canada. Now, I had a friend at A&M in Canada, and I had been a music director for a lot of years, and I knew a lot of the record promoters, and I always played Canadian music. I kind of believe that I'm spiritually Canadian. I spent a lot of time up in Montreal, spent a lot of time in Toronto, love both cities, so it wasn't a surprise to me to see something from A&M of Canada. Except when I opened it, it wasn't an A&M of Canada record. It had a little note attached from Bob Roper. And Bob Roper at the time was the record promoter for A&M of Canada. And it was basically 'Our label passed on this, but I think it's a good record for Cleveland. Tell me what you think of it.'"

As Donna alluded to, she played "Working Man" first. Her initial thought was "this looks like it's more than seven minutes long — okay, bathroom song." Meaning, if you needed to rush off to the washroom while you were on air, you had enough time to do your business without the song running out.

"But then I listened to the first two chords," she continues. "Now, I don't know who the band are. I've no idea. Rush. Somebody who knows Bob Roper, fine with me. But I just knew immediately that this record was an excellent record, okay? And I dropped the needle in a few other places. I found 'Finding My Way' and I found 'Here Again,' which I thought was a really good song. Nobody talks about that song that much, but excellent record. And I listened to a few things that sounded like your basic bar band, like 'In the Mood.' Didn't matter; 'Working Man,' I thought, was going to be the song. That was the top track on the album.

"I ran downstairs to the guy who was on the air. His name was Denny Sanders. Denny is a wonderful human being with a good ear for music. We also see eye-to-eye on a lot of stuff. I said, 'Denny, you've got to listen to this.' So he dropped the needle and said, 'Yes, this is pretty good. New Zeppelin?' And I said, 'No, not Zeppelin. Canadian band, Rush. Nobody's ever heard of them.' Now we had heard of this Montreal band called Mahogany Rush none of us could particularly stand. No offense, but they didn't do anything for us. We played some other stuff, but the audience never responded to it. This record, we just instantly felt the audience was going to respond to it. Not only because it's good music, but that the lyrics are going to relate. Cleveland is a working-class town. 'They call me the working man / that's what I am,' the whole thing."

So they played the record and listeners started calling in asking for more of the new Led Zeppelin album.

"Yes, and any time the record was played," Donna remembers, "it was 'Where can I get one? Where can I get one?' 'You can't. I have one copy.' Bob Roper put me in touch with Moon Records, and Vic Wilson and Ray Danniels, and I said to them, 'Hey, you guys have a hit song down here in Cleveland.' And they're like, 'We do?' And I said yes. They didn't know that Bob Roper had sent it out. So they shipped a box of them to WMMS, and we got them into a store called Record Revolution. Record Revolution sold imports all the time, and this of course was a Canadian import."

"I remember talking to her in the early days, and she was very excited about it and she was getting good feedback," recalls Ray. "And keep in mind, this is Cleveland forty-something years ago, before it became part of the so-called Rust Belt. That was one of the most important breakout markets in America. As was Pittsburgh, at the time. These cities had twice the population thirty-five years ago than they have now. And they were very important breakthrough markets. So we were lucky to have the two of them. And then St. Louis was probably the third major market we had. That was music that worked. The kind of bands that Rush would have followed would have done well in those areas. These were great hard rock areas. You wouldn't expect Rush to break in the southern United States or, at the time, to be a West Coast band. You really needed the Northeast and Midwest to come first, and that's what happened."

Styx, Ted Nugent, REO Speedwagon, Blue Öyster Cult, Uriah Heep, Kiss, Aerosmith . . . these were all bands that broke in the Midwest, in the Rust Belt. In fact, when Aerosmith deemed their fan base the "blue army," they were talking about concert-goers from Middle America, referring to their uniform, namely jeans and jean jacket.

Donna articulates why a song like "Working Man" might have resonated in America's hotbed of manufacturing. "Well, first of all, the listeners to WMMS were very musically savvy. They weren't just looking for three-chord rock 'n' roll, bang bang bang. They were looking for three-chord rock 'n' roll with something to say. They were very lyrically oriented; it was surprising. We took some records that hadn't been hits and brought them back and they became hits. Like Aerosmith and 'Dream On.' That had died a painful death the first time it was released. WMMS got behind it, smash hit, okay? And I have a feeling it's because the lyrics hit the people, you know, 'Dream on, dream until your dreams come true.' People working in the factories, middle-class, lower middle-class city, where the only thing there to do is either go to concerts or go to the bars. I'm not insulting Cleveland, I'm just saying it hadn't really developed as a major market. Today you go there, and it's an incredibly cosmopolitan city. Back then, it was a factory town. I mean, Republic Steel was the dominant industry. The skies were orange with pollution, and they had a mayor who was like a joke, and his name was Ralph Perk, and he was doing something with a blowtorch one day opening a factory and he lit his hair on fire. It was like that. Cleveland was kind of a joke. I didn't know about that; I was from Boston.

"But the song 'Working Man' — 'I get up at seven, go to work at nine. Got no time for living, yeah, working all the time. Seems to me I should live my life a lot better than I think I am. I guess that's why they call me the working man.' — Cleveland was not a city of sixty-three colleges and universities, okay? I'm not saying there were no universities. There are some wonderful universities in Cleveland. But the average listener to WMMS wanted a kind of catharsis; they wanted to hear songs that were about their life. They wanted to hear songs that make them think this is exactly my experience. The first Rush album, yeah, it was a lot more primitive in terms of the musicianship. Neil hadn't joined yet, and I'm not saying anything bad about John Rutsey, but it was very three-chord rock 'n' roll at that point in time. But people listened and they heard their experience. They heard their life.

"Gradually people start asking for more of it and more of it," continues Halper. "People want to hear more tunes from the record. We start playing 'Finding My Way' — it does excellent for us. That opening chord, to this day, I can't listen to 'Finding My Way' without getting the chills. It took me back to a time and place and it seemed to do that with the listeners as well. But, yes, ultimately I'm able to prevail on a local record promoter to get them down for a gig with another band."

"It's still huge," agrees manager Ray Danniels on the importance of the Midwest. "But there's been a demographic shift. When you look now, you go, Jesus, Rush is now so freaking big in Florida and places like that. Well, yeah — guess how many people from Milwaukee and St. Louis moved to Florida in the last fifteen years? So that's part of it. I've watched the shift. We were not a band that was big in Phoenix in the early days. These days, Phoenix is a very big market for us. And it is that big shift, that so-called Rust Belt, where people left the northern Midwest and moved south."

At this point, Rush had been touring hard on the backs of the Canadian release of the album, basically blanketing Ontario. Cleveland would not be the band's first U.S. show though. On May 18, 1974, they played the Northside Drive-In in Lansing, Michigan. The Cleveland show was the second, however, with Rush playing with ZZ Top and Locomotiv GT on June 28.

Confirms Geddy, "Our first American gig was in Lansing, Michigan, at an outdoor drive-in, and it was some sort of festival-type atmosphere, but low-scale. We played that gig, and it went pretty well. And then due to our popularity in Cleveland through this radio play, we got a gig at the Allen Theatre opening for ZZ Top. Which was crazy. John was with us still, and we went down, and we played the set. I guess it was a thirty-, forty-minute set that we played, and it was our first American experience. A real gig, and it was awesome. It was freaky. People were actually making a big deal about us being there and that was so weird for us."

"I had gone to New York," adds Ray, "and I was buying up shows, and eventually got close enough to an agent that I was able to get a show for Rush in Cleveland, with ZZ Top. So combined with the fact that there was a little bit of airplay and we were on our way, we actually sent enough imports there, that the record charted in the Top 30 in sales. And then after that, we went and played Pittsburgh and somewhere else in the immediate area, and it started from there. And then Donna stayed with the record and played the second and third tracks off of it. It wasn't the whole country that caught on, but bit by bit we got market after market and started touring down there and the rest is history."

"All I know is that when they came to town, people knew who they were," continues Donna. "I'm not going to say everybody knew, but people are seeing that and relating to the picture on the album cover, and people are sitting in the front row at the Allen Theatre and they are applauding and singing along with some of the songs. They looked nervous, and yet on the other hand, there was just something about them. You knew that this was not going to be like, 'Oh, they have one record and were never heard from again.' I just had a sense that it was going to be a successful career for them. Their manager, Vic Wilson, was standing at the back of the theater, and I was standing with him, and he said to me, 'Don't worry, Donna; we won't let you down.' And they never have. They never have."

Donna Halper also had a hand in bringing Rush to the attention of Cliff Burnstein, then working with Mercury Records out of Chicago.

"Absolutely, yes, of course. There are about ninety people who claim to have done that. But absolutely, when you are the music director at a major station, and when that station is known for breaking new music, other stations watch what you're playing. Sometimes they start playing it too. Pretty soon you start getting calls. You get calls from promoters. I'm not talking record promoters; I'm talking concert promoters. There was a concert promotion company, Belkin Productions, the big concert promoters in town, and they were the ones who were ultimately going to put Rush on. And they did it partially because, well, the management, but partially because the songs were getting played on WMMS and they watched WMMS.

"The same deal with the record companies. I remember very clearly four record companies calling me, and each one of them saying, 'Hey, we hear you are friends with this band. And we hear you have some influence with them.' And I'm like, 'I do? Okay . . .' And 'Would you tell them to sign with us?' And they were making their case to me, and that's not as unusual as it sounds. Again, back then, music directors and program directors had a lot of influence. Nothing was done by committee back then on who gets signed. But on the other hand, if you can actually get a name to the artists and repertoire director or whatever, it may end up getting signed. So there was interest in them."

"We could kind of see it coming, once Cleveland radio started playing so much of it," remembers Geddy, on the subject of label interest. "Donna Halper at WMMS was such a big supporter, and she really created all that excitement and the record got so much response from fans. I guess you could say she gave us the opportunity, but the fans created the excitement by phoning and requesting 'Working Man' and 'Finding My Way' over and over and over again. That's what got all the attention, and then we almost signed with Casablanca Records. We were very close to doing that. That was huge to us. We were beside ourselves. That was the Kiss label, and we were kind of close to signing with them. We had an offer from them, and we were going to take it.

"And then at the eleventh hour we got this phone call from Cliff Burnstein in Chicago; he worked for Mercury Records, and nobody was in the office apparently. He got a copy of the record and loved it, but nobody who had any signing authority . . . he was just a promo guy, the national promo director, I think, radio promo. Nobody with any signing authority was around. And he heard that we were on the verge of signing with another label. I think he called Ray and said, 'Don't; wait, please wait. Don't do that. I'll give you an offer.' And in a very short time, we'd signed with them."

Continues Halper, "Cliff and I had a very good relationship. And I played some of his records in the past. He had BTO and some others that weren't that great, but sometimes you play records because you like the promoters and the band has maybe a little bit of potential. And Cliff was a sweetheart. We got along well, and he said to me, 'I really want to sign this band for Mercury.' And I said, 'Why do you want to sign this band for Mercury? I love you dearly, but seriously? You guys don't have a lot of rock bands. There are other labels who want to sign them.' And he said, 'That's the point; we don't have a lot of rock bands. We would make them a priority.' And that really resonated with me. Because I didn't want them to get signed with a label where they would be completely lost, like CBS, Columbia in those days, or RCA. There was nothing wrong with those labels, but I just felt they would be a number or a name with those labels. But a smaller label who have made them a priority, I thought that would really make a difference.

"First he had to listen to it," says Donna when asked what Cliff thought of Rush in those days. "And when he did, he was pleasantly surprised, as many people were. Same thing, he listened to 'Working Man,' and what he said was not printable for a family audience. I think he said it was great, and you can fill in the blanks from there. But he got really enthusiastic about it. It had gone from 'We're getting a lot of buzz about this from WMMS' to 'Wow, now I know *why* we're getting a lot of buzz about this from WMMS.' And true to his word, he did make it a priority and he really went out of his way to promote the band."

"I don't know if Cliff had known at the time," reflects Ray, "but there were two labels in the States that were interested at the same time. Columbia was also interested in them, but the person at Columbia who was interested in them was a producer of some regard, and of course, he saw his imprint all over it. He wanted to produce them. And I don't think it was something the band were responsive to. Keep in mind, it was a very, very different climate. There were thirty different labels. Look at Universal today. Universal is now fourteen or sixteen of those stand-alone labels that were all bought out, bought up over the years, in a very consolidated business. So we had a lot of places we could have gone, companies who were really interested. And Cliff was definitely a cheerleader for them there. The head of A&R was not as rock-savvy as Cliff was, but he got that something was going on. And the deal did happen fairly quickly. And I thought we would be better served there at a small label, which had had a big success with Bachman–Turner Overdrive. They had proven that they could take a Canadian rock band and exploit it across the border. It seemed like the right move, and Cliff's enthusiasm was huge."

Earlier on, back in Canada, "Nobody took to it, nobody saw it," scoffs Ray, "except London Records at the time, which was one of the labels that was based in Montreal instead of Toronto. And they pitched me on a distribution deal, which basically meant that they weren't going to be the label, but they were going to put it in stores if I financed the physical records. So once again, we had to — or *I* had to — find the money to manufacture and do everything on our own. And they, for a percentage, would put the record in stores. But they weren't willing to sign them directly on London on their own. So it was interesting times. It's funny now that after forty years, the business has gone back to that model."

"I had been there less than a year," begins Cliff, who says that he first became aware of Rush in late June of 1974. "My job was promoting albums to rock radio stations in Chicago; that's where Mercury was. It was a Monday morning and I came in before nine o'clock, because I always did, and there was a note from the assistant to the president, his name was Marion Reese, asking me to listen to an album, because it was submitted, looking for a deal. And nobody else was around that day. And this was not my job, as a promotion guy. But it said, 'Would you listen to this and let the president know what you think?' The president was also out of town; he was on the West Coast.

"So I look at the package, and there's a cover letter, and it's coming from Ira Blacker, who is a booking agent at ATI, in New York, a booking agency pretty famous for its rock roster at that time. It was eight forty-five in the morning on a Monday, and I had read in *Creem* magazine about a group called Mahogany Rush, with Frank Marino, who was Canadian, and I was sure they were looking for a deal. But they were already famous. Frank Marino was supposed to be an amazing guitar player; I'd never heard him. So maybe this was actually Mahogany Rush, or maybe Mahogany Rush changed their name to Rush. I wasn't sure. Didn't make any sense to me.

"But nevertheless, I put on the record, and this was 1974, so they were real records, vinyl, twelve inch, and I put the first song on, and heard 'Finding My Way,' first track, on the first Rush album, and got so excited I didn't want to continue to listen. I called Donna Halper, who was the music director at WMMS in Cleveland, because here's Ira Blacker claiming it's selling in Cleveland — she's going to know. So I get her on the phone, probably shortly after nine, and ask her about Rush, and she says, 'Yeah, we are playing the record here. And it's already sold a few thousand imports. It's really hot.' And I said, 'Yeah, "Finding My Way," it just kills me.' And she says, 'Have you listened to the whole album?' I said no. She says, 'Wait until you get to "Working Man" — it's unbelievable. It's the last track on the album, side two.' And I said, 'Okay, I'm getting off the phone now and I'll listen to the rest of the album.'"

"And 'Working Man' was amazing," continues Burnstein. "When you heard it, and you heard a three-man band doing this, you kind of thought back to Cream, like wow, power trio, and I kind of put myself back into that headspace. And that's pretty exciting, how good these guys were. It sounded like they had musicianship on all levels. Obviously, it's always the song that kind of gets you the very first thing, and Geddy's voice gets you immediately. But when you listen to 'Working Man,' you just hear like very progressive, intricate playing, and that's exciting. That's exciting to hear that there is a three-man band that can do that kind of thing. And so I went over to the assistant to the president and said, 'Hey Marion, get Irwin Steinberg.' And I pushed him a bit, 'We should absolutely sign them.' And I actually had a conference call, possibly for the first time in my life, between Ira Blacker in New York at ATI and Irwin Steinberg, the president of Mercury, and me in the middle, and a deal was worked out by the end of the day."

"The deal was so much money per album, and two albums a year, that we had to deliver," says Vic. The advance was $75,000, as part of a $200,000 package. "And it was a five-year deal. It changed later on because we were re-signed. I think it was after *2112* that we re-signed and did another contract with them. In those days, any deal was a good deal . . . I mean, nobody wanted those kinds of bands. We were in a roster of bands like BTO. They had all kinds of Black acts that were very well known for that. And country. Huge country roster on Mercury. So we were just happy that we got a record deal. And it was sufficient money; we knew we could do the albums with that, so everything was covered. We were in heaven."

"They were in a hurry," says Donna, with respect to the repackaging of the record for American sale. "They wanted to get the damn thing out. So what they did was, they just changed the color of 'Rush' on the front and everything else was the same." Except, that is, for an added line of text in the credits on the back that reads, "With Special Thanks to Donna Halper of WMMS in Cleveland for getting the ball rolling."

"I wasn't expecting that," adds Donna. "I was very surprised that they did that. I was profoundly grateful, I've got to tell you."

"It was very exciting to get a deal," muses Alex. "I mean just to have people interested. We had a number of A&R guys come and see us play, at clubs and dances and things like that. But nobody was really that interested. And when Donna Halper played the first album, and Cliff Burnstein got wind of it and made an offer as quickly as he did, that was very, very exciting. Somebody actually wanted us. It was like we weren't fighting to get a deal. Somebody wanted us. And there was an advance, so we went out and went shopping. We went to Long & McQuade in Toronto and bought all new gear, new amps, and I had one little cabinet and a head, and that was it, and that was rented for years and years before I could actually buy it. To go in there and buy Marshall stacks and a couple of extra guitars, it was like a dream come true. That was one of the highlights of my life, that day in the music store, just being completely open-ended with everything that we bought. That was very cool. It wasn't really that big of an advance, but we managed to do some pretty good damage."

And this was a pronounced step up. Sure, a Canadian deal would have been preferable to issuing a record independently, but stories abound at how being signed in Canada could hold you back for years in terms of making advances in America.

"Well, yes, plus there was no one in Canada to sign you," says Alex. "I can't even remember the companies that we approached, but they were the K-Tel sort of companies, hoping to get some sort of deal. First of all, no one was interested in us. You had to get an American deal if you wanted to do anything. Absolutely, you had to. But you're desperate, and you want a record deal so badly, and you want to have your records out, and I think you would almost take anything. And that happens to a lot of musicians. They go for whatever the deal is because they just gotta have it. So we were very fortunate. Cliff Burnstein is a genius, and he had the foresight to see that there was something in our band that would stick around for a while, and he was right. I didn't see it at the time, but he certainly did. He's really, really brilliant, and I'm sure Cliff remembers everything vividly. He's a very bright guy, and he knows the music industry inside out, every aspect of it, and I mean he's worked with so many great people and managed some of the biggest artists in music history."

•

Simultaneous with getting the Mercury deal, Rush was working on cycling out 33 percent of its membership — no small percentage, but that's one of the problems with a trio.

"I do recall being taken aside by the band and their management," remembers Liam Birt. "And it was explained to myself and their other tech at that time that John was going to be leaving the band and were we okay with it. Not that we were necessarily given the choice, but I think it was just a courtesy to let us know that he was leaving. John had health issues, which, when the band decided that they really needed to tour very extensively, they understood the fact that he probably wasn't physically up to the task. There were rumors that other issues came into play, but I honestly don't know which of them to believe, if anything. I think it was really a matter of he just didn't want to physically continue with the touring aspect, and it was taking its toll physically.

"The closeness factor was different in those days; things happened, and life just went on. We were much younger. I was close to John too, but I'd only really known him for a couple of years. So it was a change of personnel, and a new person was introduced and the entity was continuing. Again, initially, in those early days, you went along for the ride. The overall impression that I got is that they seemed to think that unless John was replaced, he might possibly physically break down during the tour. But the communication really wasn't there. It wasn't like today when you pick up your cell phone and call someone. We didn't even have fax machines back then, which is hard to imagine. But we weren't necessarily the most informed in those days. It was just 'There's a change happening,' and 'Are you going to be good with it or not?' Well, of course you were."

"John Rutsey was a diabetic," says Donna Halper. "He was not going to be able to be out on the road very much. We forget today, but back in the 1970s, if you were on insulin, you had to go to the hospital. I mean, there you are, out on the road as a rock band, and he was not going to work out. And they wanted a new direction."

"Changing drummers ten days before the tour starts — that was exciting," says Vic, laughing. "It was exciting to get the record deal. We were all just blown away, but when you have to release someone from their duties and hire another person, and you've only got . . . well, we had a little more than that, but by the time they went through a couple of drummers before Neil was brought in, it was ten days before the tour started."

"Oh yeah, it was mad," remembers Geddy. "That was crazy. As excited as we were at getting that deal, at the same time the band was kind of imploding because it was clear that there were problems with John. He wasn't happy, and there were some mixed feelings going on. I was ecstatic because we had gotten an advance and I could buy a new bass and everybody could get new gear. You know, that was the most exciting part of it. But also there had been problems with John. His secretive side was becoming more and more what he was all about, and he was disconnecting from us more and more, from when we recorded the record and the problems we had with his lyrics and all that, the fact that he threw them all away . . . there was trouble brewing. And he was making noises like he wasn't so sure this was the kind of life he wanted to lead. And so it was kind of bittersweet happiness. And then Alex and I were ecstatic that we had this situation that resolved itself quickly when he kind of bowed out.

"To be frank, we had been looking about for quite some time. Because it was obvious he wasn't happy and we weren't happy, and so it wasn't a new concept. You know, the incident with recording the record and the lyrics and all that left a damaged feeling between us. And he was becoming, as I said earlier, more and more secretive. So we kind of resigned ourselves to the fact that he probably was not going to stay. Either he's going to make a move or we're going to make a move, sooner or later. So we were looking around, and it was frightening because we didn't know who we would find. We tried to lure one guy away from another band and that didn't work out. And that led to mixed emotions too, because he kind of said he would join us and then he changed his mind. And so then we just kept on looking until, in fact, John left the band. And then we were like, okay, I'm glad somebody made the decision here. And then we just had . . . auditions. Which is scary because, I mean, it's a three-piece band. So you miss one guy, it's a big part of the band. It was scary and we didn't know how it was going to go. But we were so young. Everything is dramatic when you're young, and again, you just deal. You just deal with it, you know? I think that kind of thing would be more dramatic today than then. I don't know, when you're younger, you just kind of go with the punches kind of thing.

"I think it's a bit of a company line," says Geddy, on the popular story that it was John's diabetes and general lack of taking care of himself that was the problem. "There's truth to that, and of course we were worried about his health, but John didn't really want to continue. He wasn't happy, and he was going through his own issues. So like I said, we were looking around. Alex and I knew that something was going to happen, and I think it was kind of a mutually agreed upon departure. But I think everybody wants to put the guy in the best possible light, so . . . It was difficult, but he was quite aloof from us in those days.

"He didn't really want to go on tour in America," explains Ged. "That whole idea was not amenable to him. And so it was like there was no choice. By his actions and his state of mind, it was clear that we had to go our own ways. If you could talk to him, he would've explained it a similar way. He wasn't in the same headspace as us. We were excited and ready to go on tour, ready to move on with our careers, and he was very hesitant. Maybe part of it was his health fears, and maybe part of it was the fact that he didn't feel as committed to the kind of music we were playing as Alex and I were. We'd already started writing some more complicated stuff, and I think he knew that and so everybody knew that it was best if we severed ties."

"First of all, when John left the band, we had a month or two of commitments," adds Alex. "And of course, he said, absolutely, I'll stay until we finish playing our gigs. And I tell you, we had so much fun. Those last couple of gigs together, we really had a great time. In fact, it was coming to the end of the summer and we were going somewhere else and John was staying behind, or going in his direction, and we all knew that was going to be kind of it. And after, we managed to keep in touch for a while, but after a few years, we didn't see each other for a long time.

"But this had been brewing for a while. Yes, John was sick a year earlier, and we had a fill-in. Jerry Fielding was his name, and he was a really, really nice guy and a really good drummer. We played a little bit together, and he was the first person that we thought of. He had other commitments at that time. We were concerned. We were together with John for six, seven years. So it was very nerve-racking. We always knew that we could probably go back to somebody like Jerry, for example, who would fill in, but that's not really what we wanted to do. And there was another drummer that had played in another band that were friends of ours that we sort of had our eyes on. But he ended up staying with that band. So it was a matter of auditioning drummers. We had a few names and we got in touch with them through our management company."

It's likely that the drummer Alex is referring to is Max Webster's Paul Kersey. "We had opened for them," begins Kersey. "I've got all this written down. It had to be '74 because that's when Rush was looking for a drummer. I remember Ray or Vic Wilson saying something to me about working hard onstage or something, harder than the other guys. And I went, 'What's that supposed to mean?' I didn't catch what he was talking about. They were just very complimentary, and I thought, 'Where is that coming from?' And then a couple weeks later, the onslaught started, where they started calling every day to try to talk me into joining Rush."

But Kim Mitchell, lead singer and guitarist for Max Webster, was less than pleased with the band's efforts to lure away their drummer. "Kim got word of it. That didn't take long, and it was a couple of uneasy weeks, maybe three weeks, where I was being bombarded by those guys. Mitchell was really getting pissed off that they would dare to break up his band. And Kim was saying, 'This is affecting our band,' and 'This is not right,' and he was getting really bummed about it. And I actually was going to do it. I almost did it. I was very, very, very close, but then I said no."

Paul never actually played with the guys in the end, but he says, "I met with them, and I met with Ray and Vic, who were saying, 'You wanna be a star, boy?' One of those deals. 'We'll guarantee you this much money, and we're going to be doing this and we're gonna be doing that. We've got this organized,' and on and on and on, just laying it on. They had an agent from New York calling me; they had people calling me from all over the place. I met the guys, 'yeah, we're gonna play here for a week, practice, and while we're playing, we're gonna get organized and tour right away.' And then it got moved up a week. 'Oh, we only have this much time. We need you right now.' Again, Kim was just flipping out. And it affected our gigs a little bit because my mind gets scrambled. It was pretty weird for a couple of weeks there."

As for Geddy and Alex, Paul says, "Oh, they were just guys in the band. They were just saying, you know, we can play. We'll be fine. Let's just go do it. It was Ray and Vic that were doing the hype. The management was doing their thing."

"We had a pretty good drummer in our band called Paul Kersey, and they asked him to join the band," confirms Kim, lead singer and guitarist for Max Webster. "And he came to us and said, 'Rush asked me to join their band.' And I'm like, 'Well, what are you going to do?' And he took a pass. So you kind of think, boy, Rush's career would have done something different had Paul Kersey come in the band. Because Paul Kersey, our drummer, was not a lyricist at all. He was just a drummer. So that whole thing . . . would they have written a bunch of 'In the Moods?' 'Hey, baby, it's a quarter to eight, I feel I'm in the mood.' I think all that other stuff would not have happened. As fate has it, it turned out pretty cool."

It seems that things were never quite the same between the guys and Rutsey. "I knew John since we were ten, so it was quite weird," says Lifeson, on dealing with John after he left. "And when I saw him, when we'd come back on those breaks, every two or three months, you would be at a party with him or something and it was always awkward. Because you didn't know what to talk about. 'Yeah, it's going great; we're playing all these places . . .' It was always very, very awkward talking to him about it. And I never really knew what his feelings were when he decided to leave. He didn't feel it was right. There were some musical differences, but he had juvenile diabetes and he was very self-conscious of his condition, and I think maybe he didn't feel like he had the strength to face the rigors of being on the road."

More specifically, with regard to the music, Alex says that "Geddy and I were interested in bands like Yes, King Crimson and Jethro Tull. We wanted to move our music more into that progressive area, and he was more straight-ahead rock 'n' roll — Bad Company, that kind of stuff — which was more of a cross section of what we were playing then in bars. And I think for a year before he left the band, we'd been pretty fed up with it. He got really, really sick; he had some other drug problems. But he got really sick at that time and we started auditioning other drummers and just playing with some other people. But he came back, and then when the prospect of signing this deal came up with Mercury — the tour, all of that — he got scared of the whole thing."

Perhaps not privy to the complicated passive-aggressive relationship Geddy and Alex had with John, Vic is firm in his belief that John had to go because of health issues. He says John was drinking and not taking care of himself, that he looked sickly and that he had to take it upon himself to make the decision.

"As far as I'm concerned," Vic says, "there was no saying that John wasn't doing his job. John was a writer in that band. So he was part of that whole family, and it wasn't for his ability to drum. Whether it would have developed like it developed with Neil, who knows? But I didn't want the responsibility of bringing him home in a box. So I said we have to replace him. For his health, or he's not going to be good to no one.

"But John was the leader because he would collect the money at gigs, bring it into the office. We would deposit it into the Rush account, pay their bills, and make sure the roadies were paid and Ian Grandy. And if there was any money left over, they got paid. If not, they can't get paid. Because they were all living at home. They worked hard, and for very little money in those days. Some days their pay weeks were five bucks. I can't tell you their feelings, but we all sat around and discussed it and they all agreed that they didn't want anything to go wrong with John. And if it meant replacing him, then it was okay. It's not that they wanted to. For me, I hadn't known him long. To me, he was just — not just a drummer, he was a nice guy — but the drummer in a band,

and we had to replace him. Now, for years after that, John would stop in and see me. So he didn't fall off the face of the earth. He would come and discuss a few things with me, what he was into, and I would talk with him, and off he would go. I'm sure he had regrets. Especially when they became successful. But in those days, there was no success. There was just a record deal, which he got his royalties from — to this day, some estate is getting royalties from Anthem Records."

Ian Grandy is pretty adamant that John was fired, saying that you can't party and have diabetes at the same time. Ian also says that his drum skills were slipping and that he relied too much on crash cymbals. As for his own lot in life at this point, he reflects, "You've got to understand, at twenty-three, I'm done school and I'm making fifty bucks a week and I'm committed to it. So I don't want the band to break up. When John was being let go, the other two came to me and told me that, and they said, 'We want you to stay, but if you want to go, we'll understand.' And I said, 'I'm in this now . . . this is my life now.'"

And even though John and Ian were friends, Ian at one point found himself living with Ray, which put him even more firmly in the Rush camp. "Oh, they were animals," laughs Ian, asked about Ray and also Vic. "It's funny, Danniels, when he started managing the band, he was only seventeen. He was actually born the same day and year as my brother, so I know exactly. And in '69, we got an apartment. It was supposed to be me, John Rutsey, some other guy and Ray. And the other guy and John didn't move in, so it was me and Ray living together for three months in an apartment. Wilson was the kind of manager that thought you should all be in a station wagon with a U-Haul behind you and don't get hotel rooms. You know, one of those guys. Like, this is the big leagues, Vic. Because I was John's friend, they were kind of wary about what to say to me. Even when they told me he was leaving. They go, 'John's leaving and we don't want you to.' I said, 'Well, this is what I do. What am I gonna do? You've finally made it from my parents' basement to potentially touring in the States, and I'm quitting now?'"

Like Geddy and Alex, Ian confirms that John would occasionally ostracize people. He also elaborates on some of John's more unhealthy habits. "I mean, I was his friend, and once in a while I wouldn't be his friend anymore, and it'd be like, okay, whatever. But he was a diabetic and involved with methamphetamine, speed. It wasn't even cocaine back in those days. You never saw cocaine or heard of it. But speed, yeah, sure. Pills that would keep you awake for fifteen hours. If you don't sleep for four or five days and you don't really eat and you're diabetic, you're gonna crash. I was always worried. I used to tell him, 'Okay, so you fall down. What do we do?' 'Well, call a doctor.' 'Yeah, but what if the doctor is two hours away. What do we do?' 'Well, then give me some orange juice,' and all that. I was concerned. If you go back and look at the famous picture after that London show, he looks like he's gonna keel over."

But Ian says the show went on, that the band didn't miss any gigs because of John. "Not that I know of. A couple of times in bars, another drummer would show up. They tell a story about this guy, that they were rehearsing with him and supposedly using John's drum kit at some studio. And see, I set up that drum kit every time it was ever set up. And if it had gone to a studio, I would have known about it. So that story, it's hard to believe because nobody used John's drum kit but John."

So it was pretty much written on the wall that John would have to be dismissed. And then one day a particularly good lead came SRO's way.

"They tried a couple of drummers," continues Vic, "and made inquiries here and there, and Johnny Trojan, from Curtis Lee, who we also managed at that time — we had about fifteen acts in our roster — Johnny Trojan said to me, 'I know this guy; he lives in St. Catharines. He's just come back from England — Neil Peart. And he would probably fit in with the band.' And I said, 'Well, where do I find Neil Peart?' And he checked around and comes back and says, 'He's working for his dad in a parts depot, a tractor firm.' So I said, 'Okay, get in the car; we're going out to see him.'

"So we drove out to St. Catharines in a white Corvette, and he was working, and we were talking and walking around, and I said to him, 'Would you come out and try out for the band?' He'd just come back from England, and he didn't know if he wanted to do anything. Neil was Neil. He was kind of vague, independent. 'Yeah, maybe I'll come. Yeah, yeah, I'll come.' He's very cautious. And he's always been that way, I guess. He was like that all the time I was there, very cautious. So anyway, I convinced him to come out and try, see how he felt."

"It was a hot July day," begins Neil "the Professor" Peart, remembering when fate dealt him a new hand behind the parts desk of his dad's International Harvester dealership. "Typical little scenario, actually, to paint. And I remember it used to be so hot in there, it soaked my T-shirt. Because I had to wear a shop smock kind of thing with my name on it, for the customers. And under that it would soak my T-shirt. And we had the old Coke machine, and you would get a small bottle on a hot day. And pulling up is a white Corvette, and another local drummer I knew, John Trojan, came in and introduced me to Vic Wilson. And John had recommended me as a drummer for what Rush was looking for. So they drove down, John was the go-between, brought Vic over to talk to me about it. Talk about a huge paradigm shift.

"And suddenly there is an offer, and they're paying one hundred and twenty-five dollars a week! I never got paid a salary in a band before. That's why I was working at my dad's farm equipment dealership and playing in clubs at night. Imagine starting work at eight o'clock in the morning, and then playing in a bar 'til two o'clock. That was doomed, one way or another, to a short-lived way of existence anyway. But that's where I was at that time. And I'd gone to England and played in bands there and played in local bands around St. Catharines. But, boom, suddenly, this is a band with a recording contract and a tour, and my big thing was they pay a salary — for music!

"That was a moment to rock your world for sure. And my dad got wind of it. This was the thing: they pay one hundred and twenty-five dollars a week to play music in a band — that's the same amount I was making at the International Harvester dealer. It's like that line out of that *League of Their Own* movie: 'Well, we get paid; that's more than we get paid at the dairy.' So that came along, and my dad was wise enough that he said you better go talk to your mom; she was always the consultant on important matters like that. Especially given that I was my dad's parts manager so he wasn't keen on the idea of me going off to pursue this, what he could only perceive as a frivolous and short-lived music opportunity. So that's the crux of how it started."

Next step had to be a meeting with Geddy and Alex, where there would be the threat of some music getting played. Neil had to use the family Ford Pinto to get to where the auditions were taking place, bringing with him a set that included two eighteen-inch Rogers bass drums. Indeed, the family's dark brown Pinto was put into service. Despite it being a two-door, it was a hatch-back. Neil's dad says that although his business had two or three trucks, they really didn't go on drum runs. "I had a Lotus Europa at the time that wouldn't even fit my little set of drums. The auditions came up, and they were at Liverpool Road in Ajax, I recall, on the east side of Toronto. It was a little series of rehearsal rooms, a typical thing they still have today, rehearsal rooms in an industrial park. We got talking, and the immediate things, interestingly, were books and humor that we started talking about. I remember talking about — you know, we were twenty-two years old in 1974 — *The Lord of the Rings* and *Monty Python*. Actually, those were probably the first two touchstones. The books we read and the things that made us laugh."

"And I remember we played together for a while and they played me a couple of the songs that they'd been working on since they'd released the first album earlier that year. So we played together a bit and lay around on the floor and talked for a little bit. If you think about, we got together, rocked out for a while and then we laid on the floor and laughed. It was obviously destined to be okay despite my misgivings and lack of confidence and all that. But that's always been another strand of my nature too. But in retrospect what was so beautiful was the fact we played well together and we laughed well together — that's the kind of thing that might last forty years."

"John left, had left or he'd been asked to leave or however you want to describe it," begins Geddy, recalling that fateful day when Neil entered his life. "But we needed a drummer — let's put it like that — and we had these auditions and that was it. I don't know if you've ever been to an audition, but it's humiliating for all concerned. It's just a terrible thing to put someone through, and we've never really been through that before so it was really awkward for Alex and I. So we made this agreement that we wouldn't discuss any drummer seriously until after we heard all the drummers."

Recalls Liam, "The last person of the day to enter the rehearsal room was Neil. I remember that myself and Ian, the other tech at the time, had been sitting outside the rehearsal room using my dad's old two-track reel-to-reel recorder trying to pick up what we could for the band, so that if they wanted to listen back to any of the drummers again, they had a reference point. We were outside of the room, so without us admitting to eavesdropping, which I don't recall doing, we were reasonably just waiting for them to make noise and we'd turn the tape recorder on. We weren't privy to any dialogue.

"Anyway, Neil comes walking into the rehearsal room and he was kind of a big gangly guy. And the thing I remember is when he first came in with his drum kit, he had a metal or aluminum trashcan full of hardware. And we were all kind of snickering behind his back thinking, well, this guy doesn't stand a chance. And I don't think the guys initially thought he stood much of a chance either. Their mind had already been reasonably made up. But as soon as he sat down and started playing, he just blew them away, and they were in there for hours. The rest is history."

"A couple of guys played, and they were okay, nothing spectacular," continues Geddy. "You know you go through this rigmarole of playing your song. The album was out, so they could actually listen to the songs and come prepared and then you just do some jamming at the end and see whether there is any spark there. So there's this kind of gangly guy, and he had all these drums sticking out of his car, and he was quite a character. And he set up this drum set with very small eighteen-inch bass drums, which I had never seen, but he had two of them, which was nice. But I thought it's a rather strange-looking kid. He was so big that he loomed over these tiny bass drums. And as soon as he started playing, I was blown away, like as soon as he started playing, he was so much better than anyone we had played with in quite some time that I started getting really excited.

"And we jammed to some of the songs and then we jammed to some stuff Alex and I had written that we could never get John very interested in. In fact, one of those was the song 'Anthem.' The beginning for that song is an odd time signature thing, and that was really not John's thing. He was a real four-on-the-floor kind of guy. So Neil started jamming along with it and it was like, dude, you are the guy. So I started talking to him seriously — 'What do you like? I love your playing, how do you dress onstage?' — stupid things like that just to get the conversation going.

"And Alex is pissed at me because we had agreed not to talk about that stuff until we heard all the drummers, and there was one more drummer coming. So he was really quiet through that whole first meeting. But as we left, I just knew that this was the guy we gotta play with. Then the next drummer came in, and the poor guy had written charts for our first album, and he was really polite and correct, and it was just so hard to play with him after playing with this monster drummer. So after the guy left, I said, 'Okay, can we agree that it's this guy?' And Alex said, 'Oh, yeah, of course.' That was how that day went."

"After he left," says Liam, "they were just totally pumped and kept talking about, 'Did you catch the triplets he was playing?' and things like that. They were just totally blown away by his style, and I think they understood at this point they had to reconsider what their decision was going to be. Fortunately, they made the right choice."

"Neil was one of the most unusual people I ever met at that time," says Geddy, reflecting on that first meeting. "There was no one in our circle that was as verbose as he was, and as well-read. He had strong opinions about a lot of things. We didn't know that at first, but that was what started to come out after the first few weeks of touring together. And Alex and I were always together, and it was hard for him if you think about that. But he's a strong guy.

"And we noticed how well-read he was, and that's when Alex and I started talking — 'We should have him write the lyrics,' because we hated writing lyrics. We just wanted to write music.

So we suggested that he try it, and it worked out pretty well. But yeah, our first impression, we were a little leery of him, took a while for us to warm up to him. But when you live together, that happens very quickly. He was funny, and he liked to laugh, and you know, your sense of humor becomes everything on the road, all the goofy things you do to each other in between waiting periods. We were the city guys and he was the St. Catharines guy, but after a week you learn that he lived in London and he had already paid his dues. And we didn't feel so cool after that. He was way more traveled and experienced in life than we were, so we stopped being the cool city guys really quickly."

Alex tells a similar story. "John left the band; we had this offer from Mercury Records in, I guess, July of '74 and everything was happening very, very quickly," says Lifeson. "We were going on the road to open for bands that we admired and grew up with in America. It was a big deal. John decided he didn't want to be a part of that, and we finished out, I guess, a couple months' worth of gigs with John, and then we started auditioning some other people.

"There were three drummers who had auditioned, and Neil was in the middle of that pack. It was really funny because he showed up — you know, Ged and I, we've got the long waist-length hair, the velvet pants and platform shoes, and we were from Toronto and we were super cool — and he was from St. Catharines and had a short haircut because he worked for his father in a farm equipment business. And he showed up and he's setting up his drum set. He had a small set of Rogers. Like the drums themselves were quite small, and we were kind of scratching our heads. 'Oh, how's this going to be?' He was really good. Neil hit his drums so hard. And they were a really small kit — small toms, small bass drum, and loud! He hit them hard. He played a lot like Keith Moon at the time. You can see in his playing where that would have come from. There was an energy in Keith Moon's playing, a constant movement. He never played time, Keith Moon. And I think that's basically where Neil got a lot of his fundamentals. Even today, you can hear so much activity in his playing. It's subtler now, but it's constant.

"But I remember we thought, 'Is he going to look cool enough to be in our band?' I mean, that was one consideration at the time. But when he started playing, it was a real eye-opener. And we had such a common interest in music. And when we started playing, we really fed off each other, particularly Geddy and Neil. And that's where it starts from, the rhythm section. It clicked for them. I think I was probably a little more hesitant. I don't know if I was so enthusiastic right off the bat. But I definitely warmed up to it quickly.

"Even back then as a local drummer, he was so passionate about drumming and about music and having a future in music," continues Alex. "He'd spent a couple of years in London hoping to make something happen. And those were very difficult, lean years for him, and he came back to the reality that he had to get a job. And so it was a great opportunity. We jammed on a bunch of stuff — he took the time to learn some of the songs from the record — and then we took a break and sat and talked about all kinds of stuff, you know, books and what's happening in the world and certainly music. And then we jammed a little more, and then we took another break and smoked a joint, I think, and talked some more. I have to admit at first I wasn't sure if he was the right guy just because I guess I had this idea of who we were and the image of the band and what we wanted to do. By the end of that night though, I was definitely knocked out by his playing and Geddy absolutely loved his playing."

And then there was the possibility of having "the new guy" write the lyrics. "Yes, because the guy was not only a great drummer, but he was willing to write lyrics and neither Geddy or I were keen on doing that. We really wanted to concentrate on the music. So we had a wonderful opportunity to have a very democratic arrangement within our framework. We write the music, he writes the lyrics and we put it all together. And to this day that's the way it exists with us. And Neil's gone a long way in his lyrics. He's touched many different areas. It's certainly one of the most important parts of the band."

"So they brought him in," recalls Vic Wilson. "The first day they were back in our office, it was 'That's it — we're going with Neil.' All three of them were sitting there ready to go, and they rehearsed all day. And they did that every day until they were ready to go on the tour. And it worked. And in those days, it was either a half-hour or forty minutes, because we were an opening act, and the bill became a three-act bill. You didn't get much time and you didn't get much PA and you'd be lucky to get three lights. But we persevered and they worked hard, and you can see the results today."

"I don't think I met Ray until quite a ways on," recalls Neil, speaking to a Rush dynamic where everyone has their role. "He had a huge operation at that time, a record label, booking agency, a concert promoter, and he was the original entertainment entrepreneur, my guess, when he was seven . . . So at that time he was running physically a big giant office with tons of people. So again, it was an overwhelming experience to walk into that office for the first time, to see such an enterprise going on around rock bands."

But as alluded to, Neil had a backstory, one that includes a fair bit of rock 'n' roll experience well beyond his commandeering of the parts desk for Dad. Neil Ellwood Peart was born on September 12, 1952, in Hamilton, Ontario, the nearest hospital to the family farm in rural Hagersville.

"In fact, at the family dairy farm for the first couple of years of my life, I was laid in a manger while they did the milking," begins Neil. "And we moved to St. Catharines before I started school, when I was about four or so. And I grew up in a part of St. Catharines called Port Dalhousie, right on Lake Ontario, an old seaport from the early, previous Welland Canal. So that was kind of the atmosphere: a small town surrounded by farmland and woods and everything so great for hikes and bike hikes. We used to call them bicycle hiking. And we had the lake there, so I learned to swim and learned to drown in Lake Ontario and still have the ear infections to prove it.

"I started getting interested in music, I think, when I was about ten. My mom gave me a little transistor radio and the notion just to have my own music was fantastic. And then she said, 'I'm going to show you where the Hit Parade is.' This is how long ago it was. She got the Buffalo or the Toronto AM radio stations, and I started listening to the Hit Parade and became just totally enraptured by it. One of my earliest memories of that time is falling asleep with the transistor radio beside my ear at night, and then I asked my dad one morning, 'Does the battery last longer if it's not turned up very loud?' Because of course even at that age, you think a battery is a precious expensive thing. So I was worried about wearing out the batteries on my little transistor.

"But that certainly was the hook that caught me with popular music. And rhythmically I remember a song called 'Chains.' I think Carole King wrote it and some girl group did it. But it had this shuffle rhythm, and it was the first time I remember rhythm really grabbing me. So that's in the very early '60s. This is all pre-Beatles. That's the kind of late '50s, early '60s pop music that was on the radio at that time. And my uncle played drums. I had an uncle just a year older than me, and he played drums in kind of an R&B band around that time, early '60s. The popular music in Southern Ontario strangely enough was R&B and everybody played James Brown, Wilson Pickett and Otis Redding. And I remember hearing Sam & Dave's 'Hold On, I'm Comin' for the first time and playing it — five white kids from the suburbs — and just being transfixed by that song and what is the saxophone line in 'Hold On.' A Fender Telecaster playing, even that melody, that's the first time I remember kind of pop rock melody having that same hook that James did rhythmically.

"So with all of that going around, I then saw the movie called *The Gene Krupa Story*. Sal Mineo played Gene Krupa and took lessons from him. I watched it several times recently and Sal Mineo did a fantastic job of drum synch, air drumming if you like; he must have really worked at it. And there's a trailer that goes with it, that I've seen in instructional DVDs of Gene, teaching him. The film I know now is completely fictional, but that musical part of it was very convincing, the way that Sal acted, Gene's drumming, and it made drumming seem so glamorous. He was always so well dressed. It set the film in largely glamorous times except when Gene gets busted for marijuana and ends up playing strip clubs under false names and all this stuff. So it was very dramatic and dangerous and all this really appealed to me.

"And that's when I started thinking, I want to do that," continues Peart. "I started lobbying my parents. I was eleven or twelve then, so for my thirteenth birthday they got me drum lessons and a pair of sticks and a practice pad and basically said, 'If you stick with this for a year, we'll talk about drums.' And that's still the advice I give to parents today. 'Oh, my kid seems to have great talent at age three.' I tell them don't get them drums, because people buy drums like it's a toy. It's like buying your kid a grand piano because they play 'Twinkle, Twinkle, Little Star' on a little toy.

"So that's what they did. It was the perfect thing to do. Every Saturday morning, I went to the Niagara Peninsula Conservatory of Music, on St. Paul Street in downtown St. Catharines, and went for my drum lessons in a little room upstairs. And it was so fortunate I had the greatest teacher who was very encouraging. He led me along the path of righteousness in reading music and learning the twenty-six basic rudiments week after week. And even in the studio, there were no real drums. It was because they were teaching guitar in the next room and saxophone and accordion, probably lots of accordion, it being St. Catharines. So it was just a practice pad drum set — click click click. But he taught me through the rudiments, through sight-reading and all that.

"If I came in with a question like, 'How do you play that bop do be bop bop?' you know, rock 'n' roll, he would show me those things. So he was very encouraging because he would say, 'Okay, just pretend you're playing a solo.' So click click click. And he said, 'Well, some of that wouldn't sound that good on real drums. But I can hear that you have a natural aptitude, and of all my students there are two of you.' So drum lessons got going, and not only did I practice every night, I would make drum sets out of magazines on my bed and beat on them and just imagine having real drums to play. And I played my uncle's drums a couple of times. 'Wipe Out' was the ticket to drum credibility in those days, so I could play that. So I could sit down at my uncle's drums or a friend's drums and play 'Wipe Out.'

"One year later when I finally got my three-drum setup for one hundred and fifty dollars — red sparkle Stewarts: bass drum, tom, snare and cymbal — that was it. I sat and played 'Wipe Out' and 'Land of a Thousand Dances' over and over again and practicing was more like obsession than any kind of drill or regime or discipline. I'd play until my mom made me stop."

Neil was studious to the point of obsessive far before he found the drums, remembers his mother, Betty Peart. "He read a lot," she says. "And even when he was a baby, he would look at car magazines rather than nursery rhymes. He was car crazy, and through the years we realized that he was different. He always had a lot of intelligence for his age. Even when he was nine months old, he looked at the car books and *Popular Science* rather than young kids' books. He just read everything. We thought he was quite amazing. And when he graduated grade eight, what he wanted was a bird, because he was interested in birds. So we got him a bird, and he's carried that on through his life. He's really interested in bird-watching. It was harder on him because he didn't conform. He took the harder life because he stuck to what he thought, not what anybody else thought."

"Certainly, as Betty said, he was always looking at my car magazines," explains Neil's father, Glen. "When something got his interest, he wanted to see it through no matter what it was. He wanted to get the end result of it and see what had happened. That was pretty well true of everything, and very true when he got to school. He was bored with school, but if they gave him a project to do, he'd jump right into it and he worked that project right to the end. Anytime through both public school and high school, all the interviews we had with teachers were always 'Neil has so much more potential. We just can't get Neil's potential — we know he should do more.' But he wasn't that interested unless he had a challenge."

"Yes, well, it was horrible coming into high school," remembers Neil, "because in those days they had different progressive ideas about kids and school. If they thought you looked a bit bored, they decided you were gifted and they bumped you up a grade — an acceleration they called it. They took me from the middle of grade three to the middle of grade four and then again took me the next year from the middle of grade four to the middle of grade five. So I was two years younger than all my peers. And yes, I was more interested in what was going on and some of those progressive ideas were good.

"Grade seven and eight they sent a bunch of kids who they'd selected as being gifted, to have a major achievement class, it was called, and we would take French and Shakespeare, once a week. And I was exposed to all these bright kids who knew all this stuff I had no idea of. And they seemed to me so urbane, knowing about politics and knowing dirty jokes and things I'd never heard before. But I was still twelve coming into grade nine. I passed my thirteenth birthday when everybody was two years older. That was a very bad idea, especially for a kid who had no athletic thing to fall back on. That was difficult."

"I wouldn't say it was that he was too smart for school, but he didn't have the interest," says Neil's dad. "The one summer when he was in public school, they had a special course during the summer and they picked, what, maybe two or three students out of the class to go to this advanced school, and he loved it. He thought it was great because the people there were all interesting like he was and interested in what was happening. It was totally different from what he was doing in the ordinary school. I think he was challenged there and enjoyed being a part of that."

As for athletics, Glen explains that "Neil's younger brother Danny was very involved in sports, but Neil just wasn't. He was interested in sports, but he was too tall and gangly, and he really wasn't good at it. He skated but he wasn't a good skater and he just didn't fit in with the other guys, not the same as his brother Danny did. Danny played every sport there ever was and is still involved in physical fitness. Neil just couldn't get involved in that. And the same thing when he was going to school — he didn't fit into the little cliques. Neil was always sort of off by himself. He was the first one to have long hair. And of course the ironic part of it is at school he was sort of the odd man out a lot of the time, and now when you go back to St. Catharines, everybody in St. Catharines went to school with Neil and thought he was wonderful. 'Oh yeah, he was my best friend.' So it's just a change; that's all."

"He had friends that were interested in what he was, like hiking," adds Neil's mom, Betty. "He loved to hike and take off and be gone all day. Anything that he was interested in, he seemed to have good work ethic. But other kids picked on him because of course he looked different, and it wasn't a happy time for him; he didn't fit in. But he got through it, and now, as Glen said, everybody knew him. Even though they wouldn't have anything to do with him, now they're proud of him.

"But once he got into music, it was strictly music — that's all there was, just music. Even when he was young, he started with pencils, drumming on anything, the dashboard, the baby's playpen, everything. He just drummed with pencils and he listened to the stations that played all the new music and liked it. And when he wanted to learn to drum, we just got him a pad to start with. And the teacher thought he had a good talent, so he went then to the drum set. And once he started that, that was his life — nothing else."

"He had his small bedroom up there which he decorated in his own style," continues Glen, "but he pretended at that time that he was doing his drum solos. He'd get thick catalogues and spread them all out on his bed and this was his drum set. And he would work through these magazines and tear the covers to shreds as he was drumming them with these sticks. But that was his imaginary drum set, and he was working on his drum solo. When he first started to talk about taking lessons, that was Walter Ostanek in St. Catharines, where Neil went for the first pad. And then when he felt he just had to get a drum set, I went and talked to his teacher before we spent the money. And he said, 'Yeah, I think definitely Neil has the passion for drums.' And he said, 'I think he's got the talent. I think that whatever money you've got, it would be well invested — get a drum set for him and go with it.'

"I knew that he was having a difficult time just because I knew that he felt like an outcast, and it was difficult for him during high school years. He knew it was a necessity, but it wasn't something that he really wanted to do. And again, whenever we had a visit with teachers, it was always 'Neil has so much potential. He could do anything he wants in school, but we can't get him to pry out of this.' We went and talked with the vice-principal and he had seen Neil's problems and I think that maybe he recognized the potential, that Neil was not intending to be a scholar, that that was not his first love in life. His first love in life was music and drums. And I think we kind of agreed at that time. Fortunately, the teacher went along with that and said, 'Well, I think you're probably right if you encourage him to follow his dreams.'"

"He was in his glory, really, when he was playing," says Betty, "but once he got into a band, it was hard on us because we had to drive him to everything. But we figured that it was worth it. He was so committed that we had to support him."

Glen and Betty were supportive of Neil's ambition, going so far as to act as his roadies, driving his equipment around. "I was in the farm equipment business then, and we always had a pickup truck and most of the jobs went in the pickup truck," says Glen. "And then we had a station wagon, and sometimes the drums would go in the back of the station wagon. And wherever Neil was playing, that's of course where we took him. And we either waited for him or made arrangements to come back whenever he thought he would be done and load everything in and take it all home again. He'd set it up in the garage at that time and that's where he worked, out of the garage. Of course, that was not a thrill for the neighbors, when Neil was pounding away in the garage. And we used to have occasional visits from the police and had complaints and that sort of thing. So actually, when he got with the group the one summer, we got them a barn through a customer of mine out in the country and they took their stuff out there. Then they could be as loud as they wanted to be and they weren't going to bother anybody.

"He had already picked it out," says Glen, concerning Neil's first kit. "He knew what he wanted, and he started out with that first small set and went from there. I really had no problem with it at all. As I said, Neil was not interested in sports; he didn't focus on sports at all like most people did. His passion, as Betty said, was for drumming. That's what he wanted to do. And even at that time, he had no interest in getting a car, which most young guys said that the first thing they want to do is get a car. All Neil wanted was a drum set, and he wanted to play on that drum set and that was his only passion. Can't fault him for that."

"I wasn't sure because I had never had any experience in something like this," adds Betty, "but as Glen said, he didn't have a car and I think he would have liked one. But every cent he got went on drum heads because as you know, he breaks them, and drum sticks. So there was no way of him having anything else because that's where all his money went."

"Once I got interested in drums," continues Neil, "this became an identity that was totally at odds with the conformity of St. Catharines and especially that high school. People willingly dressed all the same, and so once I got interested in rock bands and started to grow my hair a little over my ears and then some bangs swept to the side and wear polka dot shirts, there was the constant misfit sense and the shouted comments and all that. But I played in the high school variety show when I was fifteen and impressed everybody, and I guess my parents were there, and it was my first public drum solo and all that, and it really changed the world, I see in retrospect now, that one little variety show thing."

"All of a sudden he was a hero when they heard him play," remembers Betty, "and this was in high school. Then he got some respect. I do remember that; it was a breakthrough."

Adds Glen, "Well, actually, the first real show that they had was in our church basement hall, where two or three of the boys got together and Neil took his drum set over there and they played just this little church hall. But the talent show that Neil talks about was in the high school, and they of course asked for people to get involved. So Neil volunteered. I don't remember now who was with him in the group, but as Betty said, suddenly they realized that, hey, this kid's been walking around the hall with the long hair and maybe he's not as weird as we think he is. I just know that we were proud at the time because we could see the reaction from the people that were in there, that they were suddenly paying attention to what was happening up there, and suddenly he was a somebody."

"It gave me something to be proud of," continues Neil. "But I'd already started to build that in various ways in all the other bizarre interests I had in childhood . . . I wanted to be a professional birdwatcher first, then I wanted to be a forest ranger, so I already had my own ideas. But this was the first time I was admired for anything that anyone would understand and relate to. So, of course, my academic history went whoosh, straight downhill. And from advancing all those years earlier, I then proceeded to scrape through grade nine, failed grade ten, get into eleven, fail grade eleven.

"So I had a meeting with the vice-principal of the school and my parents because I wanted to — I was old enough to quit and I wanted to be a full-time musician — that's all I thought about. And a couple of my bandmates at the time were out of school and practicing every day. So we had a meeting with the vice-principal and they agreed I wasn't accomplishing anything there, and to my surprise and everlasting gratitude, the vice-principal said that — he said, 'He's not accomplishing anything here; maybe you should let him try it his way.' You know again though, one of those magic little moments that could have gone so many other ways. But fortunately, I was in a very serious band at the time that would practice every day. We didn't drop out of school to be bums. I took the bus to our guitar player's house — he had a very tolerant mother. We'd practice all weekdays, and on weekends we had gigs in all these kinds of halls. I had to join the union, in fact, because of those kinds of halls, I think when I was fourteen, fifteen."

The relationship Neil had with his school parallels Geddy's experience and that of so many rockers who are smart enough and wired for school but are more wired for success at whatever it is they passionately pursue. Like Geddy says, if you are doing something you really love and you apply all your smarts as well as your energy and ambition to it, you've got a great chance at success, even if it's not school. There's something about Neil's and Geddy's shared experience that makes it obvious that these guys could have done well at anything they applied themselves to. I think we're all glad they decided to apply themselves to rock. Alex, on the other hand, seems to have wound up being a rocker in a more typical rock 'n' roll way.

While Geddy applied himself to becoming a big fish in Toronto, Neil was thinking globally. "I never think of anything about me as being special," muses Neil, picking up the story. "That's a fundamental part of my personality and character. But the band was running into frustrations. And it was a good band, in retrospect, called J.R. Flood, and we were that serious that we practiced all the time, and everybody was on that same wavelength and we made some demos for record companies in

Toronto. But they gave us the classic answer of those days: 'We don't hear a single.' So we were up against this wall. And so I was kind of urging, 'Guys, why don't we move to New York or move to London or something?' But they were contented to keep doing this round of high school gigs and face rejection from above.

"So I conceived this notion that I would move to London and take my drum and my records," continues Peart. "My parents agreed to match whatever money I could raise. So I sold my record player and worked weekends for my dad at the farm equipment dealership. I came up with two hundred dollars, and they matched it, and in those days, you could get on a charter flight to London for two hundred dollars. So my dad helped build a crate for my drums and they shipped them over by boat and I went off to London. I was eighteen — that would be the summer of '71 — and I had a friend over there who agreed that I could stay with him for a little while until I got settled.

"In retrospect it was a decision and a tangent that's beyond brave. I mean it's completely naive, but at the same time it was an irreplaceable experience to go there and go hungry and starve and have to get a real job and prove to myself I could make a living other ways. That's something a lot of musicians get caught in, this trap that they have to do what the man says because they have to make their living from playing music. Even among the young bands around the St. Catharines area when I was growing up, there was already that classic divide of musicians I knew who would play anything to be a professional musician. They'd play in a polka band, they'd play in a country western band, they'd play Top 40 covers, whatever it took. They were making a living playing drums.

"The bands I was in, we just played music we liked, and if we played cover tunes, we played cover tunes that we liked. That was a firm distinction in my mind; it just seemed so natural that

that's the way it ought to be. Again, in retrospect, naive and idealistic and unrealistic wouldn't be too much to say, but that is the
worldview that I took with me to London. That all I had to do
was get good and I would be famous. Successful was really what
I was after. Fame was never a lure for me, but certainly success
was and the attainment of getting good — it was as simple as
that. And I really believed that's how the world worked. That if
I got good, I would be successful — simple."

Concerning the pilgrimage to swinging London, Betty says,
"His favorite group was The Who, and he thought if he was ever
going to be able to play like them, he'd have to go where they
are, so we did everything we could to get him there. And he got
there and had a good life there, but he didn't have a lot of gigs.
And he stayed two years, I think, and then he wanted to come
home because it wasn't very easy to break into the music there."

Neil's bands in Canada were doing well, but he couldn't shake
the feeling that his break would happen overseas. "They were
fairly successful locally," says Glen, referring to Neil and his band,
Hush. "They were playing a lot of high schools and were quite
busy. And Neil wanted to take it the next step. He wanted to get
an agent in Toronto or wanted to move the group to Toronto and
see if they could do something. And at that particular time, a
couple of the boys in the band had girlfriends they didn't want to
leave, and one or two of them had summer jobs. So Neil decided
he was going to have to go it alone. As Betty said, it was happening in England, and he felt that's where he had to go. So we
discussed it at the time and decided that we'd pack him up, and
off he went to England."

Visiting Neil there, Glen recalls that "he looked so white
and so thin being in England all that time; they don't see the
sun a great deal there. He didn't look all that healthy, especially
to his mother. We were able to get over there on this trip, and

Neil was managing this store in Carnaby Street. He had a few jobs but was not very successful with getting the drums going, and he ended up managing this store on Carnaby Street, and he was able to be with us most of the week when we were touring different places. We talked at the end of the week, and I said, 'Neil, if you're going to end up managing a souvenir store, I've got a farm equipment dealership back in Ontario that needs a parts department manager, and I've love to see you come in and do that.' So he thought that over and we got a letter from him a couple of months later and he'd decided to come home. So that's when he came home and actually came into the business with me."

"I eventually got a job first working in souvenir shops in Carnaby Street and the Piccadilly Circus area," confirms Neil. "And then one of the shops had room in the basement where I had my drums and played them. And I joined a band and the band started getting a few gigs. I quit work there and, ugh, the gigs lasted about two weeks and suddenly there was no more work. And I was sharing a bedsitting room on the farthest extreme of London with my friend Brad, and you know, not able to pay rent, not able to buy food and really facing poverty.

"In fact, my grandmother paid for me to come home for Christmas for a week or so. And when I went back, I had fifty pence in my pocket, just barely enough to take the tube to our flat and then I was destitute. Well, of course, once I somehow confessed that to British immigration, they said, 'How are we going to send you anywhere in this country with fifty pence?' 'Well, I can get a job.' And I eventually talked my way out and went back to the real job after that, highly disillusioned. When I was in the foment of London — and the professional music business was that — it was very obvious that things didn't work the way I thought they did back in St. Catharines.

© BRUCE COLE

The boys, at your service — left to right, Geddy Lee, Alex Lifeson, John Rutsey; promo shot for the debut album.

© BRUCE COLE

Rush with manager Ray Danniels, seated, 1973.

© BRUCE COLE

© BRUCE COLE

ABOVE: Alex looking young but tired in 1974.

LEFT: Another purple pose; same quest for world domination.

COLLECTION OF CHRIS IRWIN

COLLECTION OF CHRIS IRWIN

ABOVE: J.R. Flood promo shot; Neil Peart in lower left.

LEFT: Neil Peart and his father, Glen, featured in a page from the newsletter promoting Glen Peart's farm equipment dealership, 1973.

© BRUCE COLE

© BRUCE COLE

ABOVE: Geddy, 1973.
LEFT: John Rutsey, early 1974.

© BRUCE COLE

© BRUCE COLE

At the office of short-lived Toronto music magazine *Beetle*, 1974.

© RICHARD GALBRAITH

Tulsa Assembly Center, Tulsa, Oklahoma, October 24, 1975.
Headliner on the night was Ted Nugent.

An assortment of 8-track tape versions of early Rush albums, along with a U.S. promo edition 7" of "Something for Nothing," the front and back of the promo sampler conceived by Cliff Burnstein to educate radio about the band, an *All the World's a Stage* promo folder, and a ticket stub for the first night of the Massey Hall stand that produced that album.

COLLECTION OF RAY
WAWRZYNIAK EXCEPT FOLDER
AND TICKET STUB, COLLECTION
OF DONALD GADZIOLA.

© RICHARD GALBRAITH

Caress of Steel tour (a.k.a. Down the Tubes tour), Tulsa, Oklahoma, October 24, 1975.

© BRUCE COLE

© BRUCE COLE

Toronto, 1976.

© DONALD GADZIOLA

Alex and Geddy onstage at a December 31, 1976, Maple Leaf
Gardens, Toronto date promoting the double live album, *All the
World's a Stage*.

"So that was a huge lesson. But it also forced me into another life-changing decision, which was that, well, I'd rather do something else for a living and play the music I love — that was clear. I'd rather play down in the basement, play the music I like, especially if I can get like-minded musicians to do that. And I came back to St. Catharines then and went to work for my dad full-time at the farm equipment dealership and played in bands at night, 'cause that way I could play the music that I liked and make a living. So that gave me an advantage coming into it; like I could always fight for that kind of integration because I wasn't afraid to make a living some other way."

"He really was committed to both," says Glen, meaning drumming and work at the dealership. "In our parts department in the farm equipment dealership, we had just changed everything over to a computer inventory, which I knew Neil would be able to look after. Before that, it was all done manually. So Neil got quite involved when we were doing that; he was sort of spearheading that and looking after it. And he was playing the music he wanted to play on the weekend. So at the time, I think he was sort of happy with the way things were going. He was a little close to conformity then. When he went into the parts department, he was front line at that time, and he had his hair trimmed enough to make it presentable from a farmer's standpoint — he wasn't just a long-haired hippie. And Neil, as we already know, is pretty intelligent and he was great with numbers, so he fit into the parts department perfectly and was pretty soon accepted."

Even when working at Glen's business before he went to England, Neil knew how to both look and work right.

"When he was trying to collect money to get to England, Neil was coming to work in the dealership with me. But he had long hair at that time, and I said, 'Neil, I feel uncomfortable with you working in the dealership because we're dealing with farmers, rural people, who are generally pretty solid people, and I'm worried about you fitting in.' He said, 'That's no problem, Dad; I'll wear a toque.' So he worked in the back shop there with the rest of our mechanics and he wore this toque. All through the summer, no matter how hot it was, Neil kept the hair tucked under his toque.

"One of the stories I like about when he was working in the shop — I didn't watch him that closely — but we had a machinist at that time working on a project, and everything was done with intricate detail and everything was to be done right. Neil started to work with him on this project and they got along fine. And then Neil was going to be away for a few days, so I said, 'Bob, Neil is going to be away. Do you want somebody else to work on this project with you?' He said, 'No, I don't want anybody else. I just want Neil.' So I felt, well, he's pretty impressive then. If he can please this guy, as a machinist and as precise as he was, if he wanted Neil to work with him, I felt that was a pretty good recommendation."

But the contrast between Neil's two occupations would provide a life lesson moving forward. He'd done enough "real" work to realize how sacred musical life was to him.

"Yes, when we started in our early days and we were struggling with Rush, and we were getting pressure from the business side to be more commercial and to compromise our music and to repeat the chorus some more times and to write some singles and all that stuff, I was like, 'No, I don't have to do that.' I really felt that way. It was a kind of hubris again, I know, but I carried that. I had been able to protect that naivete, that . . . idealism is more of the right word. I'd been able to protect that by not caring — I wasn't afraid of them. A lot of musicians come into a situation like that with their first record deal, or they first step into the big time and they're intimidated. When people start telling them what to do, 'Oh, so that's how you do it around here, okay.' Some people, I suppose, don't care but I did — and do — so I was glad to come in armed with good reasons to do it my way as my fallback.

"There's always ironies there with J.R. Flood," reflects Neil. "Of course, when I left, they got another drummer and carried on and they changed their name to Bullrush. So the summer of '73, I guess it was, when I was first back and I was working at the International Harvester dealer, there was an ad for a concert in St. Catharines with Bullrush, Rush and Mahogany Rush — this was some agent's brilliant idea to put the three bands together. And I knew the guys from Bullrush, but I didn't go to see the show. I just saw the posters around town. I think Mahogany Rush was probably headlining because they had a record deal with Frank Marino, the reincarnated Jimi Hendrix and all that."

Neil's parents were well pleased for him when he got the Rush gig. He was initially approached about the audition at work. "I naturally wondered what it was," Glen says about that day. "They certainly weren't farmers. But they came and asked if they could talk to Neil and could take him out to lunch, and we said sure. And I really had no idea what it was at all. No thought crossed my mind as such, until Neil come back and then finally we had a chance to visit and he told me what the story was. And then it was easy to put two and two together. But certainly, we had no idea, or at least I had no idea, what was happening when they'd come up and wanted to take Neil out.

"You could tell his mind was going a mile a minute. After we locked the door, he told me they wanted Neil to join them as soon as possible because they needed a new drummer. And Neil of course was really worried because he had just come into the business and he sort of committed to run the parts department. And this was in the spring, which was coming into our busiest season. But I wasn't concerned for him at all," says Glen, who knew Neil had to take another shot at his dream. "Because with what he had gone through in England, really a lot of that was survival. Because every time we would send him a letter, Betty would go to the bank and get a few pound notes, or whatever they were at that time, and always include those in the letter. We figured if he could survive that, he could survive anything because that really was in a lot of cases a hand-to-mouth existence."

"I thought it was wonderful," says Betty. "I really was happy that he was doing something that he really loved, and he had that chance; it was great. When he came back from England, he got a flat in downtown St. Catharines, and I think he kept the flat while he went away. I can't remember, but I know when he came home from England, he moved into the flat. And I don't think he actually moved to Toronto. He went on tour with Rush and I don't think he moved to Toronto, not for a lot of years."

Now that Neil was in the band, Rush could get to work knocking down all the ducks that Ray and Vic had positioned in a row for them. The empire-building had continued, drummer or not. A record was being readied for some modest promotion in the U.S. — so that's where the band was going to plug away and play. Neil's first show with the band would have Peart jumping into the deep end in brotherhood with Geddy and Alex. On August 14, 1974, Rush supported Manfred Mann's Earth Band and headliner Uriah Heep at the Civic Arena in Pittsburgh, Pennsylvania. There would be no time to reflect, as each of the successive three nights found Rush playing again, in Cleveland, in Cincinnati and in Charleston, West Virginia.

"That was probably the busiest two weeks of my entire life," remembers Neil. "I auditioned for the band in, I guess, July of '74, and we got rehearsing by Geddy's birthday. I think I became an official member on the twenty-ninth. And that first gig was the fourteenth. We had basically two weeks to get on tour because it wasn't just the first show, there was a whole bunch after that. So we were rehearsing because we had a lot of songs to do. We had two weeks to rehearse, so we drove the band's truck down to Long & McQuade in Toronto and bought a set of drums. And can you imagine? 'I'll have those chrome Slingerlands there and new cymbals.' And the other guys: 'I'll have this Les Paul and these Marshall amps.' Doesn't get better than that. Honestly.

"And I still hold on to that spirit. In fact, many, many years later I was walking down the street, walking past a drum store in Toronto and looked in the window and saw a set of yellow and red drums and thought, 'Me at sixteen would have died to have had those drums.' So I went in and bought them for me at sixteen. But there we were with two weeks to prepare and to learn songs I had never heard before and to gel as much as we could.

"So we worked through the rehearsal time, and that first show had been so overwhelming — first travel, the first flight, the first hotel. You know, I'd flown once, twice before to England and back, but to go on tour and check into a hotel ... there's so much adventure there. And arriving at the gig, the whole atmosphere of being there . . . Anyway, we had a twenty-five-minute set. And I think that night, it was the first time they rolled back the dome during the Uriah Heep set. And standing by the side of the stage seeing this, it became day one of what became a lifetime. Especially at that age, twenty-two years old, this is the biggest adventure ever, and it might be over like that.

"Just the sheer weight of experience," continues Neil. "Ken Hensley from Uriah Heep was so friendly to us right off the bat and had us in their dressing room and looked after us in a way, which was remarkable. And when you've been around touring a little bit, and you've seen how focused people are, and how inward and blinkered they have to be to survive that, someone as out-going and gregarious as him, that's another part of it that really stood out. And the guys from Manfred Mann were really nice to us. I think we did four shows with that lineup, basically. The fourth show was their last show of the tour together, Uriah Heep and Manfred Mann, and they'd become very knit together, and they had a big practical joke party and put whip cream on each other during the show and silly string over the drummer while he's trying to play, all these pranks between the two of them. And then it ended with Uriah Heep carried off covered in pies.

"Which happened with us with Kiss. We came to the end of it and celebrated with juvenile hijinks. Yeah, they were landmark tours, which set a good example and became our model — how you're supposed to be if you're a headliner and you have opening acts. Make sure that they get sound check, which became religion for us after bad experiences. Things like that are formative. You remember that example set by the first big bands that you worked with and how you were treated. And so it does become a very good model for the future. So it was a huge experience, all of that, to be indoctrinated, boom, just like that. I hadn't played in my lifetime like that, except for a few pop festivals for a few thousand people in St. Catharines. But clubs and high schools, that was your paradigm. That is what shifts immediately. Your paradigm shifts into a whole other place, and you are just wide-eyed and innocent, and absorbing and watching and feeling things."

"I remember that crystal clearly," says Geddy, also on the sub-ject of the first show with Neil. "Pittsburgh Civic Arena, opening a three-act show for Uriah Heep, headliner, Manfred Mann's Earth Band, and us, and we were as green as you could get. We barely knew Neil. He'd only been in the band a couple of weeks. So he joined the band, we rehearsed like twenty-six minutes' worth of songs, of music, and there we were. Because that's all we were playing on this tour, twenty-six minutes. We didn't even have cases for gear. We pulled up to this gig like paupers in this little truck. We had two guys on a road crew and all our gear. All our cables and stuff was in suitcases, those little Coke carriers, those Pepsi carriers. So we were pretty green, nervous as hell, and this was show business. This was serious."

"It was a tempest in a teacup," agrees Liam, "and we got thrown into the middle of it all. We were given a certain amount of money to go and buy equipment, so we'd bought all this new gear. And of course, if you're buying any new gear, everything's going to work beautifully — or not. It was probably for me one of the worst nights ever. Things were breaking down and we were finding out all the problems with the new gear, having to run from front of house to the stage, back and forth — it was pandemonium. It was our first time dealing with unions and trying to pick our way through all those potential land mines. But I do recall staying for the rest of the show, and while Uriah Heep was onstage, they opened up the roof and you could see the stars. It was the big time. We had finally made the giant leap at that point. But we realized that we had a lot to learn, and eventually you had to increase our crew just to deal with all the issues we were having and to not look like we were total amateurs."

Geddy tells the story of how the new tour manager, Howard Ungerleider, explained to them how a rider worked and how the band could request some booze and food. Alex ordered some cheap wine and Geddy asked for a little bottle of Southern Comfort.

"We didn't know what to order. And I remember reading this article where a lot of singers used to drink Southern Comfort, and we head to the stage, and here we are playing the first gig in America, and people are just finding their seats. The place was maybe a third full, and we were the band that no one gave a fuck about; they're finding their seats and we're playing, and I'm dizzy.

It was all just adrenaline. And I never drank that crap after that. It's just like, what a dumb idea."

Geddy says that it was all over in a flash, and the guys had no idea if they played well or not. "I think by the time we finished, there were about eleven thousand people in the building. But it was a huge, huge moment in our lives. Neil didn't really know us, we didn't really know him and this was the start of our tour. This was the first show. I remember flying into Pittsburgh and it was all so exciting. We shared rooms in those days, so every night you had a different person to room with. And it was America. Traveling around in a car, a rental car. It wasn't a bus or a van. You used to sleep on luggage. But we were young, we didn't care; we were uncomfortable and didn't care.

"Every night I was nervous, and then it went away," continues Geddy. "And it does. At the beginning of every tour you're a little nervous, and then after a few shows, it's just your job and it goes away. And we looked so forward to that twenty-six minutes, because the rest of the day was just bullshit, you know, filling time, driving, waiting. That twenty-six minutes was the only time you got to do what you were there to do. So I think that's why a lot of bands get screwed up on tour, especially opening acts, because you have so much spare time on your hands. The reason you're there, and what is supposed to come, you get such a short period of time to do it. We loved to play, and we were frustrated, but it was all a big part of it."

"They were all scared, but it was a chance of a lifetime," agrees Vic Wilson. "And Geddy's hero was the guy in Uriah Heep. And so they were all working and getting together. And of course their dressing room is down the hall, four corridors down the hall, but it was fine; they went on and did their show. And the fellow from Uriah Heep came over and talked to them, and they were all mesmerized just looking at him. When your hero comes in to say,

'Guys, you did a nice job,' it's gotta work for you. And he did, and I think they played four dates with them."

Assessing the new guy, Vic says, "At that point in time, he was copying what John Rutsey played on the album. Basically, that's what it boiled down to. But starting with the next album, Neil came into his own. That's when Neil added the Peart rhythm section to the band. He basically had to learn an album of material. You can't say he was a standout or anything. He just did the job. And after ten days, you are just glad you did the job. They've got to be scared. They were scared up there. And the place was packed. It was an indoor arena. There had to be fifteen thousand people in there.

"I wasn't involved too much in North America," qualifies Vic. "And Ray and I didn't go to shows. They were out there on their own. Howard Ungerleider took care of the band, and he did a good job. Everything ran smoothly. All the logistics were done by Howard, so we didn't need to be out there. It wasn't our job to be out there. They went out and they kicked ass. I once got a pen set from the guys in the band, and it said, on the piece of marble, 'Can we come home now?' So yeah, they were out working, working, working. And that's what worked for Rush. Work, work, work. That's how they sold albums — not from airplay."

"I started off with a company in New York because that's where I'm from," begins Howard Ungerleider, remembering the early days. He was brought on at this juncture and remained indispensable to Rush 'til the end.

"Our company was called American Talent International at the time. They were one of the biggest agencies in North America, actually in the world, back then. I started as a tea boy or a coffee boy, running around bringing coffees to people, and over a period of a year worked my way up to an agent. I'd travel around with bands. One day I was told, 'You're gong to Toronto,' and I said 'Why?' And they said that you will be working for a band that's going to be the next Led Zeppelin, looking after our better interest. And I said, 'Uh, who is this band?' And they said, 'They're called Rush and if you don't go, you're fired.' So I didn't have much of a choice. I said, 'Okay, I'm on my way.' So I flew up to Toronto, and I liked the guys and the whole operation up there — that was in August of '74.

"My first impressions of Toronto were not really of Toronto because I had landed in an airport that's way out of town, and they took me to a little suburb called Richmond Hill, and I thought that was Toronto. So I was thinking, 'Now, this is a really small place.' And I met Geddy and Alex right off the top. I remember them standing next to a white Corvette, dressed up in tennis whites with rackets, and thinking, 'Wow, these guys must love tennis!' I think it was Vic Wilson's car or something. It was quite scary because I was sent up from New York to become the tour manager and to look after everything, and my first trip into the office, I went in there and I said to the accountant, Sheila, 'Hi, I'm Howard Ungerleider, here to manage Rush. I need ten thousand dollars just from my float so I can get started with this.' And what I didn't know at the time was that no one had any money back then. She thought it was a very unusual request. And behind closed doors that I wasn't privy to, there was a lot of freaking out going on. This guy from New York wants ten thousand dollars, and we don't know what to do! But over time, as you can see, we got the ten thousand.

"But they were really friendly; they were really nice people," continues Howard. "I mean to this day, out of all of the bands that I've worked for — and I have worked for a lot of bands — these guys are the best. They are gentlemen, they are fair and understand what's happening. It's unusual because you're traveling with other bands and dealing with other management, and people tend to deal with things differently. And with Rush, it's all about being forthright and honest and you are telling them what's going down. They expect the same thing. It's a give and take that's really pleasant."

"We met Howard in August of 1974, just before our first tour," explains Alex. "He worked for the agency that signed us at the time, as one of their agents. But they brought him in as a road manager. I mean, this was our first tour. We didn't know what we were doing. He'd been on the road with a number of bands, so it made sense that we had somebody with some experience going out with us. Although, you know, we were all twenty years old at the time and really didn't know what we were doing, including him. But he was our road manager, he defaulted to doing the lights, which was very simple. Remember, we only were doing twenty minutes most nights as an opening act. And we only had two other crew members. One did drums and the other did guitars. So Howard would go out and do the lights, and we sort of maintained that arrangement for years. I think until . . . I want to say the mid-'80s. When Howard just did specifically and exclusively the lighting, and we changed the whole production and ended up with a different road manager, production manager and all of that."

Howard was dropped into the mix just as the drummer situation was resolving itself.

"Yeah, it was amazing. I mean, every drummer in Toronto was coming to try out for Rush. They had a drummer from Max Webster, a drummer from another band. Neil came in unexpectedly, actually. A friend of a friend suggested the band audition him. He just got back from England. He was over there and things didn't quite work out . . . but you should really hear this guy play because he's amazing. And I remember him coming in with a silver drum kit and setting up. It was all quite interesting.

As soon as he sat in with the band, it was a done deal. Everybody went, 'Yes!' Because it was a little like *The Gong Show* before that. People were coming out and they're going, 'Okay, next! Let's see the next drummer — next!' And when Neil came in, it was like this is it, this is great and then we were on the road.

"That first show that we did in Pittsburgh," continues Howard, "we stayed in this little hotel called Webster Hall. We were also sharing rooms; we had a little rotation schedule of who shared with who. And we went in to do the show as the opening act, and it was the only time, I believe, in the history of rock 'n' roll where they actually opened the roof during the show at that building, Civic Arena, and all this air came in with birds and things. It really sticks in my mind. I'm not sure they ever opened it after that because they could never get it closed properly; it was broken and they never fixed it.

"But it kind of freaked all of us out because in the middle of the show, this roof started opening, and all this wind came in from the outside and it just caught everybody off guard. And yeah, from what I understood, it was the only time that roof had ever opened and closed. I think something went wrong and they never opened the roof again. But it was kind of cool playing with Uriah Heep, and exciting because it was a sold-out house. We had come from playing small venues in Canada to this huge place. And to us, back then, when you were really young, you go into an arena and it was huge. And you look around and you see that it was sold out and it was packed to the rafters and everything. Man, it was so powerful. And the surprise reaction for an opening act — Rush always brought the house down. They came out, it was amazing, it was a great feeling, for the guys especially. From the minute that they hit the stage, from that first night, it hit home, because they were in front of fourteen thousand people going nuts when they were used to playing small venues. All of a sudden you were on that stage and you were going, 'Wow.'

"Uriah Heep always treated Rush really well. I mean, Ken Hensley . . . Gary Thain was in the band back then, Mick Box — those guys were great. They were professionals. I had actually been their agent before I worked with Rush, so I knew them and I knew their manager, Gerry Bron, at the time. It was just a really good tour; they were great guys to work with."

"Offstage, throughout that tour, we didn't really mix with the guys," recalls Heep guitarist and mainstay Mick Box. "It was kind of like if Heep were in a bar somewhere, you would probably see Geddy and Alex on the periphery and then disappear. So there was never any of that kind of camaraderie where you sit and have a beer or whatever. They kind of kept to themselves, maybe seeing how it worked, how to work the ropes, and they did it pretty well."

This is a running theme among bands that toured with Rush. It's well known that Neil is most definitely private, but an air of seriousness and studiousness pervaded the Rush camp from the beginning. Famously, there wasn't much in the way of scandal when Rush was on the road, either as support or headliner. The band had their fair share of fun, but even when they were young, it was oddly mature, even structured fun, including Alex doing comedy skits, staged hockey games and Neil's bike and motorbike hobby.

"It was usually Alex and Geddy walking around together," continues Mick. "Never saw Neil much at all. And it was usually, like I say, on the periphery. If we were in the bar somewhere, they would turn up, look around and they were gone. We'd say, 'Oh, come on over' a few times, and they kind of backed away from it. But it was a very well-run organization we had. So doing these major venues in America must have been a big eye-opener for them. But in that peripheral position they took up, they looked around and learned, and it wasn't long before they were climbing up the ladder of success themselves, which is — power to them — fantastic.

"I guess because it was their first tour, they were keeping away from the lot of it. Because being around Uriah Heep at that time, you know . . . we were pretty full-on. There were no halos on at all. They were all packed in a suitcase and gone home. We were out there doing it to the maximum, and they were probably just looking at it in amazement, really. You walk into a bar with us, and it was like the scene in *Star Wars*, everyone swinging off chandeliers; it was pretty full-on. That's probably why they kept disappearing."

Vic Wilson confirms the band's tame reputation, saying, "Neil was quiet. Kind of to himself, much like he was for many years. The strange thing about the band is that they weren't huge partiers like everybody would think a rock 'n' roll band, or a heavy metal band, is. Most of their time was spent reading books. Kind of boring and not my idea of a wild time. But that's what they did."

"They tended to have their inner sanctum, very much so, and stayed in there," Mick Box says. "But they handled it very, very well, I'd have to say. And certainly it didn't seem like Neil was the new boy. It sounded like they'd been together a long while. So, all the power to Neil. They came up trumps there. I saw the potential immediately because as a three-piece they were very, very powerful. There weren't any three-pieces out at the time, so that alone gave them power. And there's the fact that Geddy could sing so high. And at that time, he sang everything high, although he developed some other ranges in his voice — or allowed them to come through, I should say — later on, getting more dynamic with his vocals. But it seemed like everything he sang was at full tilt. I do the high harmonies in my band, so I know the notes he was hitting. He was doing a really good job. I mean, there were some comparisons in the early days that he was a bit Planty, Zeppeliny, all that stuff, but to be honest, I couldn't quite see that. I realized early on there they had put their own stamp on it."

Mick says Geddy's vocals were unique. And with that uniqueness "comes a lot of success sometimes, because they stand apart from everybody else. And I saw that potential right there, yeah. And the fact that he was playing some incredible bass lines while vocalizing — that's hard. I think the number one guy for that would probably be Jack Bruce. But you can put him up there with that, in terms of his ability to sing high melody, sing that high, and be playing a bass line as well. Incredible. Because he had to be busy. He couldn't just plunk away and get away with it, because they were only a three-piece playing some advanced lines there, so he was a busy lad."

Acknowledging the sour reviews Geddy's voice sometimes generated, Mick figures, "Yeah, but on the positive side, no one else was doing that — he stood apart. And I thought it was great. It really was, and his voice at that register, with all the low bits coming from the basses and the drums, if you like, and where sonically Alex was chordal, it just sat right, everything was cool. So it proved the critics wrong."

ZZ Top speaks eloquently of the particular challenges of a three-piece. Bassist Dusty Hill indicates that when Billy Gibbons goes off soloing, he's got to find a way to project the illusion of both bass and rhythm guitar.

Mick elaborates, "I would say dynamically there are places where it has to come down and it can't be full-on. But you know, with Rush, the holes that were there were meant to be there, as a dynamic thing. But generally, it was just very full-sounding;

you didn't miss anything. It was all very, very well orchestrated between the three of them. And Alex's guitar was great, great big power chords and things. He was allowed to breathe and come through. Exciting. Alex was very accomplished, obviously. And he fulfills a role very much, if you want a comparison, probably the way Andy Summers does in The Police. There were nice chordal things that filled up any spaces. He just had that ability to play that part very well. They couldn't be them without him. The riffs and things he's playing . . . it's brilliant. And the sounds he gets with the effects pedals and things like that, lovely. Brings everything to life. He's kind of in the landscape a little."

Playing with the likes of Heep was a smart move for Rush strategically, says Mick, because it's a crowd that would have been amenable, ready to receive and accept a band like Rush.

"That's how they got their fan base very quickly. It was the right place and the right time to come up. And they made the right impression with the rock audience. They didn't have to play to a pop audience and convince them, or a soul audience. It was a rock audience personally built for them. And they used that to their advantage. They learned very quickly how to get across, what songs worked, the tricks of it, and you start fine-tuning things. Things you can get away with in a club sometimes are not quite the same as being in a big, major show. It's right between the eyes and knowing when to do the light and shade and where to travel and where to meander if it meanders a little bit. Where you're going to let something go for a long solo or something. You fine-tune all that stuff and then suddenly you're hitting them right between the eyes."

Adds Mick on the band's brief opening slot, "Well, twenty-six minutes can be a very long time if you're doing it wrong, and a very short time if you are doing it right. And they were obviously doing it right." But even at that duration, "It's a big step up.

You have to learn your craft a bit more. Like I say, clubs, theaters, and then you're in this vast arena and you have to point to the last person at the back of the hall, as much as the one at the front; you have to project that far. And as soon you learn how to project across, it's like a wave, and when you've got to the back, you've got there — you know what you're doing."

Flash forward to May of '78 and Uriah Heep would be supporting Rush instead of the other way around. On the band's success, Mick reflects that "one thing about their longevity is they have good songs that people still love hearing in the live arena; they've had a lot of songs that have stood the test of time, and that's brilliant. That gives you the platform to bring the new material and move on as well. So although you are very proud of your history, you can do new music and it gets heard. There's no use being a great player without good songs, because nobody's going to remember a great player if you haven't got songs. Something has to move you and touch your soul. And they've obviously had a lot of songs along the way that do that to people."

Coming full circle and summarizing, Alex Lifeson says, "We'd gone from those few hundred people in a club to twelve, thirteen thousand people, doing a twenty-minute set with a stage the size of this table. You know, there was no room — three acts. That was so nerve-racking but so exciting at the same time. I think we played three songs. 'Working Man' was over ten minutes and then a couple of other shorter songs and that was it. And I remember meeting Ken Hensley and Mick Box from Uriah Heep, and they were great, especially Ken, just the sweetest guy. He signed a bunch of pictures for me, for friends, and gave fatherly advice, all that kind of stuff. And it was really nice meeting somebody like that. They were just very genuine and helpful. And years later, they opened for us, after being out of the scene and trying to get back together. And boy, we went out of our way to make sure that they got everything, a sound check and everything in their rider, a couple of bottles of champagne from us, all that stuff."

After Rush opened for Uriah Heep in Pittsburgh, the very next night, the circus pulled into Cleveland, hometown of WMMS and Donna Halper, who, as we've heard, helped break the band through radio play.

"There were some rough edges," begins Donna, recalling that show. "They were kind of learning how to play together. At first it was Neil and the drum solos, and Neil and all the cool stuff that Neil did, and I was just sort of philosophical about it. I figured that they were adjusting, that they were finding out which particular skills were going to be put front and center. Neil was the new kid on the block, and I was just thinking as time went on, this would be like a marriage, they would find which roles each of them played. So I remember being not too disturbed by the fact that at first it seemed to have a lot of focus on Neil. I kind of felt like okay, Neil was what they wanted."

Geddy had told Donna that although Neil's style was less conventional, that's what they felt they needed. Halper says that Geddy "talked to me — and so did Alex — about the fact that they knew they didn't want to just be a three-chord rock 'n' roll bar band — 'The direction we want to go is not "In the Mood." We understand that's what we had to do to try to get played on Toronto radio . . . they wouldn't play us anyway . . . but we know we've got to do something that is more interesting than that. And Neil will help us to do that.' So they were fine about him being there and this was just sort of the shakedown cruise. 'Let's try this . . . now let's try *this*.' I didn't feel like it had gelled yet, but I felt that they would. And as a music director, I was really eager to hear their new material and hear them play it together. It was like, 'This is going to be incredible.'

"They'd been stuck as one thing for so long, and now they're finally going to take it in another direction," continues Donna, acknowledging the considerable history of Rush in the Rutsey era. "They'd been with John forever. And I often wonder what would've happened if John hadn't had health problems. I have a feeling that the band might have splintered anyway. Not that they didn't like each other, but even from my conversations with them before Neil joined the band, it was real obvious to me that they felt that they had taken that particular thing as far as they could take it. And the response they got from songs like 'Finding My Way' and 'Working Man' and 'Here Again,' which got a lot of response in Cleveland, they were thinking, 'How could we write more interesting lyrics?' 'How could we do more interesting chord progressions?' 'How could we show our musicianship a little bit more?'

"At that point, they didn't have the answer . . . and then Neil became the answer. Geddy became one answer, and each member of the band provided other answers. They didn't really start doing anything interesting or creative until *Fly by Night* where they finally had some artistic sense of, you know, we don't just want ugly fuchsia."

Cliff Burnstein, who signed the band to Mercury Records, saw Rush for the first time at Neil's sixth show, August 21, 1974, in St. Louis, Missouri.

"Back then, there were these three-act shows that would come through town every week, with three amazing bands every week," recalls Burnstein. "So Rush jumped on this Uriah Heep tour, and now they were coming to St. Louis to be on somebody else's show. It might've been Spirit in a reconstituted state because they were big in St. Louis. And St. Louis is an easy flight from Chicago. So I went out to see them at that show. I had been dealing with Vic Wilson, from Rush's management office, and I told Vic that I would be going to St. Louis to see the band and meet them for the first time. Because we had signed them, never met them, seen them, nothing, just off the strength of the record. So I told Vic that a few days before.

"And then the day before I go down to St. Louis, Vic calls me and he says, 'Cliff, I have to tell you something; I'm a little uncomfortable with this.' I say, 'Oh, okay, what is it?' He says, 'Well, we have a new drummer.' And I said, 'What?! What happened?' And he said, 'Well, John Rutsey has health problems, and we found a drummer to replace him.' And I said, 'Is this just for the tour or permanent?' And he says permanent. And Vic says, 'Don't worry. It won't affect anything with the band.' And I said to him, 'I sure hope not.' Because now my ass was on the line in a sense, because I had said to the president of the company that we should sign Rush. I didn't want anything bad to happen to them. And this was already a bad sign, replacing the drummer.

"So anyway, I go down to St. Louis, and I think I arranged to meet with a local promo manager in St. Louis, to meet him and the band, before the show, and take them out for dinner. We took them to a Japanese restaurant. I was not very familiar with Japanese food at that time, and neither was the band. And the promotion man in St. Louis said, 'How about some sake?' as we were finishing dinner. And the band says, 'Oh no, we're not going to have anything to drink. We've got to go onstage in a couple hours. We have to be at full strength.'

"And so I was impressed with how serious they were, right on the spot. So we went to the show and they were phenomenal. And Neil . . . I was seeing the whole band for the first time, but here's Neil, the replacement, and he's phenomenal. Like wow. I don't know how good John Rutsey was, but this guy is awfully good. That's what I thought.

"So after the show, I go back to the dressing room, and there is a young woman in the dressing room, who is seemingly friends with the entire band. I thought I would talk to her because I thought maybe she was in some way associated with the band. And a bit naively, I'm listening, and what she told me was that she'd been on the Uriah Heep tour and she saw Rush, and she decided to jump off the Uriah Heep tour and go with Rush instead. And then I kind of figured out what was going on. And that was the first hint to me that this band was really going to go places, because if you can immediately draw the personal entourage away from the headline act, in your first three gigs, you're doing something. You're making an impression."

Other than that rock 'n' roll wrinkle, Cliff says, "They were serious, and they were a little nervous about meeting the record company, not knowing what's appropriate, whether to be friendly or not. I think that they had their minds on playing their gig, and I think it was all happening so fast that they weren't thinking about anything except what was right in front of them. It seemed like they were very focused on the task. I mean, I think they were more nervous about meeting somebody from the record label than they were actually playing the gig. The gig was their job and that was something they already knew that they could do well. But meeting with record company people is something that nobody actually knows how to do.

"All I knew was that this girl has been out with Uriah Heep and had gotten enough of them that she was now out with Rush. That meant everything to me, okay? I thought the music was amazing, and usually in my life, when I think the music is amazing, a lot of other people also think it's amazing. I was kind of a big music fan, and an average rock listener as far as my taste went. So if I thought it was really great, why shouldn't other people think so? It also became my job to convince them that should be the case."

Once Neil joins and Rush is firing on all cylinders, the band hammers their way through the rest of 1974, blanketing the U.S., serving as support for a pile of rock greats. The band returned to Cleveland on August 26 to play the Agora Ballroom. This was the first radio broadcast show with Neil, with the proceedings handled by WMMS. On the night, besides the expected material from the debut, the band played a new original, "Fancy Dancer," and their left-field Beatles (via Larry Williams) cover "Bad Boy," both of which were heavy enough but ultimately rooted in the blues. Much heavier was the non-LP original "Garden Road." Chosen to close the show, even this one took its structure from the blues, discernable through what is otherwise a bulldozing Black Sabbath shuffle. Finally on the non-LP front, Rush also offered early versions of *Fly by Night* songs "In the End" and "Best I Can," the latter song manic to the point where you felt the band was already looking past the song before it was put on record.

A studious listen to the show reveals Neil Peart hitting everything in sight at every opportunity, and Geddy Lee's effortless, ferocious throat. Most humorous is how a frantically busy Geddy on buzzing bass manages to turn the benign "Need Some Love" into something between Hawkwind, Motörhead and punk rock.

On December 22, there was a second important radio show, this one recorded by WQIV at Electric Lady Studios in New York. The band returned to the Agora in Cleveland for a second WMMS broadcast in May of the following year.

The handful of American dates in August of '74 led into a home stand in late October. The band's first TV performance with Neil took place on October 16 when Rush guested on the new hit show *Don Kirshner's Rock Concert* filmed in LA. At this important milestone, the band played "In the Mood," "Finding My Way" and "Best I Can." Through November and December, the band found their home in America's Rust Belt, also hitting parts of the eastern and western U.S. The most memorable of the headliners was Kiss, although Rush also shared stages with Eastwind, Rory Gallagher, Law, Don Preston, Rainbow Canyon, Rare Earth and Sweetleaf.

"I think we spent more time in the north," remembers Alex, trying to map that first tour in his mind. "Those first shows were Cleveland, Pittsburgh, Jonestown, Pennsylvania and we did other gigs spread out among those big tours we were doing, all in really small venues, opening for other bands. I don't think we headed south until later in the year, after a couple of months of touring. We also did a lot of dates with Rory Gallagher in that first swing, and that was great. I was a fan of his then, and he was such a gracious guy. And I got to watch him every night; that was the best."

"There was one gig," laughs Alex, warming to the topic of old war stories. "I think it was in Decatur, Illinois, and we got there, and it was a club gig. We got there a little bit early — the truck was maybe twenty minutes behind us — and we walked in and it was a tiny club with a stage maybe about eight feet deep and about thirty feet long. And there was no way we could get our gear on there, let alone play. And we went to the owners and said, 'Hi, we're Rush, and we have a problem here. We can't get our equipment on the stage.' And he said, 'Why not? Isn't it just an acoustic guitar and some chairs?' And we said, 'No, it's drums and amps,' and he said, 'Well, wait a second . . . Tom Rush?! Isn't that Tom Rush?' 'No, this is Rush.' So obviously the gig was canceled. But he paid us anyway."

In conjunction with Rush on the winding road, there was an assault on radio.

"We knew everywhere it was being played," explains Vic Wilson. "This is where Cliff comes in. We knew all the radio stations, it was in pockets, like Cleveland, Chicago — and we knew that we had to, if we could, focus on those areas and build it up. It's like a castle — you build your base and you build up. That's what all these years they've been doing, building and building.

"But you lived life in a blur. All of a sudden, we had a record deal and the tour is booked, and the guys got in their Dodge van and off they went. And you would see them once in a while, because in those days there was no driving home. If you were in Texas, you stayed there. There was no chance to commute. It started off with four dates with Uriah Heep, right off, and they just kept going from there. The band would do about two hundred shows a year. That's unheard of. No one does two hundred shows a year. And they did that for a lot of years. Because of lack of airplay, you had to be out there to sell albums in those days. So the more you're out there, the more you sell. Come off the road, sales would slow down. Because they didn't hear it on the radio. The only time they would hear you on the radio was if you were playing locally, whether that was Cincinnati or Pittsburgh or wherever it was.

"It was a lot of work," continues Wilson, "just like going to school. But in the early days, the routing wasn't the best there because all we wanted was exposure. It cost us a fortune to do this because we were opening for a three-act show. The opening act gets booked just for, like, five hundred, seven hundred dollars. And I remember one time, we went from Florida to upstate New York and we put Rush on a bill with Sha Na Na. Now, you talk about odd, but they didn't have to put the cage up, so they didn't get hit with the bottles, but it was pretty close."

"I don't think they went down very well at that show," says Howard, recalling the September 13, 1974, date at the University of Maryland gym in Baltimore.

"We had an agent that just tried to put you anywhere, whether it made any sense or not," Geddy says. "And, yes, we opened for Sha Na Na on our very first tour, and you want to talk about the worst possible matchup: Rush opening for Sha Na Na. I mean, give me a break. They booed us relentlessly. What the hell were we doing on a Sha Na Na show? You know this is '50s grease-ball kind of rock 'n' roll, and here's this really loud, obnoxious Canadian three-piece band. It was just a nightmare."

"It was my twenty-second birthday," recalls Neil. "They didn't like us. That was one of the worst matchups in history, until five years later when Blondie opened for us. Bad choice." Blondie, who were booed off the stage, was a last-minute replacement at a Philadelphia stop on the *Hemispheres* tour. "There were those kinds of mismarriages. In thirty years of touring, anything that could happen happened. One of the early shows was a club in San Antonio, and the promoter was arguing with our tour manager about the fee and all that stuff, and at one point he just put a gun on the table."

But through war stories like this, on top of doing what you are supposed to do, character is built and the juggernaut continues to grow.

"Part of the way you promote it, since I was a promotion man," says Burnstein, "is that you go to the guy in Pittsburgh and say, 'It's working in Cleveland.' And Pittsburgh is not horribly different from Cleveland. And if you can get the guy from Pittsburgh playing it, you can go to the guy in Buffalo saying, 'It's working in Pittsburgh and Cleveland — that ought to be enough to work the album.' And it sort of radiated out. You go to Detroit and that all kind of works. It doesn't work as well when you go to New York; the guy in New York goes, 'Well, what do we have to do with Cleveland?' I would say in some ways Donna Halper is right, that WMMS was most influential in that way for Rush because I could use Cleveland to influence these other stations, from the old industrial cities — they had a lot in common.

"Everything moved quickly back then. That was at the end of June, this whole conversation and signing the band within eight hours of hearing it. And we brought the album out within thirty days. I think it was right at the end of July of '74. And my job was to promote the record to radio. That was my initial involvement, just as a promotion guy. I didn't have any involvement in any creative stuff. I mean, the album was done anyway, and I never would've been involved with them creatively. So I was a promotion guy, kind of like the head cheerleader in the company. I did the promotion job for about two years after that. I think I promoted the first four Rush albums, and after that, the next few albums, I had a little bit of a hand in the promotion, but it wasn't my primary job. But I looked out for them as long as I was with Mercury Records."

Two nights after playing with Sha Na Na, Rush found themselves on a short tour leg supporting Kiss. This wasn't famous Kiss but a band still trying to get themselves over, shocking many in the process. The band's second album, *Hotter Than Hell*, was due out a month hence. Nationwide success was still a studio album and a double live album away, although granted the pace at which both Rush and Kiss were working, that narrative represented a mere year in the lives of Gene, Paul, Ace and Peter.

Explains Geddy, on how Rush ended up on the tour, "We did an early show in London, Ontario, opening for Kiss and that turned out to be fortuitous for us. It was around that same period that we were doing the Victory and all those little theaters, and they were pretty impressed with us, I guess. When it came time for us to tour America, they were not disagreeable to having us on their show, and we got very friendly with them and ended up touring with them a lot in our first few years." The show Geddy is speaking about took place at Centennial Hall in London on July 25, 1974. Bespectacled radio DJ Ronnie Legg was also on the bill. Terry Brown, helping with load-in, and promoter Nick Panaseiko also attended the show, which was to be John Rutsey's last with the band.

"That was an exciting tour," remembers Howard Ungerleider. "We did a lot of dates with Kiss and a lot of good stories came out of that. There's one you should talk to Alex about, when he turned into a character called the Bag. Ace Frehley and Peter Criss loved that. There were some nights that were pretty wild. I remember one night when Peter Criss threw a plant off the balcony of the hotel, thinking that it was outside, and it crashed through the atrium, the glass atrium in the lobby. We weren't in that hotel very long after that.

"And it was always great because Kiss always traveled in limousines, and Ace Frehley would go to the gigs early, and he used to always call everybody Curly. You know how Ace talks. And he'd say, 'Do you want a ride to the show? I've got my limo!' So I would pop in the limo with Ace, and on the way to the venue, you would look at all the fans lined up, and he would say, 'Just look at that. It's like the Stones.' He'd be looking out the window at all the kids in line waiting to buy tickets, and we'd be in the back of the car with him and he'd be freaking out and it was just really humorous. And in the early days, everybody appreciated the limousines and all that. I guess that was short-lived, over a period of time, when the bands realized that the promoters were charging them back for the limos. They weren't the gift that they thought they were."

"We were more mature by that point," recalls Liam, with respect to the dates with Kiss. "The Kiss guys were all great and the crew were fantastic to deal with. They really helped nurture us. They were always very helpful, and they would give us anything we needed because they had nothing to fear from us — they had the Kiss show. They had the pyrotechnics, they had the flash, whereas Rush were literally going up and playing. But it ended up being a good match of artists, and it helped launch Rush into bigger and better things. But it wasn't like other artists, where you were almost treated as though you were the enemy and you might be doing something to hurt their performance or take away any kind of credibility from them. Kiss had no fear of anyone. They had their Kiss army already in place and they had their big show that nobody was going to one-up. How do you outdo pyrotechnics and flames and spitting blood and the costumes? So there was no fear of anything from an opening act. They were extremely welcoming, and they would do anything to help."

Howard agrees that the band took associations like this as a learning experience. He says, "Rush would deal with things with integrity, and they were always serious about their live presentation. Even at a young age, they were very conscious of making sure that it sounds exactly like the record. They had some bands they got on with really well, and what you would learn from these bands — aside from their bad habits, which everyone has — was the fact that it was a machine that had to be well oiled. You had to get in there and perform. And as long as you are professional and handle yourself as a professional, the learning experience is that this thing can take off and become an amazing machine, which it has over the years. You would see people using different kinds of equipment, and that's a bit of an education, and then the street itself is an education because you can get into a lot of trouble while you are walking around in a town or city you're not familiar with. And the education comes with street sense and being smart.

"And you know something? Gene Simmons is very serious about performing, and Paul Stanley as well. They were good role models at the time because they had their onstage personas. And when you see what they turned into onstage, and then you see them offstage, without their makeup, it was completely day and night. I mean, everyone now knows what they look like without their makeup, but back then, they never took their makeup off. That didn't happen until everybody was gone, the show was over and that was that. And we got to enjoy the odor of the costumes. It's like being in the back of a locker room with hockey players."

"We actually had heard the first record," begins Kiss legend Gene Simmons on how Kiss met Rush. "And Canadian bands in those days just couldn't cross the border without getting . . . well, without paying for it or somehow knowing somebody. And we didn't care about that stuff. All we cared about was that we madly loved new bands, madly loved the nurturing of them and were aware that somebody at one time gave us a break. And of course, later on, *Fly by Night*, all that other stuff, but it was that first record that got our attention. When we played with them the first time, I remember people outside were handing out newspapers that said 'the devil incarnate' or something like that, and there's a photo of myself. Thanks for telling me — I didn't know that.

"So Kiss took them on their first tour, and you know what? Besides the music, besides the musical proficiency, they were legitimately nice guys. It is true what they say about Canadians. And they knew that we liked them, and it was a mutual appreciation society; we would watch them play, when they played, obviously they worshiped at our platform heels, of course, as you should, all of you.

"But when we got to San Francisco," continues Gene, now into the tour tales, "Rush was third on the bill. It was Rush, the Tubes and Kiss. And Rush was being given a hard time. We drove all night, they didn't have any food or drink, and I remember Alex coming up and saying, 'I don't want to be a pain in the ass or anything, but we're really hungry; can we borrow a sandwich or something?' 'What's the matter? You don't have food in your dressing room?' 'No.' 'No?' 'And they're not giving us a sound check and stuff like that.' That's all I wanted to know. I tortured everybody — they got a sound check, food, everything. Kiss had always had the philosophy of anybody who plays with us is our responsibility. Because we are all in this together. Once you buy your ticket, you bought a ticket to everybody. So you get full lights, full sound, none of those crappy tricks."

Which, as the Rush guys will attest, became part of their philosophy as they moved up the ladder and became headliners. "And I'm proud to say that Rush was not the only band we took on their very first tour," adds Simmons. "AC/DC, Judas Priest, Bon Jovi, Mötley Crüe, you name it, Accept, I can't remember all the other bands, Queensrÿche, everybody. Because at the end of the day, ultimately, you have to believe that what you do onstage is not just being in a band. You've got to love the thing of it. It's one of my favorite things, to go see new bands. All the time. It's like human beings and babies. We see a little baby, you've got to nurture it. Because you were a baby once, and somebody nurtured you. You have to give back."

And then there was the comedy. Gene says of drummer Peter Criss, "Peter had this kind of profound connection with Alex. And they created this thing called the Bag, and the Bag was a paper bag with a face on it. And then Lifeson would sit on Peter Criss's knees, and they would do, like, this puppet act. And of course we tortured them; on the last date of their first tour with us, we went out and got those guns that kids use that shoot off string or something, and we tortured them on their last song. They tried to do that when we came out at the end of the night, but of course, the roadies killed them. We don't play fair.

"Criss never quite understood why Peart would play so complicated. 'Why don't you just play a simple beat?' I'd tell him, 'Peter, because you're not in that band. That's what they do and that's not what you do.' And you've got to hand it to them. You know, being in a trio means you've got space to fill, and you're not necessarily tied into the bass in terms of playing. So if you take a band like AC/DC, there's the bass, guitar and drums and they're set — you've got your locomotive. Rush is different. The guitar player doesn't necessarily follow what the bass player does, and they both don't necessarily play what the drums do. It's semi-fusion, if you will. It's certainly got rock roots, but anything is open, which is why some techno bands have some things in common with Rush that rock bands don't. And yet rock bands have something in common with Rush, which is the guitar. And every once in a while when the bass and guitar get together and play that locomotive riff, you feel that power and it veers more toward Zep. But it floats in different musical genres — it's fearless. Rush doesn't care what it is; it just is. A definition unto itself."

On the subject of commonality between his style as a bassist and Geddy's, Gene says, "I remember sitting down with Geddy and wondering about his bass licks. You know, 'When you do this in A, why do you end up in a C flat, which is really B.' And Geddy said, 'I don't know what they're called. I just play notes.' I mean, literally, they had no knowledge of what those notes were. They just played sort of by ear. So ultimately, it's what everybody should be doing, but he literally didn't know what an A note was. And look, you can say what you like about Rush — you can love them or hate them; any band that is worth their salt, their page, their chapter in history, is a band like an animal. Which is to say an animal will pee on a ground to claim its territory. And you can't make the argument that Rush isn't Rush. There is only one band that sounds like them, there is only one band that has that point of view, and that is profoundly important. What makes Rush unique, like I say, is fearlessness. It's the quality when starting to write a song, not caring what's popular or whether there are pop ballads happening or not. So, winning is good. But winning on your own terms is actually better.

"There doesn't seem to be anything particularly Canadian about Rush onstage," reflects Gene, on the cross-border cultural question. "Offstage, there is definitely something Canadian about them. They say please and thank you. They're not asshole rock stars like Gene Simmons. They are profoundly nice human beings. And onstage, they don't do the cocky 'I'm going to mount your girlfriend when you're not looking' thing. They really are there just to perform and do their stuff. But I don't see Rush as a Canadian band. I see Rush as a world band. Because if your stuff is good, it's not going to just appeal to someone who likes A Foot in Coldwater, and that's a Canadian band — do your homework. Or Headpins. You don't want something that sounds too local; you want something that sounds worldly and big."

"They were doing their own thing," reflects Liam, when asked about how a typical rock band on the road behaves. "It's not to say that we wouldn't get together occasionally with the other bands, but we just had a different outlook on life at that point. We were more grounded. We were Canadian. We weren't as extreme, and we wanted to take things a little slower. We had seen other people burning out and we didn't want to become part of all that. We all loved reading and we all liked the quieter way of life — I still do. I'm at my happiest sometimes with a book and a quiet day. But we weren't there for the party. That's not to say we didn't have fun; we just had our own type of fun. But the hard partying, it wasn't in their genes; it wasn't where we wanted to be. I think that somehow we knew that looking at the bigger picture early on, it just made more sense to us. Maybe we didn't realize why we were doing it, but we were looking at longevity. And you can tell that's something this band certainly had — they outlived so many other bands."

Following the band's dates with Kiss, plus assorted shows with the likes of Hawkwind and T. Rex, Rush did a clutch of Ontario dates with Scottish hard rockers Nazareth — a band that would take them across Canada the following year. Mid-November of '74 found Rush supporting Irish blues rock legend Rory Gallagher across America. "Very good guys and a good Irishman," recalls Ian Grandy. "We had National Sound there who took good care of us. It's one of the reasons we used them for so many years, and Rory was an interesting guy. They were a real professional band. They had played everywhere, and their top roadie, Tom O'Driscoll, was a mentor to a lot of us, actually."

And then it was very suddenly time to make a record, the first with "the new guy." Says Ian, "We came home for Christmas and our next gig was January 10, I think. And they went into the studio and just knocked it off." To get the job done, the band blew off a couple of U.S. shows with Blue Öyster Cult just after Christmas in December. "There's the picture of the three roadies sitting on the cases on the inner sleeve of *Fly by Night*. That was the next gig, because that was a gig we did in the middle of all that at Humber College. That's the only time they had. I don't know how they did it, but they were kind of ready with songs. It wasn't like later on with, say, *Hemispheres* when they were digging and digging."

chapter 3

Fly by Night

"He'll have a cigarette almost at the same time, on the hour."

"Neil is a self-professed and/or otherwise reading hound. He likes to read. Yeah, after the show he goes back . . . reads. *Anthem* by Ayn Rand, Foundation trilogy by Isaac Asimov, all that stuff. And so the lyrics, he showed me that stuff. And it's funny, Peter Criss, who came from the streets and was close to being illiterate — and I mean that in a good way — he would call him Big Head Morgan. I've no clue why, but it had to do with one being literate and well-read and the other not," so says Kiss thumper Gene Simmons, on what would be the biggest change for Rush aboard the band's all-important second album, to be called *Fly by Night*. Big Head Morgan would be writing the words of wisdom, not Geddy Lee. Or John Rutsey. Or Peter Criss.

"But if you were a fan of Rush on the first record, you probably had a problem when Neil Peart came in," continues Gene. "In 'Working Man' and some of the earlier stuff, there was a more R&B and blues-rooted feel to it. But then clearly, you can't push the guys to do what they don't want to do. And with a drummer who wrote lyrics, all of a sudden it freed up the guys to just sort of play. And this was in them. Look, you can't be convincing at doing something you're not convincing at. That's not just wordplay. You can't just get up there and be Rush if you're not. So they became what they became because that's what they wanted to become."

As mapped out by Ian Grandy, just like they were in school, Rush made the best of their time away from class and, over Christmas break, wrote their essay. But they had been thinking about what to say across all that dead time on the road, in the cars and hotel rooms, fiddling about during coveted but only occasional sound checks. The evidence is right there on the inner sleeve of *Fly by Night* — written on the road, recorded in a flash between endless tour duties.

"When we were traveling around, we worked on songs," confirms Neil. "If we rented a car, really, it was like the Monkees. You know, Alex would have an acoustic guitar and we'd be working on a song, in a rental car, in a hotel room after a show — that's pretty much how *Fly by Night* was written. I put in my little handwritten lyric sheets at the time. I wrote the cities that all of those songs were written in, and they vary wildly all over the map because very often parts of songs were composed in just that ad hoc a manner. So a lot of that was definitely conceived on the fly and so *Fly by Night* is kind of apt even in retrospect."

"I remember they were putting some songs together for *Fly by Night* one day when we were going to Cleveland," recalls Howard, confirming Neil's tale of writing songs in the car. "I was driving, and they were all playing guitars in the car, putting the songs together. And I was driving south and didn't realize that I was driving south when I really should've been driving north. It was really distracting. We were having such a good time.

"We were driving for a few hours — this is when we had rental cars that we would pick up from Hertz and drive, and we would trade cars off if we wanted to — and I kept seeing the sign for Cape Gerardo, and I'm thinking, 'Cape Gerardo? Doesn't sound familiar to me.' Going to the East Coast, and then I realized, man, I was on Highway 55 going south for hours, and now we have to sort of get to Cleveland.

"So I had an idea: let's just drive to Evansville, Indiana, right? So we'll drive to Evansville, Indiana, and we'll hop on a plane from Evansville and fly to Cleveland. So I get on the phone, made some arrangements and found what time the flight was leaving. And then we got caught in a torrential downpour and traffic, couldn't get through, and I remember getting to Evansville in time to watch the aircraft leave the ground without us. And then we just had to continue driving. It was a long, horrific process, but we managed to get to Cleveland at night and made the gig, as always. But yeah, they did a lot of writing that way and came up with a lot of the riffs. And they would flip-flop verses and choruses a lot, maybe use the chorus part as the verse and the verse as the chorus."

"We didn't have much time for improvisation," continues Neil. "We didn't get sound checks, you know, as opening act on three- or four- or five-act shows. Sound checks were extremely rare and even if, you definitely didn't have the luxury of being able to jam very long. So maybe on club dates we'd get to do that a little. Where we'd be playing longer sets, we might have had time to mess around really playing. But mostly as a whole, all of the earlier albums were a matter of coming off the road and doing it in two weeks. I think we had two weeks, ten days of studio time to make *Fly by Night* and very much had to conceive it on the fly. Probably a couple of the songs we managed to write and play before that, but the rest were arranged and orchestrated, as it were, as guitar, bass and drums.

"Learning to play with them electrically together had to happen quickly, and then we went right back on the road again from that intense creative ferment, from trying to make an album that we liked. And it was as simple as that — trying to make something that we liked. At night, we probably slept on the floor of the studio and then played in some college or high school that night and then whoosh right back out again. So they all were made that way. There wasn't much time, ironically, to explore then, not like we have now, which is interesting. But somebody said something wise once, that you have your whole life to make your first album and six months to make your second. But also most of that six months was spent on the road.

"Like so many things, it was entirely accidental," muses Neil, on how from the onset he would up being Rush's word-wrangler. "With J.R. Flood, I'd written a couple lyrics. I hadn't taken it too seriously but always liked reading, and wrote some grade two poetry, so it was just another kind of expression I wanted to try, I guess. And because I'd done it a couple times before, and neither Geddy or Alex seemed particularly interested in it, we started talking about new material right away.

"And they already had a couple of songs. I remember 'In the End' was already written at the time and we had rehearsed it in one of the first few days, so we were already thinking that way. And the song that became 'Anthem,' we were already jamming in the first audition. So a lot of that was starting to meld together. And just as in J.R. Flood, I thought, 'Oh, I'll give you a couple lyrics and see if you like them.' So it just grew from there without any intention or huge desire on my part. Drumming was all it is, the main part of my life; writing lyrics was a matter of a few weeks of a few years. Of course, I think about it all the time and make notes about it all the time now, as a discipline; but no, it really started just as 'Maybe I can do that.' Like your first band:

'Maybe I can draw the poster?' It was as simple as that and as natural as that.

"Another thing that came out of that first tour was that feeling of 'Now what?'" continues Neil. "You know, this ain't enough for my life. Beyond reading was writing." One might infer that writing was also beyond drumming and the grind of touring and meeting a constant army of people. In other words, for a guy like Neil, without word games, the road was going to get unpleasant very quickly.

"He was just so much better read," explains Donna Halper. "He knew philosophy, he knew poetry, and he was by his own admission self-taught, but he still knew all this stuff. And I think at that time, Geddy was still finding his way, no pun intended. And I think he was making the transition from 'Okay, we're a bar band' to 'We're a thinking person's band. Can I do this?' And I think that's a lot of what was going on. And the answer was 'Yes, you can do this,' and yes, he did make the transition. I don't get the sense that it was tormenting Alex so much. I think as time went on, Geddy and Neil forged a very strong partnership.

"But let's face it. When you've got a new direction, it's scary, because you know your old one. You know how things work. I mean, we've known John for years, you know? And now John is gone for whatever reason, and now we get this new guy, and who are we when he's around? I was there as this adjustment period was taking place, and I think that was probably the last time I had to play the big sister role because after that, there were other people. They had managers, tour people, and they were surrounded by people suddenly. But in those very early formative years, they were three kids from Toronto trying to figure out what they were and become what they wanted to be."

Producer Terry Brown manned the board again as Rush studio-tested the songs for their next album.

"He was great," says Alex. "He was such a nice person to be with. We really respected him, really looked up to him. He was a great engineer, he was a good producer, he understood us, we loved his little studio, Toronto Sound. It was very cozy — not that we knew anything else, really. It was just a really comfortable relationship, and everybody was doing great at it. It seemed logical that we would continue to work with him, much like most bands did at that time. I know I instantly took to him when we were doing the first record. I thought he was doing a great job. The record was really in a mess, and he managed, on those eight tracks, to pull out all the stuff and repair it. And I thought, 'This guy's a genius.' With *Fly by Night*, I think, we felt so comfortable with him that this was the way it was always going to be. So yes, it happened very quickly with Terry."

"It was completely out of my hands," continues Terry, on the replacing of John with Neil. "When the band came back to do *Fly by Night*, Neil was playing drums and introductions were done. It was a whole new band, and we just got to work. And I was pretty impressed. As soon as Neil sat down at the kit, he was a real gentleman for starters, and it was nice to see that the guys were comfortable and looking forward to doing stuff with this new member. And then we started rehearsing and I was pretty impressed — never looked back, actually."

As for what Neil was bringing besides drumming expertise, Terry says that "he was certainly bringing songwriting, which John, I don't believe, did. And really, at that point, I was involved on the outside, like I said, with the first record. So I didn't really know too much about the inner workings of the band. So it was hard for me to tell. As a player, I thought Neil had distinctive chops, which maybe John didn't have. Although John was good and certainly capable of doing the job at that time, you could tell that Neil had aspirations to take it a lot further. So that was a really good positive thing. He was a great player, back then even. And, of course, his bringing lyrics to the table, in the songwriting capacity, made a huge difference and changed the way the band was going to sound from then out. They never looked back."

Fly by Night, issued in the dead of winter, February 15, 1975, featured on its front cover an imposing and menacing snowy owl alit on a patch of ground surrounded by snow. It underscored that Rush was a band from Canada, a band that had to fly away from those long Canadian nights to visit the land of opportunity. The painting is by concentration camp survivor Eraldo Carugati, also known for the illustrations of each of the four Kiss members for the covers of their simultaneously released 1978 solo albums. From Rush's first record to the second, there was no branding: no logo was carried over — and with a four-letter name, it would have been easy to adopt one. On the back, the band is pictured as if frosted, frozen in time, the frames huddled together on a snowy expanse. *Fly by Night* was the band's first album issued in the U.K., blue and silver Mercury label, inner lyric sleeve included.

Once past the chill of the cover art and into the sonics of the record, the listener is confronted with "Anthem," a compact maelstrom of agitated playing that finds Rush summarily inventing progressive metal. A simple idea, really, hard rock mixed with prog rock. Lyrically, Peart would never live down "Anthem." It caused him to have to champion Ayn Rand, philosopher queen of selfishness, in interviews ever after. But of course, Neil read everything, and Rand (or Nietzsche, or the Beats) was a natural avenue for a young man looking to celebrate male energy — as any man will tell you looking back decades, he was most productive in myriad ways in his twenties and thirties, most sure of himself, most creative and daring.

This is why rock 'n' roll has always been a young man's game. Men inevitably look back on their twenties wishing they could have harnessed that energy and focused it. That, combined with "What was I thinking?" So here was Neil turning on his audience to big books. University students are immersed in this stuff and do it too, but Neil, as well as Alex and Geddy, were self-taught by necessity, and just like the brilliant and brilliantly stark idea of duct-taping riffs to art rock, why not use the vehicle they had to do what the university educated were doing?

As for the new note-dense directive, laid out like the war dead through the not one but two intros in "Anthem," Geddy says, "We were interested in progressive rock and more complex rock. We did not want to stay as a simple and basic rock band. We loved this whole attitude of bands like Genesis and Yes and ELP, and at the same time we liked the rough edges of Zep and the sound of Jeff Beck's albums and the Yardbirds — all that stuff is where we were at. So we wanted to make our music more adventurous, and that's what began the parting of the ways with John, and that's what made Neil such an appealing option because that's totally where he was at."

Terry was also looking forward to working with the new drummer. He felt the breath of fresh air that Neil brought was needed for the band's continued success. "I would say that given the style of material that they were doing then, and where they were going, their lifespan would have been fairly limited with John. Because when Neil came to the table, he brought with him a whole different side of the band which didn't exist before and inspired the guys to do what they're doing now. I would have to say that the chances of it being as successful would be very limited with John's health the way it was. It's a no-brainer. It wouldn't have happened. They would have broken up. Neil stepped in and saved the day.

"For starters, he came with this whole lyrical background that he wanted to bring to the band," continues Brown. "He was a great player and he gave the band a whole new lease on life. It was almost too complicated at that point, but we made it work. And we felt that it was going to be the way to go. It wasn't my decision — you have to appreciate that I was purely co-producing those records back then. We made *Fly by Night* in twenty-one days, from the very beginning when they walked in the studio to when they walked out and Vic picked up the masters. That's pretty damned quick. So I didn't have a lot of time to form opinions. I was very happy with Neil's performances, I loved the direction the tunes were taking and I felt it had tremendous potential."

"I noticed that with the rap and rock combination," reflects Neil, speaking about the idea of progressive metal, "I thought that Faith No More were so amazing when they first came out, and then there was Cypress Hill and Rage Against the Machine, and then it just kind of bubbles along for a while until it suddenly exploded. And reggae and rock was like that too. Reggae bubbled along beneath the radar and then suddenly in the late '70s — boom.

"But we just played what we liked. We were always that organic, and still are, all through those changes. It was just about trying to play the music we liked. I've made the quote before, 'I loved music so much, I wanted to play it.' That's the fundamental chemical reaction that went on. At that time, we had a foot in both camps, stylistically, as young musicians. We'd grown up with The Who, Led Zeppelin, Yardbirds and the birth of hard rock. And at the same time, we were fans of the whole progressive scene. So for us, it was just an expression of what we liked. There was no 'Let's synthesize these two styles; if we take that element and combine it with this element, we'll have something new!' It was nothing like that. We were never that self-aware, let alone that calculating. It was simply an organic response to playing what we liked. We liked to play loud and energetically, and this new complicated, sophisticated approach appealed as well."

There'd be more examples of this subconsciously arrived at credo across *Fly by Night*, but "Anthem" delivers the idea right between the eyes, in under five minutes. The song is also rife with pregnant pauses and other mathematical rhythm punctuations, which would turn Rush into one of the favorite bands for air drummers.

"Ah, we were all babies then," chuckles Neil, remembering that first progressive metal spark he felt with the band and how it came from this very song. "You know, let's remember, even though it seemed like I'd been playing for so long, I'd been playing for six years, you know? Nothing. And I'd only been in a handful of bands, and actually in terms of bass players and guitar players, I was always very lucky with the bands that I was in. Very instructive and very generous with me.

"But what I remember the most was that intensity of engagement with the music, and as we talked that day too — how much Geddy loved the music that he listened to — it was the same passion that I felt for it. The interplay started pretty well right away, as soon as we started jamming more, with more purpose, once I was actually in the band. Then we were jamming with a purpose and really melding that right away. One of the first things we ever worked on, certainly, was what would become 'Anthem.' The shuffle verses and all that, Geddy and I just automatically locked into those and gravitated toward the different kinds of changes that we would both like. There were a lot of those 'what ifs?'"

"Best I Can" is little more than a sturdy mid-intensity hard rock song, but Neil gives it energy: with snare fills, with disciplined hi-hat work, with cowbell. Geddy builds in a precise and moderately busy bass line, Alex adds a wah-wah axe solo and this older Rush song, one from the Rutsey days, is dressed up enough that it fits. Does Neil play too much for what the song is? Perhaps, but since few dared to take this approach — available in extremity from Keith Moon — all of a sudden Rush is standing alone. Some of the fills at the end would be the bane of a "tasteful," less-is-more drummer, but we don't remember those guys as much as we do the Professor, correct? Class dismissed.

"Beneath, Between & Behind" is a second very proggy song on *Fly by Night*, propelled by a wall of sound drum performance behind jazzy chords from Alex.

"I was just trying stuff out," shrugs Neil on his lyrical approach to the record, which often resulted in flights of fancy like this song. "Even the first two lyrics I wrote back in J.R. Flood, one of them was sort of a mythological thing called 'Gypsy,' where the character went around healing broken hearts, and the other one was called 'Retribution,' about being trapped in the eternal light. So the pattern, the die, was cast growing up. I loved mysteries — Hardy Boys, Nancy Drew — and English books for a sense of mystery. I've never thought this before, but it occurs to me, and it's so natural. Since I was a small boy, it so fascinated me. And when I was a teenager, *Chariots of the Gods*, all those mysteries and conspiracy theories, all that stuff fascinated me and became part of my mode of thinking. And I went through a Tolkien period. When I was in England, I read *Lord of the Rings* and a slew of other stuff like that, and Mervyn Peake was another color of that writing that appealed to me. Not very well known now, but an amazing writer — really dark, twisted fantasies.

"And all of that was an influence on, I guess, a way of thinking. Not a way of seeing the world, really, because that would be schizophrenia. But it becomes part of your own mythology, and you find these metaphors and these other stories. *Lord of the Rings* is a great example, a hero story, overcoming obstacles, a friend's loyalty. All those qualities that are important become metaphorical for you in a story like that. So all those things were formed.

"And observing too. The first travel song, it occurs to me just now, is 'Between, Beneath & Behind.' It was about the United States, and it had all this input coming in from traveling in that country, suddenly, after knowing nothing more than Buffalo, Niagara Falls and New York as a kid. Suddenly, we're traveling in that big, great big ass country. And all of that started the whole travel writing in general. Wanting to capture what I see became more important to me all the time, the way people behave and the feeling of nature, and those metaphors of human behavior and natural behavior that began then. But the mythology was just a natural thing about being twenty-two years old and being a geeky teenager and reading all the fantasy and science fiction, but also history and mystery and romances. All of that was part of my being at the time, and it was finding a way out. It's just learning to express yourself. You know, lyrics are a vehicle for expressing yourself, ultimately. But first you've got to have a self."

Adds Geddy with respect to this oft-overlooked but formative Rush song, "We were on tour during the first album, and Neil hadn't been with us long, and Alex and I noticed how much he read and how his vocabulary was rather large. And neither of us really enjoyed writing lyrics; we just were into the tunes. So we suggested that he should give it a try. And I think the first song — I might be wrong — but I think the first song was 'Beneath, Between & Behind.' And I read this one and wow, this was a song about America. He was traveling through America and he's writing this very wordy song about his observations and thinking about the past of America and the future of America and the promise of America. It was really stimulating — but really a mouthful to sing in kind of the rockin' style that we were into at that time. So it was hard. I mean, if you listen to that song, blah blah blah, I'm just . . . there are no breaths in there. It's a high-energy song, but it's nonstop lyrics. Sometimes you have to be careful what you ask for."

"I was just happy that I wasn't the singer," adds Alex. "Certainly, they were something very new and different. It took us really out of the rock 'n' roll thing and spoke in a very different way. But at the same time, you could recognize that it was going to set us apart."

"Yeah, it was good; it was just different," continues Geddy. "But they were wordy. They were a mouthful. And as a singer, it was hard, some of them. And some of them were great. Some of them just flowed. 'Fly by Night' was not difficult. But 'Beneath, Between & Behind' was a mouthful. So it was new and we had to get our heads around it. And we made it work, I think, and it's a blistering song. I'm just glad I don't have to sing it every night."

Alex has another perspective on why Neil taking charge of the lyrics was something that worked so well for them. He says, "It was a great way to include Neil at an early stage so that he felt he was part of the band — he wasn't just a hired musician. We wanted him to feel like he was one of us right from the very start." So it wasn't just that Alex and Geddy didn't want to do lyrics and Neil did or that Neil was good at them. Drummers in bands often take the reins and become the business guy. Sometimes as the wise judge, the voice of reason. Sometimes as the guy who does a lot of the interviews and serves as the official spokesman. Sometimes as a creative force in terms of music-writing — there are a lot of drummers who plunk a bit of guitar. Sometimes, as with Alex Van Halen, it's the guy who deals with the album cover art. With Rush, it just worked out that assigning lyrics to Neil was a good way to play to everyone's strengths and spread the work around.

"Well, that was a shocker," says manager Ray on Neil's impressive wordsmithing. "When you heard the *Fly by Night* album, and you got the lyrics, what would have taken umpteen records to get to, the maturity, they were suddenly there overnight. Might they have ever gotten there without him? I don't know if I was surprised. I was just thrilled. It was just blinders on, we're going for it, whatever it takes, and everyone was a willing participant. You know, certainly, the three of them and myself were willing participants. Nobody cared about much other than the band, about working and being successful. I was entrepreneurial, and they had a great drive. And they loved to play. They absolutely loved to play. As they still do.

"When Neil joined the band, I learned a lot of respect for Neil very quickly," continues Ray. "There were a couple of reviews that bothered me, and he said to me — and I'll never forget it — 'If you're going to believe the good ones, then you have to believe the bad ones, so don't read any of them.' Or something to that effect. And I took that to heart, and I still live with that. You know, later when we got predominately good ones, it was easier. Everyone has a button that can be pushed, so it's a lot nicer and a lot easier in a way, in the last decade, than it was before."

"They were writing tunes about their experiences and what was going on," says Terry. "Neil was bringing that to the table, without question. And so they had a distinct style that they were developing very, very rapidly. There were only eight tunes; it wasn't like we had this huge list of songs that we were picking eight songs from. It was all very new, and it was all very quick."

Terry touches on an interesting point there. This was not a band, album to album, era to era, with a big bank of songs from which to draw and tweak and update, to whip into shape. Rush always had just enough material to go on the record, and some-times not even that. There was no well.

"I can't remember recording one song that was put in the can, put on the shelf," continues Brown. "I could be wrong, but I don't believe they did. It was always 'This is the record,' and I mean, it would be fine-tuned and honed, all the tunes, until we were happy. And that was the record. So yes, that's weird. We never really talked about why. It was one of those things that, had they come to me with say eight or nine songs for a specific record, and there were a couple of real lemons there, I would've probably said, 'You know what? You've got to do something here; this isn't working.' But that never happened. They always came with such strong material. There was always an excitement and energy around most tunes, so it was just a question of fine-tuning them and presenting them the best way that we could. And every song was a lot of work, but for a really good reason."

Closing side one of the original vinyl version of *Fly by Night* was Rush's first full-on prog metal epic, "By-Tor & the Snow Dog," much longer than the two earlier songs on the album that were just as mathematical. All three were much more mathematical than "Working Man" or "Here Again" but not much longer than either. We now had two tenets of prog rock covered, long length and mathematical structure, three if one includes fanciful titling.

"A perfect example of using the vehicle of fantasy," says Peart of this beloved Rush classic. "Ray Danniels's dogs, a husky and a German shepherd, which were always trying to bite our tour manager Howard. So it became By-Tor. And he had a big husky that was white. By-Tor and the snow dog — it was just our manager's two dogs. So it became fun. And it really was fun, if you have the kind of sensibility that I just described, coming from all that fantasy reading. To play with that in the song, and all the instrumental exploration we did in that for the first time, trying to dramatize a story with music and using all these intricate time signatures and complicated arrangements, it was all born right there. It was born out of fun and a true sense of adventure."

Through nascent Rush workouts like "By-Tor," Neil was

getting a sense of the personalities and playing capabilities of his two new bandmates.

"Both passionate and methodical" is how Peart sums up Geddy as a student of the bass. "I think you can't find two apparently dichotomized characteristics, but in fact they work together so well. It's what lets you put all that time into working on it. And being a passionate young rock fan as a teenager, something I can totally relate to, there's nothing you'd rather do than play your instrument. Everything else was just an interruption around that main focus.

"And certainly, he was focused on bass guitar that way as a teenager. It grew out of a passion for the instrument, and then he could be methodical about parts and riffs and learning the elements of technique and so on. All of those are built over time, but they couldn't be built without the elemental passion for the instrument. That's what we share, bringing the same dedication and the same inspiration to and from the instrument, and then the application to spend time really getting it right.

"If we're working on parts together, our application is infinite. The two of us will spend forever on a rhythm section part, getting each interplay of each other's activities, and decorations, together, discussing them or just with a kind of mental telepathy, intuiting with each other, either in songwriting and recording or onstage, even. You know, that part of it certainly is the highest . . . I always say that live performance is the highest possible test."

"By-Tor" also demonstrates Geddy's ear for melody, explains Neil, when it comes to bass parts. "Sure, a lot of times, of course, young bass guitar fans, even, are going to focus on technique. And that's natural enough, but they might well miss the overall feel for melody. And Geddy plays bass like a singer, because he understands melody that way, and phrasing — very important.

The melody and phrasing grow out of that, and bass is not just a supporting instrument by any means. It's a part of his musical character, so therefore reflects strongly, this sense of rhythm and a sense of phrasing. In the same way that I write lyrics like a drummer, with the sense of syncopation, I think certainly he approaches the bass guitar with the innate greater understanding that a singer can bring."

Funny, but Geddy uses the same word to describe his new bandmate on *Fly by Night*.

"Neil is methodical, and he can be infuriatingly methodical . . . consistent; I've watched him, and when he's smoking cigarettes, he'll have a cigarette almost at the same time, on the hour. Like, he's so methodical, it's unbelievable. And he's very, very organized. He likes to be organized, and everything is considered. He doesn't say anything that isn't considered, except when we're throwing jokes around. And even then, he's such a fast thinker. And what a lot of people don't realize about him is how funny he is. And how good he is. You know, people approach him, and I love watching people approach him, because he's this god-like creature, Neil Peart, and they don't see the same guy I see, because I've seen him in every possible shape. I've seen him after a twelve-hour drive, where he's exhausted and crashing, and we're all sleeping in the same room. I've seen him good, bad and ugly. We've all seen each other good, bad and ugly. So he's much goofier in real life."

Indicative of Neil's goofy nature, according to Geddy, the By-Tor lyric was a joke that got out of control. He says the guys must have been high when conjuring the idea out of blue smoke. Also goofy is that the song is in four parts, but one of the parts also has four parts. Neil says the naming of the first movement, "At the Tobes of Hades," came from the dad of a friend who used to say, "It's hotter than the Tobes of Hades." What's also slightly amusing is that this first section of the song finds the band instantly into a verse with lyrics. Usually with a giant prog rock journey of a song — from Rush or anybody else — there's intro after intro before the wise man speaks.

Producer Terry Brown must have rolled up his sleeves and gotten his hands dirty in a protracted trip such as this. "Needless to say," says Terry, "a sort of interesting sci-fi concept needed to be explored. It was a lot of fun to make, and I think we did a good job with it. It just took a long time for it to sort of seep into the consciousness of the fans, I guess, and certainly the record labels.

"But yes, I always get involved in shaping a tune, to a certain degree, depending on how much shaping it needs. I don't remember for that album how much we did. We did an awful lot of preproduction, recording and mixing in a three-week period and finished the record in three weeks. So it was a bit of a whirlwind at that point. We had to sort of get down to it and do it, and so you were flying by the seat of your pants to a large degree and drawing on a lot of experience that you use instantly — 'This needs to be done, this needs to be done, let's do this, let's do this.'

"It was a real experience with these new tunes. With the first album there was a lot of criticism — and there still is to some degree — with the direction the band was taking. Whereas with *Fly by Night*, they had their own thing going on, distinctly. There was no question that they didn't sound like anybody else, so that was really good. Just getting more involved in Geddy's vocals and hearing him sing in that distinctive style was very exciting. I mean, it wasn't three tunes now, it was a whole record, so that was exciting. And solos too. I mean, there were so many things, bass sounds, their ability as musicians had started to really blossom. I started to realize the potential. Back in those days, Geddy's voice was one of a kind. I can't think of anybody who sounded like him. Some people loved his voice and some people completely hated his voice. So that was something special."

Now that the world was beginning to realize that Rush was establishing a toehold in pop culture consciousness — or at least in the loud rock end of the music industry, in the environment discussed in *Circus*, *Creem* and *Hit Parader* — there would be frank debate about Geddy Lee's singing.

Neil explains, "At the time I first joined the band, certainly Geddy was coming out of being a bar band singer and singing against the onslaught of distorted amps and bad amplification and PA systems and so on. So, as he tells it — and I believe it to be true — he was singing in that range and intensity just to get through all the muck. What happens when you get into songwriting and recording, you're able to explore the nuances of singing. He took quite a bit of stick too for the stridency of his voice in those days. And he was self-conscious about it. You know, anybody would be. There's nothing more personal than your voice, right? People can pick on your drumming or your guitar playing, but your voice, that's close to your heart, in a very real way.

"So he took a lot of nasty, nasty remarks about the throat. Some of them we still quote, things that were said in bad reviews over the years that came up, in the pre-tour movie and all that. That he swallowed a throat full of razor blades and stuff. You know, it did bother him. And at the same time, he was ambitious to sing on a broader palette and was able to do that, as we explored so much on those early records, using different dynamics in different types of songs without any limit. He had the opportunity to try those things and learn the craft of it, as we all did, and become better at it and be able to settle on a range that best conveys the mood and the emotion."

Alex recalls the critics say that "Geddy's voice was Mickey

Mouse on helium and we were a Led Zeppelin copy band and pretentious and sword and sorcery, all kinds of stuff. I would say probably most of the reviews were bad. But there were some that were good, and we found that we had a growing audience that didn't care about any of that stuff. They were into the band and they liked what we were doing and what we were trying to do. We were a little more thoughtful about the way we wrote music and certainly how we wrote lyrics and how we put it all together.

"We had a very strong male-dominated fan base right from the beginning, but they were culty about the band that they liked. I think most people who are into a band that nobody really knows about like the specialness. You feel like you discovered something and that was kind of how it was in the early days. I don't know if it was discouraging to read bad press. I mean after awhile it was like, 'Oh yeah, yeah whatever.' You sort of got used to it. We were certainly open to any kind of criticism because you learn from stuff like that. But usually critics back then were just trying to be smart and cool and hip.

"I think because we've outlived all those critics that existed back then and it's generations later, they're grudgingly giving us respect now that we've been around for so long. The band is different from what it was back then. Rush has always been a hate it or love it sort of proposition. I mean, it doesn't really matter to us what that press thinks. It's all about the fans and it's all about us and the relationship with them. Times are so different now. With the whole information highway, your connection is much clearer. I'd rather read fan reviews than some guy who's always hated us and didn't stay for half the show."

"Oh, they're too awful to remember," says Ray of the bad notices on Geddy's throat. "There was always this, when he would sing, he's trying to sound like Robert Plant, but at seventy-eight speed instead of forty-five. There were constant insults hurled that way. But it was never like that with the audiences. That was never the vibe in the audience toward the stage, at all."

Flipping over the *Fly by Night* record, we are invited to consider the album's title track. "Fly by Night" is the guitary enough but poppy semi-hit single that saved Rush, letting them live to fight another day. This was the first song the band ever wrote together, assembled during a three-day break in East Lansing, Michigan. Of note, many fans consider "Anthem" to be the first song they ever wrote together, but it was in its infancy before Neil arrived in the band.

The results were promising, making it clear that old originals "Garden Road," "I've Been Runnin'," "The Loser" and "Fancy Dancer" would not be moving forward onto vinyl. As with "Best I Can," "Fly by Night" is a traditional up-tempo rock song designed not to cause offense, but then the drummer throws in a bunch of things that cause offense, but only to ears that need the whole pop smorgasbord of their music to be easy listening start to finish. Neil makes "Fly by Night" just slightly eccentric, a bit wacky. As does Geddy's strange, high voice. Otherwise, the song is a solid example of a well-written and well-integrated procession of parts worthy, in the aggregate, of being a working man's moderately performing single. The Dutch issue single for the song, backed with "Best I Can," constituted the band's first picture sleeve single.

Lyrically, "Fly by Night" has Neil looking back wistfully on his attempt to strike out on his own in dramatic fashion, by going — flying — to London, England, to make it as a drumming sensation. It's a song about the rock 'n' roll dream, but he wisely couches it in the universal, making it relatable to anybody gathering up the gumption to start a new chapter in life. Reflecting typical Canadian modesty, the song didn't do much in the charts, reaching #88 in the States and #45 in Canada, but it also quietly served as the main reason the album as a whole did all right, finding #113 on the Billboard 200 and hitting #9 back home in Canada.

Next up is "Making Memories," a curious, vigorous folk rock workout akin to full band Crosby, Stills, Nash & Young.

For his slide part, Lifeson used a metal lipstick tube. Expanding on what Harold has said, Alex explains, "That was written on a drive where we got lost. It was in the Midwest somewhere — Indiana, maybe. I forget where we were going to, but we made a right and we should've made a left. We went out of our way by a few hours and we were sitting in the car with an acoustic guitar, and that's the way we wrote songs then. Pretty much everything was written in dressing rooms and sound checks. Neil's lyrics were written on the road. That one was all written before we went into the studio."

"Rivendell," named for an elven locale in *Lord of the Rings*, is the type of quiet medieval folk tune, falsetto vocals included, that tacitly props prog rock credibility. This type of acoustic guitar playing is all about demonstrating versatility and timelessness, not to mention European pedigree. You certainly wouldn't hear anything like this on a Kiss or Aerosmith album, but you sure would on a Steve Howe solo indulgence. Neither "Making Memories" or "Rivendell" became part of the ensuing tour's set list, but every other song from the record did.

Fly by Night closes with "In the End," a languid sort of roots rock epic, which is closer to "Here Again" and "Working Man" than the Rush 2.0 track "By-Tor & the Snow Dog." In fact, like "Best I Can," this one is a pre-Peart song, with lyrics by Lee.

Post-release, on March 24, 1975, Rush won their first of many Juno awards (Canada's version of the Grammys), earning a title that is jokingly considered a curse: Most Promising Group. The band, on the road in the Midwest, found out through a drunken phone call from Ray, who had been partying it up in celebration of the news; Rush did their own partying later that night. And two weeks before that, Alex had married Charlene, his girlfriend since the late '60s, already at that point the mother of their first child, Justin. Two years later, the couple welcomed another son, Adrian, to the fold.

Back on the road — because that was the formula — Rush was packaged with a bewildering array of bands, including regular show partners from the previous year, Kiss.

"Oh, we did a million shows with Kiss," says Alex. "In '75, we were playing on average three-thousand seaters, so small theaters. We weren't big bands at all. This was for both of us, our first few tours. And we became quite close, very good friends; we hung out all the time. Days off, we got together, went out for dinner. On show days, we were always in each other's dressing rooms. We corresponded when we were off the road. We really became quite close, and I think it was because we were sharing this whole new experience. We would sit down and talk to Paul and Gene about music, where we were coming from, where they were coming from.

"And it was interesting to hear them talk about what Kiss represented; it was a vehicle for them to make lots of money and to do this whole showbiz shtick. The music was part of that whole thing; it wasn't really what was in their hearts. But they knew that this was the kind of music they needed to make for this thing to work. I remember both of them sitting in my hotel room one night — I think it was in Louisville, Kentucky — with two acoustics, and they were singing all these other songs, and they were really nice songs that they'd written that would *never* be Kiss songs. And of course, we were from a whole different area, where it wasn't about the showbiz. It was all about the music and playing. And our relationship with them just soured when the live album came out and they became huge. They just became very, very distant. They were aloof. We went out to see them a couple times and they just ignored us; it was weird."

It seems also that the divide between Gene and Paul and "the rest of the band" was presenting itself even that far back.

"Ace was a riot; Ace was very, very funny," continues Alex. "And he loved getting messed up. He loved drinking and smoking pot, anything to get messed up. But he always had some new joke to tell you. For his birthday, we got him a couple of gifts, just little goofy things, and invited him down to one of our rooms. We were sharing rooms then too. And we got a bunch of booze and smoked some pot and celebrated his birthday with him, and he said [impersonating Ace's high voice], 'You know, you guys . . . I can't believe it. The band members in the band I play in don't even wish me happy birthday, and you get me all these gifts and you get me down here. Like, you guys are the best! You're the best!' I remember asking him — he got a new house — and I said, 'How's your new house, Ace?' [impersonating Ace again] 'I find it very accommodating. Yuk yuk yuk yuk.' He was really a lot of fun. And Peter was a nice guy too."

The tour for *Fly by Night*'s follow-up, *Caress of Steel*, was the last Rush would do with Kiss. "By then we were getting to the point where we were probably a little too big to tour for them," says Alex. "They were looking for something smaller as an opening act, and maybe something that was a little more in line with what they were doing."

Geddy cites Kiss when asked for examples of excess he saw on tour. "Traveling with Kiss before they started to get successful, Kiss were always very frustrated because they would walk offstage, take off their makeup, and nobody would know it was them. So it was very hard for them to get recognized and they didn't like that. So they would have these wild parties after the show and invite everyone in sight, in order to feel like rock gods. So there was some pretty serious goings-on. But we were good friends. We toured together for our first two tours of America, and we had a very good relationship. We didn't have any trouble at all. It was when they started getting really successful that they lost their grip on reality pretty quickly."

On June 7, 1975, in San Diego, before returning home for some closing Canadian dates, Rush received a memorable send-off from Gene, Paul, Ace and Peter. "We had a big whipped cream scene at the end of our tour with them. They just creamed us with cream pies; it was serious. I was getting stuff out of my guitar pickups for weeks afterwards." At the end of Kiss's set, Rush got their revenge, resulting in a stage covered in shaving cream and a turgid encore from the rapidly ascending headliners.

"We learned so much from them," continues Geddy. "First of all, regardless of what you want to say about them, musically or otherwise, or about their personalities, in the early days there was no harder working band on the road than Kiss. There was no band more determined to put on a spectacular show and give people their money's worth than Kiss. That was a great thing to see as an opening act. We were so impressionable, so green, when we first came to America to tour, and they were pretty new at it too. But I had a lot of respect for their work ethic, and I had a lot of respect for their showmanship. They really wanted to give them their money's worth, so that was an important lesson to learn.

"And you know too, back then they were rock musicians and they were interested in playing rock, and their music was quite rock. So I can't say that we learned a lot from them from a musical point of view, but certainly from a living on the road point of view, and putting on a show, and the importance of all those things. To consider everything that goes along with your live presentation, they were incredibly instructive, and they were very good to us. They took us a lot of places, so we'll always owe them a debt for that.

"But there was a lot of partying; those guys liked to have a good time, especially Gene. They had their good times, and their hotels were always fun to watch. We made some very good friends on that tour. In fact, our production manager, our stage manager, C.B., was their monitor guy and he was one of the very first people I ever met in the music business. And I look at him today and I always smile. I think he remembers those days very clearly too. It's so nice to have shared so much experience and have these people still in your life. That is a real treat of being around for a long time. If you talk to most veterans of the road or veterans of music, the people involved are really important. And when you can share that early time and our present time, it's very sweet. I love seeing C.B. because I think about the beginning and I think about now all rolled into one."

Some other members of the crew were also integral 'til the end. Says Geddy of Howard, "He was our first tour manager. He was sent to us by our first agent in the States and our first American manager so to speak. He was sent up here to teach these young Canadian guys about show business, and so it was always pretty funny, him always trying to teach us show business. And he was quite a character himself. And Liam's worked for me since he was seventeen years old. He was with us in the bars, and that's a sweet thing as well because now we've spent our entire lives together. That's really nice that we still like each other, trust each other. Yeah, those are relationships that are forged through a lot of experience.

"Sleeping on your baggage," Geddy says, thinking back to some of those experiences. "It was fun, and it was horrible. I could never do it again but that's what youth is for. When you're young, you can do all that and it's not a big deal. You hate it at the time, but you survive it pretty easily. Now you know you'd be in traction for a month if you did a week traveling like we used to travel for months. And sometimes you didn't know where you were going because sometimes your gigs would run out and you'd be in the States waiting to find out if you're on another tour. You know, the life of an opening act back then was hooking up from circuit to circuit. I remember one time we were between gigs for, like, two weeks or a month, and it felt like longer, just hanging out at some hotel in Los Angeles waiting to find out about the next tour, with nothing to do all day but play *Space Invaders*."

Getting back to Kiss, Geddy figures, "I think they kind of liked what we were about. Obviously they must have liked us because they never objected to us being on their shows. We were some of the few who got to see them without their makeup in those days. That was a big deal back then, not so much anymore. I think they respected us as players. I think they probably thought we weren't very commercial or commercial enough. I don't know if they had much respect for the way we were going about things, 'cause they were rock 'n' rollers and they wanted to make it. Hard to say how much they even thought of us to be honest, because they were obsessed with making it themselves."

San Diego along with a sold-out April 1975 support date to 4,500 at the Michigan Palace in Detroit (Kiss's home away from home; Rush's might be Cleveland!) proved to be memorable touring highlights for years to come. A headlining gig at Massey Hall on June 25 with Max Webster in tow also proved a landmark, not to mention a warm-up for the shows that became the band's first live album a year and a half later, following a shocking two studio albums in the interim. There was one more Massey Hall date six months later, on January 10, 1976, supported by folkie

Joe Mendelson, who shared management with Rush and was on Max Webster's boutique imprint, Taurus.

"We toured a lot with Aerosmith that year too," says Alex, fortunate or unfortunate enough to run into another juggernaut. "The Aerosmith tours were not the most satisfying for us. We didn't get one single sound check in, I don't know, how many dates we did, fifty dates? Never talked to them once. We got a deli tray and a bottle of wine in our dressing room, and we were lucky to get that. And their crew too. I remember one time Neil changed the skins on his drums, and he needed to tune his drums backstage. He was doing it there because we didn't have a sound check. And the crew guys came up and said, 'Shut the fuck up!' You know, he couldn't even tune his drums. He had to move his drums into the dressing room to tune them.

"They were just really . . . We just stayed out of their way as much as we could. Years later, Howard Ungerleider, our lighting designer, was on a flight to Europe, and they were on the plane, and Steven came over. This was after they fell apart and went through their dark period and reformed and came back to life. He came up and sat with Howard and said, 'You know, we were dicks. And I just have bad memories of the way we treated people back then. You know, tell the guys we're really sorry about that and maybe one day we can get together and just have a chat.'

"I thought that was pretty cool of him to have remembered that and made that effort. You learn from those sorts of things. We always went out of our way to make sure that any opening act that played with us got a sound check and everything they required in their rider. We really bent over backwards for everyone, and it was because of those experiences where you didn't get stuff. It just didn't seem right. It's just such a great experience and so much fun, and every touring band shares in that. You should be brothers. You shouldn't try to put each other off. Some people look at it as a very competitive thing. 'Gotta blow 'em off the stage tonight!' You do your own thing; that's it."

"They were one of the bands that was a good example of what not to do," Neil says when asked about Aerosmith. "They were oblivious. They had no idea. They would come on and do sound check, and fuss around with things, and Steven Tyler would yell at the drummer for not having the tempo right, right 'til the doors opened! They just had no idea."

So where did Rush stand as they went about this tour and toil? Essentially, they had now become a band with a bit of history. Despite modest record sales and a lack of radio play, people were seeing them play live by the thousands. Most people likely didn't know they were Canadian at all, and those who did know might have thought of it as only a fun trivia point because Rush always seemed to be in and out of your Midwest town.

On record, the band had established their hard rock credentials through the self-titled debut and then demonstrated a willingness to take chances with the second album. Those who noticed things like drumming or read the liner notes saw that the band had a new drummer, but behind the blinding trademark that was Geddy's voice, you'd be excused for not noticing. But yes, the drumming was more inventive and even hooky across *Fly by Night*. And the songs were more dramatic, more progressive — or half of them were, anyway. "Best I Can," "Making Memories" and "In the End" weren't a far cry from the material on the debut. Still, the sum total of all these adjustments put Rush in the camp of bands to watch, bands that could surprise you, because they seemed to be changing at a fair clip. In this light, they were doing what Led Zeppelin or Queen or even old-guard acts like the Beatles and The Who might do.

Taking a wider view of the music of the day, there was always pop and soul and R&B. Prog was doing its thing, hard rock hadn't changed much and glam was on the wane, symbolized by Sweet becoming respectable. There was no disco to speak of yet, or punk or electronic music outside of obscure synthesizer test albums. Rock was still very much an earthen experience, best heard loud across the Rust Belt, delivered by long-haired boy-men with guitars, bass and drums. And Rush fit that well enough, despite their virtuosic aspirations. In a support slot before Kiss or Aerosmith, most of that was going to be obscured in electricity gone bad. It would take the achievement of headliner status for Rush to be properly considered in the industry, not just as a curio or adjunct but as an intricate ecosystem unto itself.

But of course, life went on outside of the concerts. U.S. President Richard Nixon had only recently resigned over Watergate (in fact, within a week of Neil's first show with Rush), to be replaced by Ford. And two and a half months after *Fly by Night* came out, while Rush was tooling around with Kiss, the fall of Saigon would take place, signifying the end of the Vietnam War. There was an oil crisis and the U.S. economy wasn't so hot. It's somewhat incongruous to even mention all this because so much of rock history rolls on oblivious to world events, but that is the reality. Heavy rock — with which Rush were, sensibly enough, lumped — was in ascendance in the midst of a pretty rough time in America. Which makes a lot of sense — tough times calls for tough music. And so Rush, despite their uniquely progressive addressing of the form, were well positioned to take advantage of the tenor of the times.

chapter 4

Caress of Steel

"A young band, a little pretentious,
full of ambitions, full of grand ideas."

ollowing dates with Kiss in May and into early June of '75,
Rush was sent back to reality, playing across Ontario and
up and down all of Canada, before taking the summer to
more or less plot out their next record. *Caress of Steel* was done
as August waned, just in time for a cross-Canada tour with
Nazareth. But it was not the record that management or the
label wanted.

"Well, look at the AM hits, and later the FM hit singles,"
explains Vic Wilson. "So-called singles. You get that superstar
status. Rush are superstars, but there's that extra . . . like an Elton
John superstar. Where would he be without any hits? Back playing a little piano bar. AM radio was important in those days.
It made you a star. So that's why it's been a long haul all these
years. They just kept hammering and hammering, and I take my
hat off to them; they stuck with what they wanted to do. But
they had a mindset that they didn't want to be on AM radio,

that they were a rock band, or a quote, unquote, heavy metal band, and they just ploughed through it. And the only station in Toronto at that time was CHUM-FM. Whatever play you'd get with CHUM-FM was to your advantage, but that was basically it. There was a station in Montreal that played them. But that's it. Did you ever bang your head against a wall? That's what it was like. They had their minds set, and they weren't copping out to writing for AM radio. It didn't bother them that they didn't have any AM radio play. Give me an AM Top 40 hit! The closest we got to that was 'Fly by Night.'"

The hits came soon enough, but even achieving bestselling status would be done on Rush's terms. Still, *Caress of Steel*, and to a large extent its follow-up, *2112*, would be known as the Rush albums most lacking in a clear single and, by extension, a hit.

"*Caress of Steel* was a different story," recalls Terry Brown. "We were still developing how we wanted to do things. We went out on a limb with that record, for sure, and it almost cost me my career. But since then it's proved to be a substantial record that a lot of fans liked. It was the stepping-stone to *2112*. And after we'd finished it, we actually worked on a bunch of really good ideas which we incorporated into *2112*. It was a dark record, no doubt about that. But I still thought it had amazing potential, and I really liked it and thought it was just another phase that we were going to go through. So it didn't really bother me that much, that it wasn't a super-commercial record. It was certainly a good record, I thought. But that view wasn't shared by everybody. We got some fairly non-enthusiastic feedback, shall we say, which I thought was a shame."

"Most of that was done in the studio," explains Neil. "We came in with ideas and sketches, a little bit, and I had some lyrics written beforehand. We had some acoustic guitar ideas probably and maybe a few riffs that we liked, but that was it. The rest of it was just, you know, eighteen hours a day of work until you dropped, basically, for three weeks."

This is markedly different than the approach they took with the first two records. The debut came about the typical way debuts do. For the most part, the songs had been around. Rush had managed to avoid the second album curse by using time on the road to write. For *Caress of Steel*, that didn't happen, and if there was any clear path followed, it was to get rid of the last vestiges of rock 'n' rollsy Rush.

"I think with *Caress of Steel*, Neil had come up with this concept, and we had to put it all together and make it work," continues Terry. "This was the job; this was what we were supposed to do: put this album together and get these tunes at their best. I didn't feel that it was difficult at the time. It seemed like they eventually knew where they were going. I don't think I really knew at the time where they were headed, but we had this material, I liked it, and I thought it had potential. But most of the stuff was done in the studio."

Caress of Steel was issued on September 24, 1975, its packaging as serious and somber as all but two songs on the album. The cover art was supposed to be printed with silver ink reinforcing the steel theme and the alchemist illustration, but it wound up an intriguing mix of grayish green and copper instead. This was Hugh Syme's first design for the band. Syme was destined to make visuals central to the Rush experience for years to come, but at this point, Hugh was keyboardist in Ian Thomas's band, another Moon Records act. Syme soon switched gears and become a much sought-after graphics guy, doing covers for the likes of Megadeth, Queensrÿche, Fates Warning, Kim Mitchell, Whitesnake, Coverdale–Page, Def Leppard, Aerosmith, Dream Theater and dozens of others besides Rush.

The record kicks off with "Bastille Day," which, as well as

being a succinct history lesson concerning the French Revolution, remains to this day one of the band's most heavy metal songs — by tempo, by relatively simple structure, by Alex's riff and its distorted delivery, by shockingly shrieky Geddy vocal. Countering the briskness of the track, the band cut the speed in half for the chorus. Both speeds are used for other musical passages as well, but the overriding sentiment is that this is a headbanger of a song more straight between the eyes than anything on *Fly by Night*, a match in metal intensity to "What You're Doing" and "Working Man," but with the added advantage of speed.

Next is the curious case of "I Think I'm Going Bald," a boogie rocker similar to "In the Mood" and a host of blues-derived hard rock hits and also-rans from years such as 1972 and 1974. "We were touring a lot with Kiss in those days," explains Geddy, "and they had a song called 'Goin' Blind.' So we were kind of taking the piss out of that title, by just coming up with this. Pratt [another nickname for Neil] came up with this line, 'I think I'm going bald,' because Alex is always worried about losing his hair. Even when he was not losing his hair, he was obsessed with the fact that he might lose his hair. So he would try all kinds of ingredients to put on his scalp. And I think it just got Neil thinking about aging, even though we weren't aging yet and had no right to talk about that stuff yet. It would be much more appropriate now. And it just became a kind of funny song. And even though the song is not funny, in terms of the sentiment, it kind of is, and the music is really goofy. A lot of people mistake us for being deadly serious, but some of our songs are just plain goofy."

For years, people speculated that the song was about band buddy Kim Mitchell from Max Webster, who definitely was dealing with a thinning mane early. Also, Donna Halper seems pretty sure Geddy told her that it was about himself.

"Lakeside Park" was likely the record's best shot at a single, except its success is hampered by two factors. It's a little bit stilted and proggy — smoothed out, it would sound more like "Fly by Night," or at least be in that mid-tempo Goldilocks zone amenable to radio play. Second, it's very Canadian, mentioning the May 24, Victoria Day weekend in Canada, traditionally celebrated with fireworks. And even though many prospective Rush fans could relate to a "lakeside park," this one is in Port Dalhousie in St. Catharines, Ontario. Neil is reminiscing about his youth and, in particular, the summer job he had as part of the fair, hence the "midway hawkers." This wistful quality links "Lakeside Park" to "Fly by Night," which also tells a chapter in Neil's pre-Rush life.

It's the number one favorite Rush song of Neil's mother, Betty, who remarks, "We had that in Port Dalhousie, where we lived. I asked him to write something that I would understand, and he phoned me one day and he says, 'I wrote one that you will understand.' So naturally I like that one. *2112* I didn't understand much; it was outer space and black holes and all that stuff. When he had time, I used to ask him to explain them to me. Like 'A Farewell to Kings,' I had no idea it was about kingly virtues. It just . . . it had to be explained to me, because it's really deep. I'm very interested in his lyrics and where they come from, but I have to have them explained. I thought it was marvelous, the way they played and the way they put things together and the sound, but I didn't understand it and still don't."

Closing side one of the original vinyl is "The Necromancer," the second full-on prog excursion of the band's catalogue. There is shockingly one more to come before *Caress of Steel* is over.

"It was a stepping-stone certainly," says Alex of this three-part, twelve-minute assemblage. "It even started a little earlier with 'By-Tor & the Snow Dog' on *Fly by Night*. That was the start of writing in more of a thematic, multi-pieced idea, and then with *Caress of Steel*, we did that whole side of it. I mean even 'The Necromancer' was kind of like that. It was the start of those longer pieces and getting more involved — we were searching for something."

Snapped to attention by the opening low-cycle word, the listener can hear what sounds like a foretelling of the debilitating tour grind the band would experience trying to sell this record to the masses. Three men of Willowdale fording the River Dawn to journey into the land of the Necromancer where they become "empty, mindless specters." Rush was from the northwest Toronto burb of Willowdale, and one of Toronto's biggest rivers is the Don River. Geographically, for our three travelers, it's not necessary to ford it on the "southward journey" to the States, but what happens in the story sure sounds like the "thousand-mile stare" that hits bands on tour, especially at the lower rungs, something Geddy has talked about at length.

Part one of "The Necromancer," "Into Darkness" is about as slow as Rush ever played, the band creating a bluesy mellow vibe with Alex soloing through various effects, exercising his acumen for textures. The spoken word is back for part two, "Under the Shadow," which also marks the return of the metal, Geddy turning back to his shriek in tandem. After the initial exercise in math rock, the band falls into a jam, Geddy and Neil playing busy and Alex taking center stage, letting rip with a fuzz pedal solo that pans back and forth, left channel to the right. A huge Sabbath-like riff leads to a second, more intense jam that sounds even more like Sabbath, circa *Paranoid* or *Vol. 4*.

For part three, "Return of the Prince" (which saw limited issue as a single), the band opts for chords straight out of "Sweet Jane" to represent the happy resolution of this *Hobbit*-like story. The character By-Tor returns and slays a foe, which doesn't seem to be the Necromancer himself. Not spoken or sung, there's a Latin phrase printed in the gatefold at the conclusion of the song's lyrics that translates to "As the hour ends the day, so the author ends his work," which comes from *Doctor Faustus* by Christopher Marlowe.

That might have made more sense after the end of the entire album, for the author's work is far from complete at this point. Side two is swallowed up entirely by one song, "The Fountain of Lamneth." Presenting in six parts and spanning twenty minutes, it is the tale of a man's life and achievement-steeped tribulations from birth through to an end marked by a kind of fugue state, an awareness that despite great accumulation of wisdom through advancing years, there is even more that one can never know — and then the curtain falls.

Part one, "In the Valley" comprises three different musical passages, a drumless, Zeppelin-esque soft rock intro, a progressive metal section with full-throated singing from Geddy and then a sort of West Coast rock "idyllic" soft prog feel.

Part two, "Didacts and Narpets," is arguably the most avant-garde "song" Rush has ever done. It opens with a drum solo and then blasts into sharp, geometric chords over which Geddy barks single words, some discernible, some not, none of which are volunteered in the gatefold's presentation of the lyrics. Neil has explained that the words represent viewpoints of the seeker or hero that oppose those of his "didacts," which is an anagram for addicts and "narpets," an anagram of parents. Peart can't recall the full text but says that "Work! Live! Earn! Give!" is part of the back and forth. In effect, this search for the fountain is turning out to be an allegory for the unfolding life and lives of the band and its members, something that can be read into "The Necromancer" as well. The combative feel intensifies with a more musical but just as dramatic power chord sequence followed by a simultaneous low frequency and high frequency "Listen!"

Part three, "No One at the Bridge," is dark, mellow music with lots of words. For parts of the verses, Neil plays only hi-hat and snare. Geddy sings most of it extremely high and full of throat. Alex has said that the main influence for his very electric solo was Steve Hackett, who he had been listening to a lot at the time.

Seagulls and ocean waves give way to part four of our tale, "Panacea," a quiet song of medieval or renaissance-type music, Alex on nylon-stringed acoustic at first, after which the band enters electric, collapsing into something like mainstream soft rock. Interestingly, this is one of two sections of six where the music is not credited to both Geddy and Alex but to Geddy alone.

Like "Return of the Prince," part five of "The Fountain of Lamneth," "Bacchus Plateau" (the second song section for which music is credited to Lee alone), makes use of sunny, predictable chord patterns from the '60s to turn the tone of the story hopeful. Much wine-drinking and weary travel later, part six, "The Fountain," has the band returning to the prog metal musical architecture of the opening segment. Reversing the order though, the tale ends with the same drumless acoustic music that opened the song twenty minutes ago. Lyrically, there are many clues that the journey has not resolved itself, that now there are more questions than answers, that the birthing at the beginning merely put the hero into a cycle of perpetual motion.

"It was just something we had to do," reflects Geddy, summing up "The Fountain of Lamneth" and echoing Alex's sentiments. "But it's kind of absurd. I mean, it's just where we were at. We were a young band, a little pretentious, full of ambitions, full of grand ideas, and we wanted to see if we could make some of those grand ideas happen. And 'Fountain of Lamneth' was the first attempt to do that. And I think there are some beautiful moments, but a lot of it is ponderous and off the mark. It's also the most time we ever had to make a record. I think we had a full three weeks, and we were just indulging ourselves. And we were just languishing, indulging ourselves, oodles of time. You know, *Fly by Night* was made in ten days. Now we had three weeks and there were a lot of funny aromas in the control room too."

"'Necromancer' was an extension of 'By-Tor,'" figures Alex, "but 'The Fountain of Lamneth' became even more of that experimental, full side, thematic . . . I don't want to say opera, but concept kind of record. I mean, we were experimenting then to see what would work, and that was very challenging. It was really important for us to do that. The record company, I think, hated it. It was the least commercially successful record that we've done.

"You smile and you shake your head and you go, 'What was I thinking?'" continues Lifeson. "You look at all that stuff, and you can't help but smile. It was all growing through a period that we shared with everybody else. Everybody else was into the same sort of thing and it's a big generational group that kind of moved through those different fashions and different sensibilities. I look back with a bit of nostalgia and good nature and smile. But that has always been important to us: that we are serious about what we do and about the music we play. Even when we are onstage goofing around, I mean, that's on the outside. But on the inside, we're hearing every note that's being played, and where we are in relation to those notes being played by each other. That's very, very clear to us every night we play. But to be able to remain relaxed and goof around with the audience is an important part of that marriage of being serious and being loose."

Alex recalls playing *Caress of Steel* for Paul Stanley in the van one night and realizing that there was a disconnect there. "It was an important stepping-stone for us, but you could see that those guys thought more in rock hits and selling lots of records and making gazillions of dollars, whereas we were more about the music and hopefully making hundreds of dollars and doing our own thing."

Adopting a similarly semi-dismissive viewpoint, Neil says, "Those were the growing years, and I often equate that to children's drawings on the refrigerator that hang around too long, you know? I really wish that they would just go away. I think we really started . . . wow, given my druthers, I would make our first album *Moving Pictures*. I can't think of a single reason not to do that! It's like even with book writing. I wrote probably ten books before I published one. And I'm really glad to have had that luxury, doing all my experimenting and getting it all out of my system, doing my stream-of-consciousness writing and doing my six-adjectives-per-noun writing, getting that out of my system privately. And then by the time I was ready to publish, I had a book that I can still live with years later. And music, unfortunately, isn't like that. You do your growing up in public, and it's there forever. I still turn on the radio and there's a song that makes me cringe. But that's the reality of it. A lot of it I have a personal affection for just the time it represented and what we were doing and the men we were and the people we were. But I don't necessarily think it ever needs to be heard again."

Despite the hard sell of an album, the band was nonetheless getting a few reviews, including one by Geoff Barton at influential music weekly *Sounds* over in the U.K. Barton was not particularly impressed, pointing out Geddy's vocal similarity to Robert Plant but also to Burke Shelley, which is interesting, because not only did Geddy sing somewhat like the Budgie bassist, he looked like him too. Barton also pointed out the Tolkein-inspired lyrics and suggested that Alex was sounding derivative as well, although it's telling that Barton doesn't actually compare him with anyone. *Sounds* competitor *Record Mirror* reviewed the album as well (albeit in 1977), establishing dialogue and debate about Rush that would be ongoing from this point, introducing the band to many musicians who would populate the coming new wave of British heavy metal.

"I had a great time making that record," reflects Terry Brown, years later. "And I was extremely disappointed when it got bad reviews and everyone was really down. Looking back, it was a tough time for the band just getting their feet planted on the ground. And it was a little ambitious. In the record business, what we should have done was a couple of covers and made a really commercial record so we sort of grabbed a bigger market. But that's not what the boys wanted to do — and me neither. We had this crazy, cockamamie scheme that we could do original material and everyone would just flock to the stores and buy it. Well, it kinda backfired on us. I remember the reaction, and the reception wasn't very good, and it was concerning. Initially we were hoping that we would keep on this trajectory, but we were sort of falling off at that point.

"It's a dark record and that probably had a lot to do with it," continues Brown. "It's really hard to know, sometimes, why records take awhile to be accepted. You see it happen a lot, where a record will come out and it might take a year or two before all of a sudden it becomes part of the consciousness, and then it becomes a hit. But sometimes these things take awhile. During that period, you can read all manner of different reviews from good to bad, and it's a question of persevering and working hard and trying to give the record some coverage. They bounced back quickly, which proved that we weren't completely crazy. But it was a scary moment, no doubt about that. Not so much for myself, because I had other things on the go. I wasn't involved with them on a day-to-day basis at all. But certainly, in retrospect, from a management standpoint and a record company standpoint, it was not good for them."

"I'm just going to set the historical record up here," begins

Cliff Burnstein, offering the lay of the land with respect to the Chicago offices of Mercury. "The first album, in its promotable life, did about seventy thousand, and then continued to sell after that, so it went over one hundred thousand. The second album, *Fly by Night*, which came out six or seven months later, did about one hundred thousand in its promotable life, and then continued selling awhile. So in reality, *Fly by Night* was, on a timeline basis in sales a little bit ahead of the first album, *Rush*. *Caress of Steel* was yet another six months after *Fly by Night*.

"When *Caress of Steel* came in, nobody thought it was particularly commercial, in a sense. But I have to say that nobody actually thought that *Rush* or *Fly by Night* was particularly commercial either. Rush was gaining fans from their live shows, a certain amount of word of mouth and the barely adequate job of promotion that I did on them. There were a lot of radio stations that should have been playing Rush that didn't want to because they thought that Geddy's voice would be an irritant to people listening.

"So, one thing we used to do — and this is the thing that I got the record label to do — is buy radio ad time on stations that weren't playing the record. This is exactly the opposite of what people usually do. You usually advertise where it is getting played. We advertised where it wasn't getting played, and we would do a sixty-second radio spot of one song and just kind of play a good chunk of the song on the air and just identify the album and that was that. And immediately you would get reorders from distributors in most markets, where they had never sold any Rush albums before. Just off that advertising.

"And I believe in the long run that made the radio guys more comfortable with Geddy's voice. Because they were playing it as a commercial and hearing it. And that was the first step in acceptance. I don't think anybody . . . I certainly didn't think when *Caress of Steel* came in that it was either harder to work or easier to work than the other two albums. It was only after the fact, I think, if my memory serves, that *Caress of Steel* didn't progress the band's sales curve on a timeline, the way *Fly by Night* had over the first album. It actually maybe regressed a tiny little bit from *Fly by Night*. But meanwhile the *Rush* album still sold every week and *Fly by Night* still sold every week. So you can see that the audience was still growing anyway, even if *Caress of Steel* didn't seem to be advancing it in a large way. Rush was advancing even if *Caress of Steel* wasn't advancing."

Which is a phenomenon you often see with the follow-up album to a massive hit. Sometimes the tour for the ensuing dud becomes a tour for the previous record or the back catalogue in general. Rush was demonstrating this on a tiny band level, when they took *Caress of Steel* on the road — and in effect, even that's not accurate, because on the road you are playing your catalogue to date. However unquestionably still a back-up band at this point, Rush clutched a set list that was none too long. Yet all of the short snappers from the album, plus "The Necromancer," made the grade.

The *Caress of Steel* campaign, dubbed derisively the Down the Tubes Tour, was mercifully somewhat short, spanning a pretty intensive three months — essentially just the fall of 1975. However, things got off to a cracking start, with Rush opening for Nazareth across Canada.

"We did a coast-to-coast tour of Canada and it was completely sold out," recalls Nazareth bassist Pete Agnew. "Donald K. Donald, big Canadian promoter, did that tour. I think we had three albums in the charts, in the Top 20 in Canada, so you couldn't get any bigger. And we took this young band as our opening band. We met them at the first gig and their name was Rush. And they were absolutely overawed to be playing with the mighty Nazareth. And when they came on, they were getting their gear on, and we said to them, 'Well, you can use our gear if you want.' And of course, that blew them away. We said, 'You can use this,' because we had all these massive stacks. But they were too nervous to use it. So they played their own.

"And when we got to Vancouver, I remember taking them out on a fishing boat to go shark hunting, because *Jaws* had just come out, and we'd become very, very good friends on the tour. They were lovely young guys. They were innocent young guys, when they started the tour — I don't know what they were like when they finished it. But we started in the east and we finished in the west. And the next time, it was funny enough, many, many years later, we were over in Germany, and Rush had a gig in this big, horrible-sounding thing in Frankfurt, the big glass dome thing, and they needed somebody as the opening act. And we did it. So Nazareth opened for them many, many years later. By that time, they'd had gold albums and they were huge throughout the planet. And then after that, I remember taking my kids to see them in Edinburgh."

When asked for a first impression of Rush back in August of '75, Pete says, "Even on the very first night, we thought they were a great young band. And what anybody thought at that time was that they were like Zeppelin, that vibe, and that was the kind of thing they were aiming at. Well, that's what it sounded like they were aiming at at the time. I think they wanted to be the Canadian Led Zeppelin. Right or wrong, that's what we thought of them.

"But, yeah, I remember the shark fishing. A guy we knew there had a big pleasure cruiser thing and used to take people out fishing. It was a great day, good fun."

Ian Grandy says, "We finished in Vancouver, had a day off and they kindly invited us on this fishing expedition. There was a lot of drinking and there was some fishing. I caught a three-foot shark and nobody caught anything bigger. But otherwise it was mostly a drunk. There were a few things caught but not a lot. There was a lot of sitting around drinking."

"Dan definitely played a good part in the corruption," continues Pete, referring to Nazareth vocalist Dan McCafferty — the members of Nazareth were notorious boozers in the '70s. "But they were young. To us, they were like the kids on the tour, and they were really nice around us and quite quiet. We treated them well. Like I said, at the beginning of the tour, we offered them our backline. I mean, not every band would do that. Especially then, you've got to remember, Nazareth was probably the biggest band in Canada at the time. So you can imagine, it was quite awe-inspiring to these young guys. They were so delighted to get on the tour because they knew what was at stake here. They were playing to sold-out arenas all the way across Canada.

"And they did very well — that's the other thing. They availed themselves very, very well. They were a great band to have as an opening band because they got the crowd right up there. And that's what you want. You don't want a bunch of donkeys on before you. You've got a reputation to think of. Somebody comes along to buy a ticket for a big show like that, they're expecting class all the way through. And those guys were great. We'd see them for a couple of numbers each night, and you saw they'd gone down with the crowd and you'd think, 'Oh, these guys are going to do it.' And by the end of the tour, they'd got a lot of good press. You could see it was going to happen for the guys. They got mentioned in every review, which was always a good sign."

An even longer spate of dates was spent with Kiss from November into December, with one-offs with the likes of Blue Öyster Cult, Aerosmith, Iron Butterfly and Frank Zappa also taking place. Any support bands were selected from within the general area Rush was visiting; therefore, on their home turf, they played with likes of Leslie West, Artful Dodger, Queen City Kids and Max Webster.

"We did have some really good times with Mott," recalls Alex, with respect to another occasional pairing. "They were sort of on the back end of their career; Ian Hunter wasn't in the band at the time. They were just trying to make a last stab. We got along really well with them and had some really fun times. Ted Nugent, we did a lot of shows with Ted, all over the country, mostly smaller sorts of arenas or secondary markets. He was such an interesting guy, but he was crazy at a time when crazy meant drinking, that sort of crazy. He was nuts, but he was super straight and very conservative. Even though he had really long hair, he had really conservative ideas about things. But he was always full of energy, and he was great to us. We hung out with Ted. We were special-guesting, and somebody else was opening. We always got our sound checks, we always got our encores, never a problem."

Offering a glimpse into transportation logistics on that tour, Howard says, "We had a series of rental cars at the time. Our favorite was the Chrysler Newport, where we had a little fluorescent light in the back seat where everybody would be reading. Afer we'd finished our dates in eastern Canada, we had to go back home to Toronto. And I remembered them selling lobsters on the street. So I decided, well, it'd be great to get some fresh lobsters and take them home. So we opened the trunk to the car and I filled it up with ice and we threw all these lobsters in there, not thinking it'd be a twenty-four-hour drive. And by the time we got to Toronto, it sort of melted and became a real unbearable situation. Literally it smelt awful to the point where they could never rent the car anymore; I think we had to buy the car. It was really bad, but the lobsters were great.

"I was the driver, and when I got tired, we'd share," continues Ungerleider. "We'd actually draw for who was going to drive and there are lots of great stories about driving. We drove all over the place. But I did the majority of the driving; I enjoyed the driving. The station wagon . . . we'd usually put corkscrews into it and all sorts of hood ornaments, and by the time it was over, the car was quite decked-out. We had a lot of interesting times in that car.

"We went across Canada and played every little city possible because that's what you have to do when you start. When I flew in from New York originally, I had that New York attitude, where you know everything. And here I am up in Canada, and we're going to a place called Cochrane. And I'm wearing a denim jacket, and we hop in this station wagon to go out there, and it's like minus thirty or forty. And Alex turns around and says, 'Where's your warm clothes?' And I'm like, 'This is it. I got it.' And they said, 'Well, if you go outside right now . . . if we had an accident and actually something happened, you would probably die.' And I'm like, 'No way! That's bullshit. There's no way.' And they said, 'Okay, pull the car over, and you go outside. And when you start to breathe the air, take a nice deep breath — it'll feel like someone took razor blades and sliced your nose open.' I'm like, 'No way, I've been in cold weather before.'

"So we pull over, and I jump out and I took this deep breath and he was right. It felt like someone took razor blades and sliced my nose open. And I was freaked out at how freezing cold it was. I'd never experienced that. And I went to grab the handle of the car and my hand stuck to it. And they all laughed, of course. I got in the car and we drove away. 'You need to get some warm clothes. We've got to stop and buy a parka down the road or something.'

"And we continued on that journey that night to Cochrane, Ontario, and we got there, and there's a big statue of a big white bear there, and we were staying at this hotel that didn't have enough rooms. So we had to move to another one. I remember it was called the Albert Hotel, and upon arrival, in the lobby, there were the locals hitting each other over the head with logs, and they were all drunk out of their minds. And there was one bathroom on every floor and we had to share. And the fire escapes were ropes out the window; it was a pretty classy place.

"But to us, it was an experience. That was the same gig where Rush was supposed to be playing a dance, and so after they played their set, which was about an hour, everybody said, 'Well, when are you going to finish playing?' And we're like, 'We are finished.' And they're like, 'No, you've got to play another hour.' 'No, we're only contracted for an hour.' And the whole place got upset and they wanted to run us out of town because we had only played an hour, and it wasn't enough. It was a dance, and we had to play for another two hours or something. Those are the kinds of things we had to deal with in the early days."

Howard's story refers to the band's gig in the St. Joseph Gymnasium on February 8, 1975, on the *Fly by Night* tour, but the band indeed played Cochrane again on the *Caress of Steel* tour, September 15 of that same year, at which point they were supported by Max Webster even before they had an album out.

"Rush are great guys," recalls Max Webster drummer Paul Kersey. "Really, they are. They deserve what they've got, for sure. They worked very, very hard. Their touring schedule was very tough. I remember I was amazed at their touring schedule. Because we played Cochrane with them one night. I remember we left right after a gig to go to Cochrane, and there was a little bit of grumbling going on, saying, holy cow, we're a little tired, we're a little worn out getting there, and thinking, yeah, this is a little rough. We got there, we're trying to sleep in the van, bouncing around, lying in the back, and Rush gets there, and they'd come in from Thunder Bay, and they're headlining. All we had to do was play half an hour, forty minutes. We just walk up and do our thing, we're done, we leave. They've got to shine — we didn't have to shine. We just had to be there. I thought, 'Wow, now that's tough.' And they were like that a lot. They had a grueling schedule at first. Ray really put them through it. And I appreciate that. They worked hard."

Paul got the notion that the Max guys were resentful at the resources spent on Rush. He says that "Kim was never happy. Just because it was always Rush, Rush, Rush, never Max, Max, Max. That's about all I can say about that, because no matter what, Rush was always number one in Ray's mind. Just because they were friends and they were whatever they were, and Max was second, simple as that. Kim didn't like that. That wasn't sitting well. But we also knew that Ray was the guy. So what are you going to do?"

"We were quite fond of them and they were fond of us," reiterates Pye Dubois, Max Webster's non-performing lyricist, concerning relations with Rush. Still, he admits there was a rocky start to the rock 'n' roll marriage, though he's unclear on exactly what happened. "Yeah, Max's first tour with Rush was almost sabotaged by speaking about Rush in this restaurant we were at. Someone from Rush was in the restaurant, and it got overheard and it got back to Rush, or someone, and Max is off the tour. I don't know how it was resolved. But someone said something in the restaurant. Something was said, and it was considered pejorative, and Max was off the tour. But then it was resolved. I don't know who said it — I don't think it was me . . . I'm sure it wasn't me. But someone said something."

"We also did a lot of dates with Ted Nugent," says Ungerleider of this time. "Ted strangled me because we brought our own lights and he didn't know about it. He didn't like that very much, but those were the good old days. Because in those days, Ted Nugent was driving around in a Lincoln Town Car, with his brother John and a CB radio, and we used to communicate, driving around the United States in our rental vehicle. We would be talking to each other all night long, keeping each other awake as we were driving around from city to city."

But specifically, as Howard relates, this record's tour was a letdown. They were supposed to move forward, but Rush was in danger of flaming out. "It was frustrating," explains Ungerleider. "You had the first Rush album followed by *Fly by Night*, which was a huge success. And then they did an experimental album in *Caress of Steel*. Which had a lot of great songs — 'Necromancer' was pretty amazing. But as far as mass appeal, it wasn't one of the most popular albums, after those two. And they became very disappointed, and I believe that fueled the fire for *2112* because they were not very happy. They called it *Corrosive Steel* because it wasn't as successful after it came out, and it put doubts in their minds back then — should we continue or not? It wasn't what they were used to for the last two albums, especially after *Fly by Night*; it was hard to follow that. The songs that they put together for it were, I guess, a bit self-indulgent. But I felt they were great songs. I love the album, but I guess the masses didn't take to it as well as the other two.

"Psychologically that can play games on you because you're not getting the action you got with the other albums. Back then it was all about radio airplay and exposure, so with radio airplay decreasing during that time, you're used to what you're used to, so it is discouraging. And I believe they were thinking about possibly packing it in. So I think that fueled the fire for *2112*. *2112* came out and just blew everyone away. That was what they needed. That was the turning point, I believe, to launching them into the next level."

Liam also remembers the *Caress of Steel* campaign as a grind. "It was a hardworking band out there hammering away. Third album, the record company wasn't that impressed with it. Radio, as usual, wasn't impressed with it. I think it was coming to the end of a cycle potentially with the record company where we could have been dropped as an artist at that point. Fans weren't showing up and there was no airplay, which was normal. It just became a really depressed period for everyone. I think the crew might have been three or four people at that point, maybe five. But between the band and the crew, there was just a general malaise going around. It was difficult because there was nothing radio-friendly there," continues Birt. "I hate that term, but it is what it is. There was nothing that radio was interested in, the record company had lost interest and it seemed like the fans had lost interest. It really felt like it was the end of the line. But fortunately, they came back from there."

As to why the tour was derisively deemed Down the Tubes, Liam says it's "because literally we thought it was all over. I mean, they as artists and we as people were going down the tubes. We were being flushed out the gutter. It was all basically over with. I forgot that we were out with Ted Nugent, but yeah, it wasn't going good. When we did break off to do our own gigs aside from opening up for Ted, no one would show up. We just thought, 'Well, I guess we've run it and that's it — it's become a dry machine and it's going to grind to a halt now.'"

Liam brings up a good point. A place like Cochrane might have been more a touring reality for a band this size. They might have work between the "glamorous" shows, because like a shark, if you stop moving, you die. Explains Neil, "Fortunately, of course, opening act in those days — our set was twenty, twenty-five minutes long. But on days off, we'd go play clubs and we did need a longer set too. So in between the opening acts, of course what you should do is when the headliner takes a day off, you go play a club. That's the strategy that we always followed, not to mention the economic necessity that we followed.

"I've come up with the subject lately, 'roadcraft,' that I really want to write a book about. Not just touring, obviously, as a rock musician — because that really doesn't have much broad appeal — but everything I've learned from traveling by motorcycle, traveling by bicycle, hiking, just roadcraft in general as a metaphor for life too. You think of the road less traveled as a metaphor, but there's the roadcraft on that road too. So that's a concept I've been messing around with lately. But that's when I first started to learn also that it wasn't enough . . . it wasn't a life to be schlepping around all day long and then playing twenty-five minutes, and then schlepping around for the next twenty-three and a half hours and playing twenty-five minutes. Already within a month it was like, 'This is not a life.'"

And so Neil embarked on a self-tutored arts degree, reading heavy books, earning himself the title of "the Professor."

"As I mentioned earlier, I left school very early, so I had a lot to catch up on. By that time, drums had been part of my life long enough that I was starting to open the blinkers a little further, and I wanted to know things. And, well, what more perfect portable education is there than having a lot of free time on your hands and books too, everywhere? So for the next few years, basically, I started filling those hours with reading. So that too was a negative that turned into a positive.

"And through the years, I found many other hobbies to fill up that time. I took up model car building at one time and carried a road case with airbrush and model car building equipment and would sit in my room doing that. We had roller skates, we used to race radio-controlled cars backstage, and then bicycling in the '80s — I bought a bicycle and just kept it in the luggage bay of the bus and pretty soon started riding every day. And then if the cities were a hundred miles or so apart, I started riding from city to city, going for distance. I'd get the bus driver to drop me off a hundred miles out of Denver or wherever, and I'd ride the rest of the way in, on the back roads, of course. And that led to getting around the cities and seeing the cities too.

"And going to art museums became another part of education that those empty hours on the road could be filled with. It was the best education because I've seen probably all the best art museums in the United States. Because if it was a show day, I would get my bike off the bus, ride around town, finish at the art museum, wander through the area. Plus, I started collecting the books and putting together a knowledge of American and Canadian painting. So yeah, I absolutely got a first-rate education that no one anywhere could get. Okay, your education is going to be to go to all the best art museums in the country — that's a wonderful start.

"And then the broader education of being on the roads every day on my bicycle," continues Neil, touching down again upon the hobby he famously wrote about, followed by similar books about motorcycling. "I was out there among people. The thing that I still preserve today on the motorcycle and riding through their towns, I go down roads every day that nobody goes down unless they live there, all these back little parts of the United States and Canada that I've come to know and still hunger to explore every day. I go by people that work, and I keep a perspective on my life with that. And yes, I might have sore hands and the show might be a tremendous physical ordeal, but every day I'm walking past people who are working in the fields, working on the roads, all the things that normal people do. So it keeps my perspective so much more rooted in that."

Ironically, Neil later purposely took up the lifestyle that was a necessity back on the Down the Tubes Tour. "I go to gas stations every day. I sleep in cheap hotels and go to cheap restaurants. Just thinking, last night I stayed in a sixty-four dollar motel and ate at Smitty's family restaurant. These are the kind of things that mean you can't help but stay rooted. And then I stop at the truck stop gas station. I sleep on the bus after shows and wake up in a truck stop. Again, you can't be more democratic than that kind of thing.

"So yes, and I'm keeping this under the umbrella of education because it absolutely is. People talk about travel broadening you. Well, it doesn't on a rock tour when you go from the airplane to the arena to the hotel or from the tour bus. You wake up on the tour bus in the parking lot of the venue and go inside and play and go to a hotel. You know, I did that for twenty years, so I'm not being dismissive — I know of what I speak. And I thought I knew something about America, but after twenty years, when I did get out on my bicycle and then my motorcycle, I knew nothing. I saw nothing compared to the country that I know now."

chapter 5

2112

"We wanted to be the world's most
complicated three-piece band."

ush's situation at the end of 1975 wasn't out of step with industry standards. Kiss wasn't setting the world on fire at their third record. Aerosmith didn't have a hit for three albums. Blue Öyster Cult took at least three. Ted Nugent took almost a decade to break, and then, finally, after having a hit with *Free-for-All* marked a bit of a letdown. Heck, even the mighty Van Halen spent records two, three and even four trying to recapture the mania that celebrated their debut.

Alex explains, "The problem was we were in such an early stage of our development in the record company's point of view that suddenly we were on the third record and it wasn't going so well according to their plans. Maybe we were better off to go back to something like the first record, a little more hard rock, with that straight-ahead sort of appeal. I know we had a lot of meetings, but there was one in particular. Again, it was in that one Funcraft van that we lived in for 500,000 miles."

This was when the guys decided that they would rather go back to their jobs than to give in, that it would be full speed ahead into realms as fanciful as those explored on *Caress of Steel* or nothing. And so in the dead of winter — note that 21/12 marks the winter solstice — fresh off the Down the Tubes Tour, Rush reconvened with Terry Brown in February at Toronto Sound and knocked out *2112*, to be issued April Fool's Day, 1976. Also on that day, Rush received their first Canadian gold record, for *Fly by Night*. It must have served as an additional reminder that *Caress of Steel* was a stumble.

"*2112* reflected all of that," explains Alex. "I mean, that's what that record's about: declaring our independence, our individuality. We came back fighting . . . if we go down, as long as we go down in flames, it will be fine."

"*Fly by Night* had outsold the first record," says Ray, setting the stage. "Rush has never had an unsuccessful record. It was degrees of success. So the first record was moderately successful, *Fly by Night* was more successful and then *Caress of Steel* took us back down to what the first record had done. So some of the people at the label — Cliff wasn't there anymore — but some of the people at the label saw that as a sign that we were going down. I saw it as a sign that we had a base. If the first record did one hundred and fifty thousand, and the next one did two hundred thousand, and then the next one went back to one hundred and fifty thousand, we had a core audience of one hundred and fifty thousand people, and that was something to build on. I remember Terry Brown and I meeting with the label about two things: continuing to work the current record, not abandoning it, because there was a sense they were doing that, and that we were going to continue to tour on it and not to give up on the band. I was telling them that the band wants to sell more records. And then of course a year later, I had to go deliver a concept record to the same people."

In bringing news back to Geddy, Alex and Neil, Ray says, "I would have filtered it . . . they would have known that there was some pressure. I know the band didn't feel good about that. They never wanted anyone in their face about what they were going to do. They believed it was their career and their music and their art, and they didn't welcome anyone telling them what to do, in any regard. I was caught between knowing them and knowing that they were going to do what they wanted to do and that no one was going to interfere with that.

"And the reality is that I didn't particularly want to be dropped," continues Danniels. "Mercury was a decent label. It was fairly comfortable there. I was starting to work with other acts on the other labels, and I understood that the whole hit single thing was everywhere. There was nowhere that we weren't going to hear that, in that era. And so it was the devil-you-know scenario, and my goal was to just keep it together one more record and see what happened. And as it turned out, they were right, because that's the record they wanted to make; that's what they felt artistically they *needed* to make. I don't think there was any great calculation on anyone's part."

"I had a contract," says Vic, on the possibility that Rush might have been dropped by Mercury. He says it could have happened, but "not without a big stink. Or they would buy out the contract. That would be a windfall. By then we had three albums done, which was something that you could present to the next record company. And we were very careful because Ray and I owned the production company, and we owned the masters. We always had that ability to hold the masters. So any deals that were changed, the masters would all come to us. They didn't belong to the record companies that made the deals. That's just smart business."

When asked why Mercury would have consented to that

arrangement, Wilson shrugs. "If you don't ask, you don't get. First of all, they had Canada — we gave up Canada. And they weren't performing as a company, and we just said we want Canada back, and they gave it back to us. And also we got Japan back because they weren't doing anything there either. And I went over to Japan, and I had five record deal offers in one day. We ended up with CBS in Japan. I don't know if Rush are still with them or not. But it was in the renegotiations. They didn't own the masters, but they did own the territories, under contract. But we eventually started getting all the masters back."

Famously, Rush made *2112* without management knowing much about what they were doing. "You don't have a choice with them," says Ray. "They know what they want to do, and they're one of the very few bands in the world that I know of that have never gone into a studio and not completed a record. If they write twelve songs, those twelve songs are going to make the record. Because they don't have it in them to walk away from something. If they start it, they have to finish it. It's this middle-class work ethic. I hear that U2 claims to have written sixty songs to come up with the fourteen songs on their record. If Rush wrote sixty songs, that's the next five albums . . . Rush would have found a way to make all of those songs work. And not work in a commercial sense, work musically."

Ray recalls being surprised at *2112*, saying, "When I got the record, I didn't know that it would be as conceptual as it was. You get caught between what the band wants to do and what the label expects and is pushing you to do. And then there's the third component where you go . . . you know, I love *Dark Side of the Moon*. The moment I heard it, I loved it, and the moment you saw it performed live, the reaction from the audience was thumbs-up. So I knew very early in the cycle that our record was going to be a bigger record."

"*Caress of Steel* was a problem for the record company," says co-manager Vic Wilson. "I personally like the album, but Mercury were on the edge whether they were going to continue. We had one more album to deliver because that was the third album — it was two albums per year. So we were in the second year of the contract, and they pulled it off. They delivered *2112*, but they worked. They had to work. And after *2112*, things started to roll. We could see the light toward the end of the tunnel by then. I had to accept that there was no AM hit coming from Rush. *Caress of Steel* — there were no AM hits. 'Fly by Night,' I think that was the last AM — possibly AM — hit. But we still had a contract. We knew we had to deliver another album. So they did what they had to do and they pulled it off. That's where your faith with the people that you work with comes through. A lot was riding on it, and it worked.

"But it was a five-album record deal," clarifies Wilson. "If worse comes to worse, what are you going to do? Give them three more records of nothing, or take a chunk of money and leave? Those weren't options. We wanted to be successful, the band wanted to be successful, we all wanted to be successful. *2112* was a huge album for Rush. It was the turning point in their life. But the attitude of the band was 'We're going to do what we want to do.' And they had carte blanche on what they wanted to record. I didn't interfere with the recording and Ray didn't. And eventually they went overseas. And when the band went overseas to record, no one went to bother them. They went away, rehearsed, did the preproduction work, recorded and then they delivered an album."

Explains Geddy, framing the personality of Rush's fourth record, "I don't know how well versed I am on what my fellow musicians were doing in '76, but certainly *2112* was part of a progression to us. It was surprising how everyone received it, because we felt we were moving in that direction for a number of years. And we had this concept in our minds that we love progressive music, but we also love to rock. We liked The Who as much as we liked Genesis and Yes, and to us, The Who were still a progressive band even though they were more of a hard rock band. They were not afraid to put challenging influences in their music. So our dream was to combine the feeling and the emotional rock potential of The Who and even Zeppelin and bring the complexity of a band like Genesis and Yes.

"And we wanted to do that in a three-piece format. We wanted to be the world's most complicated three-piece band. That was kind of our dream. Just to play purely progressive music didn't satisfy us. And I think there were a lot of people like us, a lot of musicians like us, a lot of listeners like us, that liked heavy music. But just regurgitating the twelve-bar blues thing was boring. It was not something we wanted to play, and it was not something we wanted to listen to. So it was a perfect opportunity for us. We saw this combination of all the different branches of rock that we liked, the complex and the simple."

The Who, of course, could be stronger and more conceptual on a song-to-song basis than most prog rock bands. After all, this is the band who brought us *The Who Sell Out*, *Tommy* and *Quadrophenia*, and all of that by 1973. Drill down to Pete and his Lifehouse project and his synthesizers, and later *The Iron Man*, and The Who could be kind of futuristic and visionary as well — "2112" as a tale wouldn't look out of place scribbled in Pete's notebooks.

"I guess it was being termed as progressive in a certain way, and it was definitely metallic," continues Lee. The record was subtly designed to be heavier but also less layered than *Caress of Steel*, more easily translatable to the stage. He says, "I think we objected a little bit to the idea of being considered a metal band, just because we felt our roots were more in hard rock than metal, and to us there was a real clear distinction. Maybe not so much to an audience, but certainly to us the difference between Black Sabbath and The Who was quite profound. The Who were rock, and Sabbath was metal, and we were kind of an amalgam of that edginess, the guttural power those bands had; we were in between that. And yet the influences were much more complex. So yeah, we did consider ourselves to be a progressive rock band, in the way that those words truly mean. We wanted to rock, so we never wanted to lose that aspect of it, yet we wanted it not to be mundane rock or boring rock or ordinary rock, so what else are you going to call it but rock that is progressing? It's trying to be more than it is. People interpret that phrase, progressive rock, as rock with pretentions. We never saw it like that, and I think our fans and fans of that kind of music don't see it like that. It was just adventurous rock.

"I mean *2112* sounded like the record we'd been trying to make for a few records. I think the first record obviously was an amalgam of X number of years playing bars and high schools and gave a particular sound. *Fly by Night* was a new influence because Neil was now in the band and we were kind of still seeking our identity. With *Caress of Steel*, I think the sound we were after was *2112*, but we weren't there yet. The material wasn't there yet, the style of writing was still too experimental, too wandering. We were too high to deliver that. And somehow all those experiments and all that imagining what we should sound like, and Terry Brown's skills, all came together with *2112*. It very much felt like our first record."

Neil calls the period leading up to *2112* "a nadir. Of course the excitement level of starting to tour and playing all these big places with big bands, going to Los Angeles for the first time, all the towns were exciting to go to for the first time. So that wave carried us certainly through the *Fly by Night* period. Really the first three albums all sold about one hundred and twenty-five thousand copies, which in those days was just respectable enough to keep going. The first one was like a solid beginning, the second was solid, but the third one selling the same amount, the record company wasn't so impressed. Everything took an awful downturn around the time of *Caress of Steel*.

"But we had explored so much and so deeply into what we could do in writing and arranging and in playing. That touring was the greatest crucible for improving as musicians, just playing night after night especially when we had longer sets than just twenty minutes. You just grow and learn so much. Even to this day, I still feel such improvement in the craft just by doing it night after night for a period of time. So we were getting better — we were. It was all tentative, and yes there were experiments that didn't quite work out on *Fly by Night* and *Caress of Steel*, but we loved it. That's all the mattered; you know, successful or not, smart or stupid, we loved it.

"And then toward the end of that period, it was getting so bad. First we couldn't pay our road crew, then we couldn't pay ourselves or vice versa, probably couldn't pay ourselves and then couldn't pay our road crew. Coming up to do *2112*, there was zero confidence anywhere except from us. Even the road crew — you know, it was they who called it the Down the Tubes Tour. I don't think we made that up."

And getting back, Neil says, "My car didn't run. I had to borrow a car to be able to get to the studio when we were working on *2112*. I lived still in the St. Catharines area, so I was sleeping on a friend's couch. It was a Toronto winter, had no money, no car, but again had that dedication to make the best record that we could. And also anger. I have said this before, but it bears repeating, that we were really mad when we made that record. Of course, few things translate as well to young people more than anger and sex; put either of those prime movers into music and it will connect. And that's certainly what was in there, just this desperate anger to do what we wanted and to express it.

"In fact, we found out later that the record company had completely written us off. They'd made their financial projections for the following year, and we weren't even in it. So we were just fortunate the record company was in a bit of upheaval. I think we had three or four different record company presidents in that time, which was very common through the '70s and '80s. So we fell through the cracks. Never mind nowadays, in those days, after three records you would have been dumped. The fact that we got to make *2112* at all was just a fluke. We just kind of got ignored and we managed to get through."

"When I delivered *2112* to Chicago," recalls Ray, "I remember distinctly, I already knew at this point it didn't matter. It's either this record was going to be successful — and it was going to be successful because it's really good and because the band had a core audience now and we'd tour behind it — or it wouldn't. And if it wasn't successful, we would get dropped. And I would've succeeded, in the best-case scenario, with getting one more record. Until you are a superstar, you are only as good as the next record anyway. So you're always, from a manager's point of view, trying to get one more. It was going to be what it was going to be.

"But the record? They didn't get it. But in fairness, there was a sense in the room that this was good. It wasn't necessarily what they ordered, what they wanted, what they really understood, but I don't know how anyone can listen to that record and not go, 'This is a good record. This is good play.' They were puzzled as to how to sell it, and if memory serves right, I did the best I could to show them how to sell it, and where to go, and that we would get whatever radio we could. We would tour like crazy,

© RICHARD GALBRAITH

© RICHARD GALBRAITH

Tulsa Assembly Center, Tulsa, Oklahoma, with UFO and headliner Blue Öyster Cult — Mott was also billed but didn't play.

© RICHARD GALBRAITH

The Professor professing, Tulsa Fairgrounds Pavilion, Tulsa, Oklahoma, January 16, 1977. Also on the bill was Artful Dodger and headliner Ted Nugent.

© DONALD GADZIOLA

ABOVE AND BOTTOM LEFT: Maple Leaf Gardens, Toronto,
December 29, 1977.

© DONALD GADZIOLA

© RICHARD GALBRAITH

RIGHT: Neil, *All the World's
a Stage* tour.

An assortment of memorabilia purchased mostly at Flash Jack's head shop in 1977 and 1978. The top belt buckle is the original from 1977, with the belt buckle below it being a reproduction from the early 2000s. COLLECTION OF DONALD GADZIOLA

COLLECTION OF RAY WAWRZYNIAK

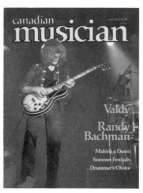

Canadian music magazine covers. *Cheap Thrills* is from January of '77, *RPM Weekly* is from December 9 of '78 and *Canadian Musician* is from June '79.

© RICHARD GALBRAITH

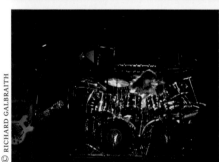

© RICHARD GALBRAITH

October 14, 1977, Tulsa, Oklahoma; supporting on the night were UFO and Max Webster.

© RICHARD GALBRAITH

© DONALD GADZIOLA

© DONALD GADZIOLA

ABOVE AND LEFT: December 29, 1978, Maple Leaf Gardens, Toronto.

A Farewell to Kings World Tour tour book, printed in the U.S.; *Hemispheres* European tour book, printed in the U.K. Collection of Donald Gadziola. At right, *The Words and the Pictures*, a rare tour book-type release which was available only in the U.K. during the *Hemispheres* tour. COLLECTION OF RAY WAWRZYNIAK.

Varsity Stadium at the University of Toronto, September 2, 1979.

State Fair Arena, Oklahoma City, Oklahoma, February 24, 1979. Support on the night came from fellow Canucks April Wine.

© RICHARD GALBRAITH

State Fair Arena, Oklahoma City, Oklahoma, February 24, 1979.

Colour ad for *A Farewell to Kings* and German black-and-white ad for *Hemispheres*. At right, industry ad that features the original photo that was altered and used in the gatefold of Rainbow's 1978 album, *Long Live Rock 'n' Roll*. BOTTOM LEFT AND MIDDLE: COLLECTION OF RAY WAWRZYNIAK.

BOTTOM RIGHT: COLLECTION OF DOUGLAS MAHER

© DONALD GADZIOLA

© DONALD GADZIOLA

© DONALD GADZIOLA

The boys performing a warm-up show in advance of their *Permanent Waves* tour. Varsity Stadium at the University of Toronto, September 2, 1979. Support on the evening was the other "baby Rush," namely FM.

and we would, in spite of the fact that we got terrible reviews in magazines, continue to do print magazines and rock magazines at the time. There was *Creem* and *Circus* and magazines that don't exist anymore, and we'd pursue it with blinders on, as we always had."

And, of course, *2112* was be the album to save the band's listing career. Punchier but nearly as conceptual as *Caress of Steel*, *2112* benefits from a thicker, warmer sound, an effect that really drives home the increased levels of power chording. In fact, "A Passage to Bangkok," "Something for Nothing" and "The Temples of Syrinx" rank as the band's heaviest compositions ever. In other "Solar Federation" news, Alex penned the lyrics to the pert, poppy, then crunching (and vaguely BTO-ish) "Lessons," while Geddy word-smithed a haunting, ambitiously arranged ballad called "Tears."

"*2112* was written on the road just before we recorded it," explains Alex. "And you know, that came from a different place, more from a place of defiance and anger that things were sort of going the way they were around us. So we were fighting back. That was quite a spontaneous record. Obviously, there was planning and work done beforehand. We went into the studio armed with all the material. There was a lot of pressure from us, from the record company, and to some degree, from management, to go back to our rock roots, make another *Rush* album.

"And we basically said, 'You know what? That's not what we're about. If that's what everybody wants, then that's what they're not going to get. If we go down, we're going to go down in flames.' And I remember having this discussion in our van. We were so despondent. We thought we were doing what was right and learning and that this was a stepping-stone. But there was no support anywhere for us. So we were pissed off. We thought, 'You know what? We're just going to do what we do.' And we started writing *2112*.

"And there's a lot of passion and anger on that record," continues Alex, using the same word we heard from Neil. "And we couldn't have done that without *Caress of Steel* and feeling kind of alone. And *2112* turned out to be our ticket to independence. After that, the record company said fine, do whatever you want. You guys have proved that you know what you're doing, for you. So there's never been anybody from the record company in any of our sessions ever. Ray's never been at any of our sessions. It's always a closed-door thing. We write the music, play it, whatever we feel is right, and it's up to them to work with that. But I don't think we could have accomplished any of that without cutting our teeth on *Caress of Steel*, which was a very important record for us creatively."

Digging a bit more into the logistics of the album, Alex recalls that the band "didn't have a lot of time to record; we were always touring. So most of our material was written on the road. Very little of it was left to the studio. At least we had very clear sketches of what we wanted to do. *2112* was recorded in about a week and a half, something like that. Quite a difference from an album like *Vapor Trails*, which took fourteen months. But we were prepared; everything was really direct, we plugged in. You didn't have a lot of room to do overdubs and get all crazy; it was very, very straightforward.

"But yeah, everybody had invested a lot of time and money in us, and there was a real concern that it wasn't going to work out. And we had decided we can either make another *Rush* album, like the first album, or we're just going to stick to our guns and do what we think is right for us. I think we all felt very strongly that was the kind of writing we wanted to do and that we felt that was unique to us and that's what we wanted to pursue. We were into that mode of wanting to write a more conceptual piece for the whole record. So with the backing of 'Fountain of

Lamneth' from *Caress of Steel*, which was our foray into writing in that mode, that's really what *2112* came out of. And like I say, that really bought us our independence from everybody. After that, everybody left us alone to do what we thought was right."

Technically, *2112* is less conceptual and long-form than *Caress of Steel*. That record contained about half a side of conventionally structured short songs, one prog epic to fill out the side and then a second side with one song. Here we get the one long song, but then five selections on side two of near uniform length.

But *2112* feels as conceptual as *Caress of Steel* or even more so for a number of reasons. First, it's named for the side-long epic song itself, and the cover ties in with it. The red pentagram on the front represents the oppressive Solar Federation of the tale, the elders who dismiss our hero's finding of a guitar and the music it brings. This seeker of soul through the lost art of music is represented by what's been deemed "Starman" or "Naked Man," dressed down to represent man without trappings, pure humanity, who has been suppressed by the stern runners of the futuristic world of which Neil writes.

"What we stand for is signified by our logo of a guy reaching out in the star," Geddy told *Record Mirror* in 1978. "We're a capitalist band; we come from middle-class homes. So although our parents maybe didn't approve of what we were doing in the early days, there was always a warm bed for us at night. We chose the name Rush because it represents a positive force or feeling. It means that you can achieve anything you really want to by your own efforts, whether it's music or anything. We're very much into power for individuals for each person to express their own minds."

Added Neil in the same U.K. interview, after showing writer Robin Smith his radio-controlled model car, "I like noble virtues, the difference between right and wrong. I also don't like people telling me what to do. And that can happen with some bands — they become puppets of record companies. You have to make your own decisions if you want your ideals to come across. Britain's in a strange state at the moment because you have a socialist government. I'm against socialism because again it stifles the individual. It tries to wrap him up not letting him think for himself."

Even the back cover, which finds the guys in matching robes, kimonos of sorts, tacitly suggests that they are somehow characters in this drama. On the back, there's a quote topical to the tale, in a red font that matches the lyrics presented on one page inside. Finally, the very act of putting the side-long song first tempts a kind of continuity to the second side, where one finds songs that many listeners feel could be included as part of the sci-fi narrative, except "A Passage to Bangkok." Geddy, in interviews, suggested as much himself, further noting that "Something for Nothing" goes so far as to express the moral of the story.

"'2112' obviously wasn't the first rock opera," says Geddy, addressing the success of the first track on the record, presented in seven parts. "I mean, there's *Tommy*; there were tons of them before that. *Thick as a Brick*. But maybe because this was the first kind of mini–rock opera from a power trio from Canada. Maybe that made it unusual. We were always referred to as a power trio, and it's a strange phrase if you really kind of isolate it. What is a power trio? When I think of a power trio, I think of Blue Cheer, first off, who were one of our first influences. Were they progressive? They tried to play fast. That was one of the important ingredients when you were a rock fan: How fast did they play? Could they play complex stuff? I guess you couldn't really call Blue Cheer progressive, yet they were a power trio. So we were like a power trio–plus, with benefits, trying to make it more interesting, more complex. It's hard for me to see why '2112' is regarded in that light, aside from the fact that maybe it was the first attempt at that kind of concept by a power trio."

As alluded to, "2112" is a tale about a future where music is banned after being deemed superfluous and against logic. In a wider sense, it's more so about oppression, the question of freedom and how much of it we should have. This was an area of study near and dear to Peart's heart at the time, given his Ayn Rand readings. *Anthem* was a particular inspiration for the story. In a narrower, and cheekier, sense, "2112" can be read simply as a criticism of the music industry.

The crowning graphic image for both the record and the tour was the lurid red pentagram, which became an enduring Rush symbol. "If someone gets something else out of that, you know, that's their problem," laughs Alex. For Peart, the sign had nothing to do with Satan, representing instead the creativity-suffocating authorities of the tension-filled tale. Pre-release, Geddy spoke of the song as being a science fiction tale concerned with individuality, and how society's leadership — consisting of priests and computers, hence the circuitry on the left side of the gatefold — prefer everybody programmed to be homogenous.

As Neil explained in 1976 to *Circus* magazine, "*2112* is a cycle of songs based on a development and progression of some things I see in society. We come across a lot of weirdness on the road, and it comes out in the music. The cycle begins with an 'Overture,' then the discovery of the guitar and music. Guitars don't exist in the Solar Federation because the computers won't allow music — it's not logical. Then there's the 'Presentation,' where the hero brings his guitar to the priests in the temples of Syrinx. But the acolytes smash it up and send him away. And he has a dream about a planet, established simultaneously with the Solar Federation, where all the creative people went. He's never seen anything like it before, this alternative way of life; even the way they build their cities is totally different. And he gets more and more depressed because he realizes that his music is a part of that civilization and he can never be a part of it. But in the end, he finds that the planet is real and things do change for him."

Speaking in the same year to *Creem*, Neil promised a "surprise double ending" and in total "a real Hitchcock killer," adding that with respect to parallels to modern times, "Things aren't all that bad now, but it's a logical progression from some of the things that are going on. All of the best science fiction is a warning. We want to let people know what's going on so they at least have a chance to change it. It's not going to change anybody's life or anything, but if you just put the germ of an idea in someone's head, then you've done your job."

Included in the show flyer for their Toronto Massey Hall stand (from which the forthcoming live album would be generated) was the following summary: "In the year 2062, a galaxy-wide war results in the union of all planets under the rule of the Red Star of the Solar Federation. The world is controlled by computers, called Temples, which determine all reading matter, songs, pictures . . . everything connected with life during the year *2112* ('The Temples of Syrinx'). In the midst of this assembly line living, a man discovers what was once known years before as a guitar ('Discovery'). The man begins to pluck the strings and turn the knobs, discovering that he can make his own music — a music much different than that of the Temples. He rushes to tell the priests of his discovery ('Presentation'), but to the man's dismay, the priests dismiss the instrument, saying it doesn't fit the plan of the Solar Federation. The man returns to the cave in which he found the guitar and, during a dream, is led by an oracle to a land of incredible beauty and serenity ('Oracle: The Dream'). Upon awakening, he cannot believe it was a dream — the beauty was so real. He remains in the cave for several days, becoming more and more depressed with each passing hour ('Soliloquy'). The man decides he cannot go on as part of the Federation and takes his life to move on to a better one. As he dies, another planetary battle begins ('Grand Finale') with the outcome to be determined in the mind of the listener."

Neil reiterates that one of the big real-world lessons from this fanciful tale spanning 2062 to 2112 is that of the individual against the masses, importantly not just a power cabal like the Solar Federation but *any* mass psychology. "That's definitely the way we were feeling too," says Peart, "this crushing weight of the recording industry and even other musicians. All these bands we'd worked with talked about their product and talked about playing in a market and so cynically milked the audience for encores and said the same things onstage every night: 'This is the greatest rock 'n' roll city in the world!' or 'You're the best audience we ever had!' And it would work. So you're thinking terrible things about these people, but also the people are falling for it.

"This world of cynicism was crushing us. I remember Geddy and I came up with a saying: 'the sickness.' These bands that pander, we said they had 'the sickness.' That they have sold out, in a '60s way of putting things. We retained that purity, and it was shaky at times to keep that vibe, but we did keep that vibe — always. This was going to be music that we loved so that other people would like it too. That remains simple truth to me. But it's easier to say that now than it was in the winter of 1974."

It's not just speculation that this work has ties to Ayn Rand's ideas; Neil went so far as to include right after his lyric credit, the missive, "With acknowledgment to the genius of Ayn Rand." This was done in part, he admits, so as to not be accused of plagiarism. *Anthem* was the main inspiration for "2112," but *Atlas Shrugged* also had some influence, and Neil was often asked to defend Rand as a personality, as well as her contentious politics, in interviews, much to his (and Geddy's) annoyance. But more broadly, "2112" is most richly read as a cautionary tale of political and cultural oppression, and most amusingly read as a shot at the record label.

"'2112' is probably the most important thing we've ever written," reflects Geddy firmly. "Because without that song, we probably would not have continued as a band. It was largely written in the studio and in rehearsal, and I think we had four weeks to make that record. So we got an extra week out of the deal, from *Caress of Steel*. And it just came together. Even some of the heaviest parts, Alex and I wrote just sitting down together with acoustic guitars. The concept came together very clearly, very quickly. We had these riffs we wanted to put together, and it just started to click for that song. And that whole album is very much like that. Alex had a turn of writing on his own. We just wanted to throw everything into the mix. My memory of it is that we were all very much in the same direction. Whenever we talked about what a song should be . . . 'Yeah, that's right!' We knew right away. There wasn't a lot of second-guessing; there wasn't a lot of 'Should we treat it like this? Should we treat it like that?' We all knew how we wanted to play that song and write that song. And we really just dug the concept Neil had come up with."

The best remembered part of the song's nearly twenty-one-minute duration is part two, "The Temples of Syrinx," emboldened by the equally heavy metal instrumental part one, "Overture."

"I believed that we could do something special with 'Overture' / 'The Temples of Syrinx,' that opened the album," recalls Cliff. "I thought those two segued together made a huge statement and would be very popular on radio. And it turned out, in fact, that that was the case. And if you could point to any one track in Rush's career that kind of made it a certainty that they would become an arena-headlining act, I would say it's 'Temples of Syrinx.' And you'd have to say nobody would have thought that at the time — or since; that was pretty wild. But in the time that we promoted *2112* in its regular life cycle, it did about two hundred and fifty thousand in sales, way more than any of the first three albums, and then continued to sell at a much faster rate than any of the other three albums had."

"The Temples of Syrinx" is a majestic and pounding heavy metal classic; "Overture" would be too if the guys had figured out a way to write some lyrics for it, other than the amusing and ironic "And the meek shall inherit the earth." But once "The Temples of Syrinx" explodes onto center stage, the band is firing on all cylinders, Neil crashing his crashes, Geddy full-throated, Alex robust of power.

Cliff is still a bit incredulous at the turn of events from one record to the next. "They were under pressure, but the pressure manifested itself on the album that followed *Caress of Steel*. That was the real problem for Rush — *2112*. They responded to the pressure that they received coming from *Caress of Steel* by doing *2112*, which, I would say, is very counterintuitive. What they actually did was, well, we're just going to blow this out even further. Too bad, that's what we do. And that's what *2112* is all about. And the real record company panic, not on my part by the way, but overall, set in when they received *2112*, as the fourth Rush album. With only a six- or seven-month gap between albums, *Caress of Steel* was a step back and now this one . . . there's no hope for this one at all. I begged to differ, actually. And I take a tiny little bit of credit for that.

"I think the ambition had a lot to do with it," continues Burnstein, on what he thought *2112* had going for it that its predecessor didn't. "I think also that when a band is really good and they are different, like Rush, it takes time for people to catch up to them. And there's a little bit of a — I don't know — compensatory factor, where people are thinking, 'I missed this, I should get on board now.' And really, 'Temples of Syrinx' was so heavy and so amazing, and anybody that was into heavy metal, certainly at the time, could not say, if they heard it, that this wasn't something they had to have."

Following nearly seven minutes of crunching, full-bodied Rush metal (most of which is "Overture," not "The Temples of Syrinx"), the listener is greeted with waterfall sounds and an out-of-tune guitar being plucked and strummed. Both "Overture" and "Grand Finale" reference Tchaikovsky's "1812 Overture," but additionally, one might describe "Overture" as flamenco in structure, albeit fully metalized. The drumless "Discovery" gives way to part four, "Presentation," which is a mix of quiet rock and full-on power chords, Geddy singing boldly, Neil killing it with memorable, musical fills. As well, note the presence of a character called Father Brown.

The "Temples" theme returns, and Alex rips off a spirited wah-wah-drenched guitar solo. This transitions into more pensive vocals and spare guitar, as part five, "Oracle: The Dream," cranks up into geometric prog and dramatic hanging chords, affording Neil more opportunity to create fills and demonstrate the high-fidelity production job applied to all his drums and cymbals.

Next is part six, "Soliloquy," which is near Sabbath-like heavy blues, with Alex sounding massive, drenched in electricity. "Alex was constantly searching for something new," notes Terry, "and changing amps fairly regularly between albums and trying to come up with something that was maybe not quite there for him on the previous record. And Alex would not play something sloppy. If it didn't sound the way he heard it or I heard it, we would work until we got it sounding right. He was very specific. We took hours to do those things, you know, doubling guitars and laying down rhythm tracks. They had to be right. Solos, I was very specific about what I thought we should do for solos, and he worked very hard to bring that to fruition."

"2112" closes out with "Grand Finale" (original title: "Denouement"), distinguished by the obligatory epic-ending "sunny" sounds. But soon the listener is immersed into a cauldron of swirling, rhythmic doom metal at high speeds, chaotic and strafed by effects-laden soloing, culminating in the iconic "We have assumed control" spaceship wreck. The Big Brother voiceover during this sonic collage of an ending was done by none other than Neil Peart, who had also provided the spoken word bits in "The Necromancer" one album previous.

Side two of the original *2112* vinyl opens with "A Passage to Bangkok," a heavy metal classic exploring those Middle Eastern tonalities pioneered by Led Zeppelin and then Rainbow. Helping Rush with their street cred, this one is about a worldwide whirlwind pot-tasting tour. Alex admits the song's Kashmir influence, and a little higher up the intellectual food chain, the title is a play on E.M. Forster's classic novel *A Passage to India*.

Remarks Geddy, who would chafe at the Led Zeppelin reference, "We were, if anything, too aware of our influences and trying to obscure those, and trying to be ourselves and trying to break away from the obvious Led Zeppelin comparisons: the singer has a high voice so compare them to Led Zeppelin and Humble Pie and all that stuff. Those are the comparisons that haunted us constantly and what we were trying to move away from. I don't think we really knew that we created an original sound, 'cause to us we still heard influences. And we still had those comparisons. We still had those bad reviews with 'poor man's Led Zeppelin' and that kind of thing. If you listen to *2112*, there is just no way you can compare that to Led Zeppelin in any way, shape or form; it's a very different animal. But it was easy to if you've got two paragraphs to write about a band — you're gonna grab the first thing."

Beyond the voice, beyond the Moroccan musical conceits of this one track, the smartest comparison that has some validity is the light and shade, the whisper to a roar aspect of both bands. Rush ended up doing a lot of that on both *Caress of Steel* and *2112*, but oddly, as their sound was found in the late '70s, the decibel levels found a tighter middle range, even as the complexity picked up.

Notes Geddy, setting the contours of this record's second side, "It was more focused, and the songwriting was very strong, I think. Regardless of the '2112' side of it, the individual songs on the other side were more focused. They were better recorded, there was better playing, there was better singing. *Caress of Steel* was a weird record, there's no escaping that; it's a very unusual record, I mean . . . it's still . . . some people love that record. But *2112* was more of a coming of age for us in that period. Even though one song was a whole side of a record, it was more concise. Our sound was more concise, and I think it was the first record that really sounded just like us and nobody else. So all of the influences of the past were less visible and there was more of our own kind of personality on it."

Next is "Twilight Zone," Rush making good on their dedicating of *Caress of Steel* to Rod Serling — "one of our great teachers," says Ged — by writing an actual song celebrating the classic sci-fi show of the early '60s. The *Caress of Steel* dedication had been prompted by Serling's death on June 28, 1975, just previous to the start of the sessions for the album. "Twilight Zone" is presented as a 4/4 shuffle with creepy parts added at slower speeds. There's whispering, there's a spare and bluesy solo from Alex and Neil proves his ability to groove when asked to do so. This was the last song written for the album, once they realized they were coming up short, setting a pattern for a perennial frustration — not only using everything but *having* to use everything. Then again, as Terry Brown articulates, for Rush it was never a case of throwing filler on the record, but more so nurturing and kneading a song until it's done, knowing it's going to get used and so working the hell out of it. Still, it seems more sensible to commend a band for having two records' worth of songs from which to pare down to forty minutes, or in Rush's case, less than forty minutes.

"Lessons," lyrics by Alex, alternates cheery, up-tempo acoustic folk with a heavy chorus placeholder on which both Geddy and Neil get to apply joyous, accessible fills. Both the mellow verses and the hard-charging chorus section feature Geddy high and roaring.

Says Terry of recording Neil and Geddy, "I had a background in drums too, not even close to Neil's of course, but it was something that I loved. So I loved recording drums and getting the best sounds and the utmost energy from the drums that I could. He was very happy with that. Because there was something we did: unless it sounded amazing, we didn't record it. Geddy was always developing his bass sound and had a damn good bass sound right off the bat. But then it was a question of capturing it for a record. We spent quite a bit of time fine-tuning the way we did that, like miking half of his Rickenbacker bass with an amp and then recording the other half direct to tape back in the early days."

"Tears," with lyrics by Geddy, is a somber, elegiac ballad featuring textural Mellotron work from the band's graphics guy, Hugh Syme. Again — and I'm sure many will chafe against the comparative — Black Sabbath comes to mind, "Tears" sounding like any number of that band's nearly inaudible dirges. "It was a sci-fi record so you had to have some sci-fi keyboards on it," chuckles Terry. "Otherwise it would not have worked. It was an extremely important element to that record. And I was totally into the sci-fi rock thing at that time, working with Klaatu, so this was just a natural progression. It needed those keyboards. Delays were also very much a part of what was going on and using the technology in terms of delay lines in the recording. I was using keyboards a lot at that time, so it came fairly naturally. We got the right sounds, and it stood the test of time. Hugh also got involved in the intro to '2112.' It was a vital aspect of a sci-fi record. I mean, for texture, you couldn't do it with bass, drums and guitar."

2112 ends on a rockin' note, "Something for Nothing" being up-tempo hard rock, based on stacked chords more than riffs, save for the chorus, which is very riffy. The band expertly builds tension throughout the song, jamming more urgently as it progresses, hitting the punctuations harder. It's as grand a finale as "Grand Finale," and another song that contributes to the idea of *2112* as a concept album, start to finish. With respect to the core philosophy of the track, Neil says that the idea was touched off by the band seeing graffiti on a wall at the Shrine Auditorium in LA stating that "Freedom isn't for free."

"We came back with *2112* and never looked back," reflects Terry, summing up his experience with the record, which represented for him "a more fine-tuned version of this direction that we were heading in. We felt that it was going to change everything, and I think it did. The attitude when we went in for *2112* was extremely positive. I never really got into the whole aspect of 'this could be the last record . . . or how can we make this commercial?' I mean, that never even entered my head. I treated them all as individual works of art. The material on *2112* was a little bit more succinct, it was more 'up,' the vibe was a lot better on that record if you want to compare it with *Caress of Steel*. There was a similarity, except I think we nailed it with *2112* — if we were to accept the fact that we didn't quite nail it with *Caress of Steel*. But *2112* is a classic sci-fi record, and it's got great sounds on it and is just a really complete record."

In terms of the sonics across the band's breakthrough fourth album, there's no question: *2112* was in possession of a fuller, more muscular sound. "Yes," continues Terry, "and this is sort of a small detail, but on the last day of making *Caress of Steel*, we got a hold of a digital delay line, which were pretty hard to get your hands on in Toronto at that time. And I remember we played with it for an afternoon and laughed so hard we were all in tears because it would be so funny. Because you can do all the octave jumps with voices and just do crazy things. And that was really going to be the tool that sort of got us through *2112*. So when we did *2112*, we got one of these delay lines and used it as part of the production. And I think it really did make the difference. It was a very experimental kind of idea, but it worked really well. So there were things we had learned, obviously, from doing the last two records together, so it became more efficient."

Says Howard, "When Neil came up with those powerhouse lyrics, and they put *2112* together, it was almost like the band was reborn. It's a combination of everything being put together and it gelled. It broke and it broke huge. That just opened up the doors for so much that happened after."

"Whether you could call it stubbornness or whatever, I think all three boys took the same attitude," reflects Neil's father, Glen, on the reversal of the band's downward spiral. "If they were going to go down in flames, they were going to go down their way. And that of course is what brought *2112* to the front. They did it their way, and they had all made the decision. We're going to go down together playing the type of music we want to play, and . . . we'll go back to other lives. But that didn't happen, of course. But Neil never expressed any real thought that 'maybe I'm not going to make it.' He certainly never mentioned that to us."

Helping make sure things didn't go pear-shaped was the band's solidarity, says Glen. "Yes, and their organization and the way they put things together; they all work the same way. They had a passion to do things together. And that's one of the things I've heard over the years about Rush is that they're the tightest group there is. The way that they did it, and the commitment they had, certainly won my respect.

"There's a security guard that said that the only rock group he would work for was Rush because they were organized, and when they said they were going to do something, it was going to be done. I was proud of that fact, that that's the way they were viewed and in a world that was totally alien from that way of operating as a business. I think it influenced their people over the years because a lot of their key people have been with them on every tour."

"All of us were just happy that the tables had turned and that people were interested in us again," explains Liam Birt. "I wasn't trying to read too much into it, from my personal perspective, because after you've been slapped down a couple of times, you tend to take things with a grain of salt. I just was happy with the fact that we were actually having people show up; it was just good from that perspective. It was a sigh of relief that maybe there's light at the end of the tunnel. That was the beginning of a rebound for us, but I probably knew that more in retrospect. It really wasn't until a few years later when we'd actually built up a little more steam that you felt like maybe this thing has a shot. You know, maybe we can actually go out and do headlining tours. But it wasn't specifically on that album, at least not from my perspective.

"They've never wanted to do things the easy way," continues Liam. "They used to joke amongst themselves that if they were ever to have a hit single, it would be the end of the band, because they would have sold out somehow and wouldn't be able to live with themselves as musicians at that point. So as far as them always wanting to take the hard road or the high road, whether they did it intentionally or not, that was always the way it went.

"Even many years later, jumping ahead a bit, the concept of sponsorship on tours came up. But it was always 'How can we endorse a product we wouldn't use ourselves? Why would we take someone's money for the sake of taking it?' They've always wanted to keep their credibility. They just don't want to sell themselves out. Because if they would have done something that was too bubblegum, too whatever, and if it sold too well, it would be the end of the band. They are a players' band. They're musicians — they love playing. People say to me all the time: they must have enough money and wherewithal not to need to continue touring. And whether the answer is yes or no to that is secondary. They love playing. It's what they are. They're musicians and they love it. They love the challenge, they love getting out there every night and just testing themselves, and that's what makes them great to work for."

2112 succeeded with the public where *Caress of Steel* did not, selling 160,000 copies by June and certifying gold in America for sales of 500,000 copies a year and a half after release. In Canada, Rush notched their second gold record when the album was certified October 1, 1976.

But why was it a success? Perhaps, as Cliff says, when you are that original, it takes some time for the public to catch up. Or one might argue that the public had no problem with a record like *Caress of Steel*, but a slightly improved version was required to break them. Because really, *2112* isn't appreciably more accessible than *Caress of Steel*. Its best bear-hugging songs — "A Passage to Bangkok," "The Temples of Syrinx," "Something for Nothing" — happened to all ring long and loud in the ears of fans. In other words, as Vic might put it, there was no AM hit. Stacked against "Bastille Day," "Lakeside Park" and even the amusing "I Think I'm Going Bald," it's not so obvious that *2112* should go gold and *Caress of Steel* might have gotten the band dropped.

"I think it comes back to the songs," muses Geddy. "We hit the right combination of chord progressions and we were starting to become accomplished at writing and all those things. I think it's the songs that make that album. Why has it endured? It's gotta come back to the songs. Sure, it's a good-sounding record, and we play real fast on it and people like that, especially young musicians, but the concept of what the album says and the sound of the music and the chord progressions are what make it endure."

"I think it was right place, right time," adds Ray. "I think Mercury Records at the time wasn't acknowledging, or didn't realize, that their first three records had carved the base of that one hundred and fifty thousand. And it meant that the next record was probably going to do one hundred and fifty thousand — and the good news: it was going to do it quicker. It's a business that rewards momentum. *2112* came out, and the band toured a lot off of *Caress of Steel* and the first two records, and so it started to sell quicker. I think any record they were going to do was going to sell quicker because they had just carved that base — momentum was on their side. And word of mouth. It was very much a word-of-mouth business back then. You heard from your friends, and if you had friends who were Rush fans, and it was their turn to play something in the car, they reacted to it. And that record still sells eight hundred copies a week, every week, until this day — it's never not sold that."

Further charting this happy sense of progress, Danniels says, "We had gotten to the point where, in some markets, we could headline our own shows. And that made it easier because they could do a longer set, and they could expose more music to their fan base and people in the building who weren't necessarily big fans. I think it's because the record is that good. How do you still sell a record thirty years later unless it's that good? It obviously was the right place, right time. And of course, after *Moving Pictures* — which did even better for them — *2112* became the record that suddenly had sold three million copies. A lot of those people became fans, and they went to the back catalogue, and *2112* was the record they went to. And now *2112*, most weeks, outsells *Moving Pictures*. Those two records totally stand the test of time. And yet there is not a song on *2112* like there is on *Moving Pictures*. You don't hear 'Tom Sawyer' in a movie or whatever and run to *2112*. You hear about *2112* because it's a passage of youth, like *Dark Side of the Moon* or *The Wall*. It's like the first time you smoke a joint, that's one of the records you must hear. It's a passage of youth. It's in that short collection of records that if you are a young rock fan in your early twenties, late teens, you've got to get."

But Ray acknowledges that the critics again weren't exactly on board. "They weren't a critics' band. I'm sure there was some positive press, some good press, but I'm sure it was much more throwing stones at them than anything else. That was just the way it was in those years. Every now and again, you would find a closet Rush fan that wrote a review, or on the live side, we would get reviewers that would be objective and talk about how the audience really liked them. But the critics themselves liked to throw rocks at this band."

"Oh, I don't know, nothing nice," answers Neil dismissively on how *2112* got reviewed. "I made a decision early on never to read anything. *Skinny Legs and All*, I think, was the book . . . I'd been a big Tom Robbins fan and read all of his novels, and I saw just the most scathing, snotty review of it in the *New York Times*

Book Review, so I wrote Tom Robbins a letter, and I said, 'I just wanted to let you know as a reader, whatever these "unmentionables" say, as a reader I was totally satisfied with the story and thought that every one of your novels continues to get better, just the way it ought to be.' And he sent me back a very nice letter saying that 'I stopped reading my reviews years ago because I realized if I believed the good ones, I'd have to believe the bad ones too.'

"And yeah, bing, the tuning fork goes off — what a great idea. So I never read another review again and still don't, because, well, for a multitude of reasons, none of them arrogant. I read the *New York Times Book Review* every Sunday, and I read every single one because these are intelligent people writing about intelligent people. If music reviewers knew more than I did about what I was doing, of course I would read it — you could learn things. Like when we worked with co-producers, you learn things from them because they know what you're trying to do and maybe they even know more than you do — that's the collaboration process for us. Reviews do not offer that. So I know that of course we did not get good press through the '70s and even for much longer. But it ceased to be a factor. Honestly, that's another thing we were free of — we had an audience. We weren't dependent on media of any kind. Our audience was there, and we built it on live performance because we were so dedicated to that. Every show was — to live the old Broadway thing — you live and die by your last show. We just always played that way; every show was the best show we could possibly do on that night. It seemed to us that's how you do things. I've seen other bands that maybe don't work that way, but we always did. So we had a reputation as being a hardworking, good band live who was really there playing for you that night.

"And people would come back even if they didn't like our latest record. As we started to go through changes, that would happen and the fans became factionalized . . . 'Oh we like those records but not these ones.' I think that has smoothed out a little over time as people have grown into our music as part of the soundtrack of their lives and there's less of that disparity. But there was a time when they were very fragmented. But again, we were free of that, free of that restriction or even that concern. We were really trying to follow that path: making music that we like, and other people should like too."

And so it's back to word of mouth — Rush was a people's band, thriving beyond any critical barbs and reflecting that back by doing well in cities where there were no magazines. For years, you never thought about Rush and the U.S. coasts. "Why do they play Omaha and Des Moines and all these places?" asks Ray rhetorically. "There's a rock station, there's an audience, they're not as picky and they're not as aligned with one kind of music. It's an event when someone comes to town. If you can afford a ticket and you are at all interested, you want to go."

"It was word of mouth that saved us," agrees Neil. "It's the same as when I was a kid. It was the way I knew about The Who, the way that I knew about Jimi Hendrix, the way I knew about the Grateful Dead. I mean, all I knew about these bands was word of mouth. You didn't hear those bands on the radio in St. Catharines, Ontario, in the '60s. Kids told other kids; musicians told other musicians. A perfect metaphor for those times . . . that was the network that carried *2112* to its audience. And then the sheer spirit of anger and rebellion conveyed it once it reached those people — 'Whoa, they mean this shit.'"

"What happened was the album did really well," says Alex, his recollection of the sense of relief palpable. "It was a success both artistically and commercially. And it really bought us our independence from the record company. The record company has never been in on a single session that we have ever done, and in fact even Ray wasn't in the studio until *Vapor Trails* when we happened to have a meeting at the studio and he came down. That was the first time he'd ever been in the studio with us. So it's our territory; whatever we do there is what we do and when we're done it moves to the next stage. It gets packaged and it goes to the record company and they accept it the way it is. They have no choice. So when I hear stories about young bands that are influenced by us, I think that's really a lot of what that influence is. They look at us and they see a band that's managed to stay for decades and done things on their own terms. And that's the great hope every artist wants to have. It's very rare. It's very hard to do — now it's virtually impossible."

Neil notes that at this time the band started climbing the ladder with respect to the venues they were able to play. "The Michigan Palace was an old vaudeville type music hall theater in Detroit, and the first time we headlined there was magical. The first time we headlined Massey Hall in Toronto . . . those are stepping-stones, never to be forgotten. And those are the times too that you say if I never do anything else, you know, I played at Massey Hall, I played at the Michigan Palace and toured the United States.

"I was always prepared for it to end at any time. That's kind of a life philosophy for me too, that every day should be spent such that if it ends now, well, I spent today the best I could. That was definitely my guiding philosophy at that time too: whatever happens, I had this. So people say, 'Did you think you were going to last?' Of course, you didn't think you were going to last thirty years. 'Was your ambition to play at Massey Hall or Maple Leaf Gardens?' No, my ambition was to play at the roller rink, the high school — these are realistic ambitions. If you're a dreamer, I think you're automatically doomed to a sense of failure. If you're taking drum lessons in an upstairs room in St. Catharines, Ontario, should I be thinking about Madison Square Garden or the Los Angeles Forum? It would be stupid. I dreamed of being good enough to play at the roller rink and the high school, and as our growth came, same thing: 'Gee, if we could headline this club or that small hall . . .' These were the dreams. Or even to open on a bigger tour. All of those things meant so much — they really did — that you didn't waste time or energy dreaming of the impossible.

"Certainly *2112* was that turning point. No one could tell us what to do anymore," continues Peart. "Before that, they had been thinking, 'You guys should do this,' and 'You should write this sort of song.' People thought they could tell us what to do, and it drove me crazy because, as I described before from teenage years, I don't work that way. There's the music and there's the business, but I never accepted any involvement either way really. Music shouldn't bother business and business shouldn't try and meddle with the music. So there was never any more questions, fortunately. As we continued to grow from there, the decisions were ours."

Adds Geddy, "We did have a chance to make another record, so we went in and tried to make the best record we could. It was really us and them back then, and we weren't going to give in. Fortunately, we were young and idealistic enough to stick to our guns. And geez, guess what? Everyone didn't hate it. Well, a lot of people hated it, but a lot of people liked it. And it was such a pinnacle accomplishment for a young band because there could not have been *2112* without *Caress of Steel*. All those experiments of the previous album bear fruit on *2112*. And ever since that record started getting attention, the record company never bothered us again and our management never bothered us again in terms of our direction. They figured either that we knew what we were doing, or we got lucky once and 'let's see if they can get lucky twice.' But everything changed with that record — everything.

"It was us as individuals saying we don't want to sound like everyone else," continues Geddy. "We're prepared in our own small way to risk everything to not sound like everyone else. So is that a small thing? Not to us at the time. It's a large statement because, honestly, we believed that regardless of what happens to the record that we were not going to get another tour and we would probably end up breaking up. So in a way, this was our swan song, in our minds, in our hearts.

"Of course, you think, yeah, we'll convince people. But on the practical side, we thought that by doing this we were risking all of our futures. But we did it anyway; it just felt like we had to do this. Is that what we represent as a band? I don't know; it certainly was at that moment, and how that reflects on our career as a whole is hard for me to say or see. But I do believe that the sentiments of that moment are what a lot of fans got from that record, and they were able to identify that in their own lives, feeling in their own way that they've always had this choice of conforming to someone else's rules or not. And in that way, that's no small part of our success with our fans."

chapter 6

All the World's a Stage

"In the encyclopedia, there's his picture
next to the word 'polarizing.'"

ush's tour in support of *2112* would, halfway through, produce the tapes used for the band's first live album, a double record called *All the World's a Stage* that was issued September 29, 1976. But the band logged dozens of shows before rolling home for the historic three-night Massey Hall stand that documented this hard-driving road band. After a few Ontario dates in February, *2112* already in the can but not issued, the band was off to California for a four-day residency at the Starwood in Hollywood. This kicked off an intensive U.S. tour up, down and sideways, with a week off around the record's release date on April 1. The guys were up there with the likes of Ted Nugent, Sutherland Brothers and Quiver, Starcastle, Kansas, Aerosmith and Thin Lizzy, with multiple dates logged with Styx and Starcastle.

"Those are three very nice people who are wonderful instrumentalists," recalls Styx singer and keyboardist Dennis DeYoung.

"All three of them. And Neil, he's a drummer's drummer. And Geddy, liking somebody's singing is so personal and so outrageously subjective. Certain people, there'll be millions of people, I guarantee you, who tell me I'm the greatest thing that ever lived and there'll be equal or more who say I'm the worst thing that ever happened. There is no accounting for what you like or don't like about singers. And Geddy Lee, in the encyclopedia, there's his picture next to the word 'polarizing.' It says, 'There's a voice that's polarizing.' Geddy is like if Robert Plant and Tiny Tim had a baby. So he's an acquired taste, and he's a lovely man. It's just not my thing. That doesn't make me odd. I know Rush fans will now go run to my Facebook page and call me all sorts of names. Save your breath. I think Rush are a terrific band, but they certainly were and are very, very specific. And I also remember the period where they tried to get synthy, like we did with 'Mr. Roboto.' But they're sensational, and yes, Neil Peart is indeed a drummer's drummer."

Geddy says of Styx, "In some ways they were more progressive pop than they were progressive rock, and they were very operatic. Styx was very operatic, and then there's 'Domo Arigato, Mr. Roboto,' you know? That was a different thing than what we were trying to do. We were darker. I think that was the difference. But Kansas had very much the same mentality as us. Complicated stuff, but they were a Midwestern band, and their bluesy roots were quite evident in their music. We were big fans of Kansas when they came out. We thought they were brothers in arms in a way, that they had a very similar mentality. And the first time we saw them — we did a number of gigs with them — we were blown away by their precision and their complexity, and yes, very much they were coming from the same place we were."

"I remember Dennis DeYoung once, at the Montcalm Hotel," notes Howard, "sitting down with Geddy and getting fired up on baseball. That was one of the first times I heard them talking a lot about baseball because I guess he was a baseball fanatic and Geddy was also into baseball, quite heavily. But I remember that conversation. It was a very, very intense baseball conversation in that hotel. The guys in Styx were very nice guys."

Progressive rock was a very British style of music, with almost all the big bands coming from the U.K. and a secondary scene coming from Germany, what was known as Krautrock. A terrain as vast and populous as North America coughed up only this tight fistful of major label acts — Styx, Rush and Kansas — and all three of them had qualifications or asterisks that took them away from U.K. prog: Kansas had the violin, Styx verged on what at the time was called pomp rock and Rush had two: they were from Canada and they hammered heavy metal into their prog.

Geddy's voice aside, the band was destined to be doomed with critics outside of the *Creem/Circus/Hit Parader* axis for two reasons: they didn't like prog rock and they didn't like heavy metal. Strikes two and three — and you're out.

"Generally, at that time, yes, that's what they hated," says Cliff Burnstein. "I mean, Led Zeppelin got trashed by *Rolling Stone*. There were some horrible cases out there. But I'd say generally the national magazines were not supportive of Rush. But back then, there was quite a chain of regional magazines that sometimes were only devoted to music. Remember, here are these rock shows that are going through towns almost once a week, it seems, with two or three great acts on them, and so the business was booming, even though the economy was not great. The music business was booming. The baby boomers were all turning twenty-one and twenty-two and everything, and they had their first jobs and were making their first money and going to shows and buying records. So there was a lot of advertising directed toward the baby boom or kind of the edge of the baby boom coming up.

"Lots of these music magazines existed on a local basis, and they were not critical. What they wanted was to spotlight bands that were coming through town and write something supportive of them. And the people who worked on these magazines were not actually worried about whether they were going to have a national reputation and be quoted in national magazines. They were more on the level of the local rock fans and heard music and saw music pretty much the same way. And so as time went on, and Rush had played in more markets, more of these magazines, local and regional ones, became more interested in them, and I think treated Rush very, very well. You would go from mentions to features to covers. That's how it pretty much progressed."

"The press in the early days shunned them," agrees Howard. "The press didn't even want to know about Rush — and at that time, Rush didn't want to know about the press. But over time they just bucked the odds by playing live. When you play live and you go from city to city, that's your best selling tool. That's how you established yourself years ago. If the media didn't want to help you out, you did it yourself. And Rush worked so hard. I mean, we went everywhere. We even played Lake Okoboji, Iowa. Does anyone even know where that is? I do. We played Estevan, Saskatchewan. I mean, we went right across. We were in places I'm sure no North American band would ever go to. It was great! And that's because those tiny places are where your most loyal fans would be. And the fact that you are coming to their towns, they respect that. And Rush is a band that really wants to please their fans. They care, and they really care about their music. And when you care about your music, you will go to those places."

And again, as the blanketing of Middle America in April and May of 1976 attested, this was Rush's bread and butter, with the guys returning again and again. As Burnstein says, there were practicalities associated with the strategy.

"Well, the circuit was different back then," explains Cliff, "because there were more bands going out. And the money certainly wasn't as great, and nobody expected it to be so great. And you want to play five or six times a week, and the crews were smaller, so there were actually less mouths to feed. Not everybody had their own personal bodyguard, personal stylist, personal this or personal that. It was a tight-knit group. And there were markets that had all these great, oh, call them war memorial coliseums that were built in the '30s with WPA money. And that was another stop on the road. The booking agent, who I believe was Marsha Vlasic, at ATI had a circuit that was very, very detailed. You could play markets — and everybody did play markets — like Johnson City, Tennessee, or Yakima, Washington, and places that are much less played today. You would talk about: how many shows in Iowa are you are going to do? And now a lot of the bands skip Iowa entirely, or maybe they just played Des Moines. But there are other good places to play in Iowa. And in South Dakota. Everybody did that. Blue Öyster Cult did. That's what you did if you were serious."

To help the cause with radio, in January of '77, Cliff concocted a promo sampler. "Yes, we sent out an album that we made ourselves for promotional purposes only, which I called *Everything Your Listeners Ever Wanted to Hear by Rush ... But You Were Afraid to Play*, and I sent this out to radio stations. It was my own compilation of Rush's greatest hits from the first few albums, and my idea was to get this in front of people who are not familiar with Rush, or who refuse to play Rush, and get them to feel like they were way behind the curve. Ultimately, I think that turned out to be very helpful for them. We started wearing them down, bit by bit."

The full-length promo album — regular Mercury label but plain black and white jacket — consisted of tracks from the three

Neil-era studio albums, including excerpts of "Bacchus Plateau" from "The Fountains of Lamneth" and "Overture" / "The Temples of Syrinx" from "2112." The back cover reprinted a *Circus* magazine headline announcing that "*Closer to the Heart* will be the group's sixth LP."

Like the guys from Kiss and Styx, Thin Lizzy guitarist Scott Gorham remembers Rush fondly from this time as well.

"I'd never heard of Rush," begins Gorham. "I never knew who these guys were, never heard their music. So I was quite interested to see what everybody was talking about. I remember we had done a sound check and I was at the side of the stage and watching them build — never heard anybody say build — the drum kit. They were building Neil's drum kit with the cages and all that. And I'm thinking, 'Who the fuck does this guy think he is? Oh my God, look at all the instruments he's got hanging off of it. There's no way in hell this guy's going to hit probably half of those, right?' So I made sure that night, the first time after we did our set, went out there and watched them — and they absolutely slayed me. Neil hit everything that was put in front of him, and in a really great way, and he probably hit them twice. It really put me in my place in a big way.

"And you know, the really cool thing about them is they're not only great musicians, they're just really cool people. You know, even if they didn't play any instruments at all and I met them somewhere, I would just want to buy them a drink as they're just funny guys. They have a great sense of humor and they're a great hang. We're all really lucky that they played really great music at the same time.

"I'll tell you, I had the whole band come into my hotel room one day. We were pretty stoned and there's about eight of us in the room. Alex is dressed in a red smoking jacket with his hair all slicked back. Geddy is in this pink ladies' nightgown with two pigtails. And Neil's wearing a shirt that's two sizes too small for him with his pant legs rolled up. And they're 'Excuse me, Scott, do you mind if we come in and join your little soiree?' So I'm kind of stoned; 'Uh, yeah, okay.' They came in and immediately started to do this skit. I didn't get it right off the bat, and everybody that was in the room kind of had their jaw on the floor because nobody knew what was going on.

"And then it hit me — they were doing *Leave It to Beaver*! In my room. And as soon as we got it, we all just started roaring with laughter. They probably spent like fifteen minutes. I couldn't tell you to this day if it was like a memorized skit or just off the cuff or whatever. And then they were gone — wow. They left the room and that was that. And then I thought, first of all, 'That was great,' and then, 'How fucking weird was that?' What we just witnessed.

"But yeah, they were doing great and they were the headliner. That was the stupid thing, that I didn't know about them. What the fuck rock am I living under? But yeah, 'The Boys Are Back in Town' is how we got on a lot of those tours and got to know bands like Rush. That one particular song enabled us to tour with a lot of different bands and meet a lot of different great musicians. It was very cool."

Alex says of Thin Lizzy, "We got so tight with them; I love those guys. They were great. Brian Robertson and I became really close friends, and we hung out all the time. Talk about drinking; it was not unusual to drink almost a bottle of Scotch a night, just because you were fired up and that's the way it was. And they were coming from the same sort of place we were musically. They cared a lot about their music."

Blue Öyster Cult were also at that same place on the career ladder, having finally broken right around the time of their 1975 double live album. "They were really good to us and were really nice guys," says Alex. "We got along really well with them, no problems with us that I can recall. I really respected Buck [Dharma] a lot. We spent time together and we did a lot of dates with them. The crews got along really, really well. And we opened for them, I think, through that whole time. They opened for us for a series of shows in the Midwest, '84-ish. One thing, they have a song called 'Godzilla' that started off with that stomping, and the tape of Godzilla coming, and they do the whole rap before it: 'As he rounded the corner and he looked down, and . . .' And we substituted their tape where he roars or whatever, with a tape of Mr. Ed. 'And he said . . . Hello, my name is Mr. Ed.' And they all stopped onstage with their mouths open, speechless, stuttering . . .

"We did some shows with Bob Seger that were mostly Midwestern shows," continues Alex. "I remember one night, in Flint or Saginaw or someplace like that, we got an encore and came out and played the song and we left the stage, and people were still going mental. And the band were on the side of the stage going, 'Come on! Come on!' to get us back on and do another encore. I mean, that never happens! House lights usually go on immediately. But they were so cool, those guys. I remember them as being probably the nicest people we ever worked with. They were all such gentlemen, really, really good people."

Geddy figures that *2112* marked the germination of the monster cinematic presentations that would increasingly accompany Rush's music onstage. "In our history, I think we went through every kind of possible projection system that anyone's ever used, from the early days when we actually had almost like a Grateful Dead–like system using oil and colors, things like that, which originate from our very, very first tours when we used lights. There was a guy Tim, out of Virginia, who used to work with our sound company, National Sound; he would bring out some extra lights. This is when we were just starting to headline a couple of gigs here, a couple of gigs there. It must have been early *2112*. And we wanted to project the *2112* logo on the back of the screen. And I think that's how we started getting into this whole visual thing, this whole filmic thing, just with those few ideas. We actually, I think, used a little projector, like one of those ones you used to use in school."

At the time, Geddy remarked that the band had considered an expansion in membership but that, after a vote, decided to learn more instruments themselves, in addition to experimenting with slide shows for the live presentation. Geddy mentions sixteen-string and twelve-string guitars, double-necks, vibes, orchestra bells and bass pedal synthesizer. Neil said at the time that the bass pedals were for "Lakeside Park." Geddy also lamented the fact that Canadian border laws made it difficult for the band to bring their full light show north of the border.

"Just building, building, building" is how Vic characterizes this point in the band's touring career. "I mean, the snowball just kept collecting more snow and got bigger and bigger. And the venues got bigger and the performances got bigger and the production got tremendously wild, as did the cost. But you know what? That's what sells tickets. They had carte blanche on what they wanted to do onstage with their lighting and sound. We never bothered them at all. Never even questioned them if they wanted to change the sound company or get a bigger sound company. We never pushed. At least I didn't. They had free rein of what they wanted to do."

Right after playing with Thin Lizzy in San Antonio, Rush got down to business, loading in for a three-night stand at Toronto's venerable 2,200-seat Massey Hall theater to play the shows that would constitute the band's first live album.

Terry Brown says, "From a creative standpoint, obviously the tunes had already been established, the arrangements and preproduction and everything, and they didn't really change a whole lot on the live record. But we had to get that magic performance and all the little details straight. Both the live records we did, quite often fans say to me, 'It's the first record I ever bought, and that's how I learned about the band.' I think when you've spent that much energy putting tunes together properly and you have something that is successful, making a live record can be a lot of fun. It certainly wasn't drudgery. It's not an easy job, but it was a lot of fun. Now, we're talking about making a movie instead of just making a record. But it's the same kind of thing. There's a lot of detail that has to be looked after, and it takes a lot of energy. So it's certainly not boring."

"We brought the truck in and had a very in-depth sound check," recalls Alex. "I think we might have even set up the day before and did a good solid sound check. And I just remember how nerve-racking that was. Playing your hometown is always nerve-racking, always crazy. Knowing that the truck was out there and the record button was on, you were so nervous and so afraid of making mistakes."

"I don't think we did anything," says Alex with respect to touch-ups. "That's such a long time ago. We might have done a couple vocal things ... maybe? But even that doesn't sound familiar to me." The record, however, did go through three remixes.

"The first live album was very raw; it was the first time we ever recorded the band live, over three days," says Geddy. "We basically took the best of what we had, which to some fans is very exciting, and from our point of view it's a little difficult to listen to because it sounds a little crude. But that's the nature of that album. In terms of the work on it, I think we were all pretty involved, us and Terry Brown because he co-produced it with us."

Neil says that by the third night, he was experiencing some frustration and anger over how the shows were going, and this resulted in extra energy shot through the selections on the final night, something they were pleasantly surprised to discover once they were able to review the tapes.

All the World's a Stage was issued as a resplendent triple gatefold, albeit as a double album. Introduced by roadie Skip Gildersleeve with "I want you to please welcome home, Rush!" the band tear into "Bastille Day," tight but loose, as they say in Zeppelin parlance. Every instrument and Geddy's voice are in place, the production raw but essentially correct, save for a bit of boxiness to the bass drum and mud to Alex's solo guitar. And yet Ian Grandy says of the record, "I listened to it one time, I went, 'That sucks,' and never listened to it again. And I've heard Geddy say that he can't even listen to it." And it's true, this live album is somewhat ignored by the band, as are all of them, really.

But no point raining on the parade, *All the World's a Stage* is beloved by the fans, and it stands shoulder to shoulder with all the classic live albums of the day, which, at the hard rock end, includes the likes of *Live and Dangerous*, *On Your Feet or On Your Knees*, *Strangers in the Night*, *Unleashed in the East*, *Double Live Gonzo!*, maybe even *Frampton Comes Alive!*

Next up is "Anthem," played and sung perfect — look at old video, and you'll be shocked to see that Geddy doesn't have to contort himself in the least to hit those notes. Two minutes' worth of "Fly by Night" transitions into "In the Mood," where on record we hear for the first time Neil drumming all over a Rutsey-era track and frankly overdoing it. Closing side one is a ragged "Something for Nothing," a song built for this kind of jam spirit. Again, it becomes apparent that Alex is buried in the mix come solo time, but on the positive, Geddy's bass sounds appropriately unarticulated for regular bass parts and slightly Lemmy-like for his licks. "Something for Nothing" was issued as a single from the record, backed with the "Fly by Night"/"In the Mood" medley.

Side two features "Lakeside Park" (more than half the *Fly by Night* album, mathematically, is represented), with Geddy continuing this stylistic thing he's been doing on the record of occasionally coming in late with his vocal. The rest of the side is devoted to "2112," with "Discovery" and "Oracle: The Dream" removed and the parts renumbered. It was twenty years, up into the *Test for Echo* tour, before the band played the entire thing live.

"By-Tor & the Snowdog" is next, a groovy, jammy twelve-minute version replete with a long atmospheric sound collage section, followed by "In the End," which has Geddy throwing in a "one, two, buckle my shoe." Side four practically invents one of Rush's side-long concepts, the band creating a medley out of "Working Man" and "Finding My Way" that also includes a drum solo. Closing the album is "What You're Doing," making the side a dedication to the debut album's three weightiest songs — this early heavy metal classic wasn't heard live again until the R40 tour of 2015.

"Probably the funniest thing to do with that album was the way we ended it," says Geddy. "We had this long applause and in the end we faded the applause into this sound of Alex, Neil and myself in the parking lot clapping our hands. We put it long into the thing so you really have to let the applause run to the end of the groove to hear it. The applause fades into the three of us in the parking lot clapping and then we say, 'Okay, see you later,' and then we get into a car and you hear the car door slam and then we drive away."

Reflecting 1976's love-in with live albums, *All the World's a Stage* cracked the U.S. Top 40 (exactly at #40, arriving there in November), the first Rush album to do so, and was en route to a gold certification along with *2112* and *A Farewell to Kings*, which it got November 16, 1977. Taking two weeks off in late June/early

July, Rush was back on the road touring nonstop for almost a full year, into June of 1977, going to the U.K. for the first time, supported by Stray. In the world of personal news, a month after the Massey Hall stand, Geddy married Nancy, sister of early Rush alumnus Lindy Young, in a traditional Jewish wedding. The couple was able to steal away for a two-week honeymoon in Hawaii, in contrast to the chaos of scheduling afforded Alex and Charlene's nuptials during the much bleaker *Caress of Steel* days. Neil and Jackie, on the other hand, remained common law until Jackie's death in 1998.

Neil's parents, Glen and Betty, can't agree on whether the first time they met Geddy and Alex was at Massey Hall or at the band's first show headlining Maple Leaf Gardens, December 31, 1976, but it was one or the other. Glen thinks Massey Hall, but Betty says, "Wasn't that at Maple Leaf Gardens? I know at Maple Leaf Gardens they had a big party afterwards to honor the fathers, all the fathers; that was fun."

"Offstage they are fairly quiet young men," adds Glen. "We had no problem at all having a little visit with them and getting to know them a little bit. And I think on their behalf, getting to know Neil's parents, maybe trying to figure out where he came from. And we got along fine and have ever since got along really well."

Glen was never worried about his son running off and doing the rock 'n' roll life, and with these marquee shows, all of it was working out just fine. "I don't think it really ever bothered either one of us because we had, I think, supreme confidence in Neil and his ability to be able to handle himself. It never really caused me any concern for a moment that he wouldn't be able to do it or wouldn't be able to handle it. It definitely was a career. It maybe took a few years before the viable part of it kicked in. They were busy touring and they were determined to do what they wanted to do. So I think the career path was there. It was just a question of when it was going to kick in and be viable."

Betty, on the other hand, did worry a bit about Neil "when I knew he was traveling and traveling; you know, the law of averages. But no, it was a great opportunity, and I knew he could do it. As soon as I saw the name on the marquee at Maple Leaf Gardens, I knew he had made it."

The "traveling and traveling" was about to go international. The band began to tour more extensively, and given the inclination toward the intellectual inherent in Geddy, Alex and Neil, it was mind-expanding.

Recalls Vic, "When we first went to the U.K. with our lawyer, we did England and we did France and we worked our way to Holland, where PolyGram Records' head office was and discussed the future tour with them. And I shocked them because I asked for tour support. And the international guy said, 'What you're asking for is my whole budget.' And I said, 'I don't care. That's what we need.'

"And Mercury came through in the end with that tour support. We had only sold fifteen hundred albums in the U.K. when we got there, but we did very well with the live shows. They were jammed, they did very well, and within the next six months, we went back. And the houses were packed. Mind you, we were doing venues like a thousand, twelve hundred, fifteen hundred people, and then the third tour is when we started at Hammersmith, and then went to five dates at Hammersmith, where they did the recording of the second live album. And then the sky was the limit from there. But every town, like Birmingham and Manchester, has these agricultural halls which are fairly big, and they were eventually playing all those halls. The reception that they got in England was that big. They went from selling a few albums to silver and gold albums. But yeah, when I went out, I went ahead of the tour and whatever we did in Europe and England. I never toured with them. I've been on the road with the band, the first tour they did of the U.K. and Scandinavia. I was with the band just because I handled all the money and took care of everybody, made sure all the hotels were paid. Make sure nobody wanted for anything."

"I was so impressed in Britain with the audience and how they listened," says Alex, adding his impressions of that first overseas mini-tour in June of '77. "During a song, they would just stand there, or sit, and listen, and then at the end of the song, 'Rooaaarrr,' and then we were on to the next song. Very seldom did you hear anybody yell during a song unless it's one of those big stops where the whole crowd kind of cheers. That's really what impressed me with all of Europe. In Holland, it was the same thing, the way people responded to certain parts of certain songs — they have a whole different appreciation. When you talk to people about music, they can be fans of ABBA or some heavy metal, Black Sabbath, to use an early example. They were so diverse in their musical interests, and that really, really impressed me. And they're more of a polite audience to play to. Whereas in America, especially if you're playing the Detroit area, there's stuff whipping around, and people are going mental all the time."

Which leads to the inevitable subject of onstage injuries. What's the tally? "I think Geddy got hit with a bolt once, a bottle once, a bullet, like the shell case. I was hit with glow sticks. In terms of real injuries, actually, Geddy got hit one time pretty hard with a bottle. I think it glanced him, and I think it cut his forehead or something. We had to stop the show for a few minutes. I don't think Neil was ever hurt. There was a PA horn that fell off the stage at Nassau Coliseum. We were playing with Blue Öyster Cult, in fact. And it had fallen back off the stage-right stack onto the stage, fell back and decapitated my double-neck, sheared the head stock off the double-neck, and it fell over on an old Gibson that I had on the road with me, that I retired after that. It was just too valuable to me to have on the road."

"Those were the days when everything was new and exciting," reflects Howard, who paints a picture of Rush on the road at this juncture. He explains that by this time, they'd had a long association with Max Webster. "Because we were all really young. I guess when you're really young, your eyes are open and everything is great. I mean, they are still great now, but when you're really young, I think you can appreciate it more because you think how lucky you are. And with Kim Mitchell, he always had amazing musicians around him, and he was an amazing musician himself. So touring with Max Webster was great back then. People in the United States didn't really know Max Webster very well, but up here in Canada, it was huge. And the two bands together played off each other."

"The guys in Rush were amazing," remarks Max Webster bassist Mike Tilka. "And they were diligent. They were wonderful to be on the road with. But we didn't hang with them and that. I know that Neil practices more than any drummer in the world. The guy has a work ethic that nobody else has. Remember the big fuel crisis in the '70s? There was a huge fuel crisis in the States, and I remember playing in Tennessee, and it was an extremely cold winter, and it was really hard to get gasoline. We're driving in the van and we'd put a piece of cardboard in front of the radiator so the water gets hotter, because we were driving with blankets on our knees. Because the front of the van is just tin. It was freezing! And the guys in Rush would sometimes . . . Kim and Gary would sometimes ride in their bus."

Then there were shared shows with UFO. "They were nuts," comments Mike. "Phil Mogg was crazy. And what's his name, the guitar player, Michael Schenker? He practiced all the time. He never talked. He didn't socialize. In rehearsal, you could hear him practice; if you're at a gig, you would see him practice; the guy was scary. And Pete Way? Yeah, he was drunk all the time. He used to fall over onstage."

Howard remembers the UFO bassist all too well. "Oh, Pete Way used to come out and tell them, 'We'll be dining on honeydew tonight,' and they used to make fun of Rush's long silk gowns that they used to wear. But Yes and all these progressive bands used to wear all this flowing . . . and so did Rush. Everybody has their role model somewhere, and the Rush guys were into Yes and Genesis and that was it. They were pranksters, Pete Way especially. I remember they had these Malibu racetracks with these little Malibu cars, and they would get out of their minds and get into these cars. And Pete Way would get especially out of control and would go off the track and roll. We would get thrown out of places all the time. But Pete Way used to fall off stages when they were playing. They used to hang out with Rush and get in a lot of trouble. It was UFO and Thin Lizzy as well. I mean, it was incredible, the amount of classic bands they played to. It's even amazing to me now that I'm recalling all this. You think back and go, 'Wow, those were some amazing times.' But yes, UFO used to sneak around the stage when Rush were playing and just distract them, tried to distract them a lot. Their outfits were classic. I mean, Pete Way with the circus pants."

Back to the Massey Hall stand with Max Webster, Tilka says, "It was three days and it was phenomenal. The guys in Rush, even then, they were a pretty slick band. It wasn't like everybody was nervous. They had three nights, which is wonderful. They had a really good-sounding venue, not the Gardens or something that's big and boomy and echoey. But they had three nights of material to pick from. And I certainly don't know which nights the majority of it is from, but I do know having read a lot of rock magazines when bands do multiple nights there, it tends to be one magic night over the other two."

"It clicked, over time, like anything else," continues Howard. "There is a catalyst and a blending that happens, and all of a sudden, boom, Rush started accelerating, and they've mastered their performance. But they did have great mentors. They were watching a lot of different bands at the time. But even just hearing them for the first time, just playing, you knew that they were special. They had a powerful sound, they really could play and the energy was unbelievable. Prior to this, I was working with a lot of bands like Savoy Brown, Deep Purple, Badfinger, Fleetwood Mac, Rod Stewart, and you see all these bands and then you hear Rush, as an opening act, and you just knew it. I remember telling Geddy's mom, 'Your son's band is going to be huge.' And to this day, she comes back to me and says, 'I remember when you told me that in the kitchen. It was pretty funny.'

"But the first ten years of Rush were pretty excruciating. We did about two hundred cities a year. We always toured and basically never stopped touring. Because you had the stamina to tour back then. We would always share the driving, which is pretty funny because one day, I think it was Alex's turn to drive, and he'd lost his wallet and he couldn't find it anywhere. And he had a bunch of money in there. We would pay each other off to take turns driving, so, 'You take my shift — I'll pay you fifty bucks if you take my shift tonight. Because I don't want to drive.' And I remember Alex took three shifts one night to make the money back when he lost his wallet. And at the end of the shift, I remember, I was lying on the floor — at the time we had a van — and I opened my eyes, and we're at the end of the drive. I look to the right, and behind the passenger seat, on the floor, was Alex's wallet, after he'd taken all this money to drive like twenty-four hours."

Charting the evolution of the band's transport, Howard explains, "The very first vehicle, we rented a Chrysler Newport, and I remember Neil put a fluorescent bulb in the back of it so he could read in it while we were driving. So we were always driving down the road, at high rates of speed, with a fluorescent light in the car. It was such a dead giveaway for the cops to pull us over. But we were lucky. We went across Canada in that.

"Alex and I used to go out a lot. We used to walk around Regina and Saskatoon. And it was definitely in Saskatchewan somewhere, but we were walking around and we saw a Dodge Funcraft in this lot, and it was a van where you can actually sleep a person above the driver and passenger side; it had a raised roof. And we were looking into it and thinking, 'Wow, imagine if we could have something like this. It would be so amazing!' Well, about a year later, we did have it. We had a Dodge Funcraft, and it was like a dream come true. We used it for over two hundred cities."

Alex remembers this advancement in the band's travel arrangements fondly as well. "We were in a rental sedan for the first year and then we were in a station wagon for, I guess, the following year. And then we got a van, maybe around the time of *2112*. It was a Funcraft van, a Dodge van with a cab on it, and a back seating area you could fold down into a bed. It had a table and two bench seats and this little area over the driver that you could climb up and sleep in. There were five of us in there, I guess. And we took shifts driving. We all took three-hundred-and-fifty-mile shifts, and it was smelly and a mess but it was sure a lot of fun. We had that thing for a couple of years. We went through, I think, three motors and we traveled, boy, a hundred and something thousand miles in those couple years.

"And then we graduated to a Barth motor home. I mean, it was the ugliest thing you've ever seen. It was a big shoebox on wheels. It figures that we would pick something like that, instead of one of those more elegant Winnebagos or those other ones that were more streamlined, Gulfstream or whatever they're called. We had that for a couple of years and then finally we got a bus around the time of *A Farewell to Kings* or *Hemispheres*. You know, we just couldn't afford it. But there weren't many buses around at that time. And when you get in a bus now . . . boy, it would've been nice to have one done up like that back then."

"We got the Barth motor home in Elkhart, Indiana," says Howard. "We went from that Funcraft to a motor home, and the motor home was a thirty-foot tandem axle. I drove it for a while before we hired a driver, and we all slept in it. It had a kitchen, it was air conditioned, it was great. I think we were in the motor home for a couple years, maybe three years. And we called it the Beirut Bomber because at one point it was painted gray. There were a lot of fun stories with that. Neil used to lounge across the dashboard as I drove and look out the window and tell stories."

Rush's next uptick in terms of roving accommodation didn't take place until the *Moving Pictures* era, figures Howard. "There was a company called Rocket's Silver Train that makes buses, these Silver Eagles out of wood. And they were woodworkers. It was like a hippie commune, and they would just be building these buses. And we would see them on other tours, and we'd say, 'Oh, we've got to get one of those buses eventually.' And Rush's first bus was a Silver Eagle, and it had three state rooms built into it. The bus was great, and we traveled everywhere, and that was our biggest upgrade. And then eventually we had better buses. And then over time the band just said, 'We're sick of going on the bus; we're going to fly.' So that was a whole new ballgame."

All this came from necessity because there was no money in the beginning. "Yeah, that's right — it's usually five to seven years," figures Ungerleider. "I mean it's no less than five years.

And it's actually five years on until you're generating any cash. You're not making any money as an opening act. So the first two years, you're exposing yourself and you're taking a loss, actually. You're losing money because you're spending money on fuel, transportation, your crew, salaries, hotel rooms, and the money you're making as an opening act doesn't cover anything close to that. So Ray Danniels bankrolled it for many years and took the loss and had to wait to recoup and wait to recoup. It's an investment. I mean, managing is a rich man's sport. We didn't have the money to do that, and with a manager who believes in the band, who gets behind it and does that, whatever resources you reach out to, if you have to mortgage your house or whatever, you know down the road, it's going to pay for itself. And Rush worked so hard. I mean, it was amazing. And I was there with them — we all worked hard.

"There were some tricky times out there. We rolled into Wichita, Kansas, one day and went into a hotel where a bunch of cowboys were in the lobby. One guy says to the other, 'Hey, Riley, look what we got here! Horse shit on legs!' And we all looked around going, hmm, welcome to Kansas. We're ready to play here now. We played with Hawkwind in Kansas.

"I had guns to my head a few times, in collecting the money to try to get paid for shows that were done outside the mainstream. We played a club in Detroit for a guy named Denny McLain, who used to be a baseball player. And he had a club and Rush were so successful in his club that he padlocked the doors and wanted us to stay and do another night. And we were actually going to play with James Gang in Evansville, Indiana, and we said no. And he padlocked the doors and wouldn't let us go. It's like, no, we gotta get out of here. I had to make a phone call to New York, and he had to get on the horn with some people who I knew in New York City to get us out of there."

"We played there the Friday night," confirms Ian Grandy, "and we were supposed to play in Evansville on the Saturday night and then come back and play again at this club on the Sunday night. So after the Friday, I don't know, we went and saw him and Howard tells a story that he pulled a gun and stuff. It's not surprising. I mean the guy's a mobster. Do you know Denny McLain? Won thirty-one games for the 1968 Tigers and then he's been in trouble ever since. Anyway, we played there and went to Evansville and the gig was canceled, and we played the Sunday night. One of the weirdest things, the first night somebody slipped behind the amp line, which is about a foot away, and stole Alex's Les Paul. So we're obviously in great stress. Go to Evansville, come back to the club and his guitar's there. Apparently, the kid went home, and his father said, 'What the fuck are you doing with a Les Paul?' and brought it back, no questions asked. So we're one of the few groups who's had something stolen and got it back two days later."

Ungerleider relates another tall tour tale. "There was another place in the early days in Texas called Randy's Rodeo, and I guess they oversold. It was between two major cities. And they got a gig in this old bowling alley that was now a country and western bar. So we got there a couple days early, and when I arrived there, I saw that the stage was like a country and western stage, for a guitar player. It's a little square. Neil's drum kit wouldn't even fit on it. The place could probably hold two, three thousand people, and it had a bunch of glass windows in front and a huge bar that went the length of the whole place and a wide-open floor and this little tiny stage.

"So we had to get a local shop class, this guy named Charlie Applegate and these students, to make a stage overnight. So we put a stage in there, and I guess whoever was promoting the show decided to sell too many tickets, as always, because it was selling so well. And he oversold the show by probably over a thousand tickets. At one point in time, half the audience was in the parking lot pressing against the glass windows to where they were bending. And I saw that all the employees at the ticket window were stuffing money into their pockets. It was out of control, and I got one of those big green plastic garbage bags and got everybody to empty their pockets and put all the money in the green garbage bag.

"And I go up to the office and started counting it. And the people who were promoting it, with a bunch of guns, came up there and basically put them to my head and said, 'Give us the money!' And then the next six hours were very interesting. But the band were taken away from that whole situation while this was going on, by the local radio station guys, at the time, from KMAC/KISS, which was Joe Anthony and Lou Roney, God rest their souls. And they went to a party at their club, having a good time, while I was sitting in a room sweating it out, getting the money.

"And I finally did. I got out of there with the help of some of the people, and I got in my car and I wanted to get pulled over by the cops because I was so paranoid I was being followed with this big bag of money after I got out. I was speeding through Texas doing a hundred miles an hour plus, and do you think there was even a cop? No, so I got away and went to the hotel and then finally hooked up with the band at the party and told them what happened. It was the Wild West."

chapter 7

A Farewell to Kings

"The sun never shines in Wales, for weeks."

"**T**his album to us, signifies the end of the beginning, a milestone to mark the close of chapter one, in the annals of Rush."

Geddy, Alex and Neil put it in print right there on *All the World's a Stage* and then put it into action on *A Farewell to Kings*. To be sure, the band's fifth studio album — with titling that gives a nod to both Hemingway's *A Farewell to Arms* and (nominally) Rush's own "A Passage to Bangkok" — marked the opening of a new chapter.

Still, the band continued to operate more or less in the world they created and live in that world pretty well alone: that of progressive metal, or progressive rock where the guitarist usually has his fuzz pedal on. In this way, *A Farewell to Kings* wasn't such a big change. But beyond the general similarity shared by the new record and the ones from the past — and I'm going to be contentious here and say that we're closest to *Caress of Steel* — the new music was be leaps and bounds ahead in terms of sophistication, especially with respect to deft use of new instrumentation and sonic textures. In essence, what we got with *A Farewell to Kings* was something much more akin to *Relayer*-era Yes, old Genesis, heavy Tull and conservative King Crimson.

"We started going to England," says Geddy. "We were so obsessed with the English sound of those great bands. We went to the same studios they used; we went to Advision, where Yes recorded. So we were still trying to absorb all that progressive rock mojo. So where to get it? Get it from where they come from. It's not going to give it to you — just as an aside — but it was inspiring and that's what mattered, I guess. That we went to England, we were inspired by the environment, we were excited that we had found a sound of our own and wanted to keep pushing that sound. We wanted to keep pushing the boundaries; we wanted more influences.

"So *A Farewell to Kings* was a big experimental record for us. We started then bringing in textures of some of the bands that we liked growing up, like Strawbs and even Amazing Blondel, who were kind of interesting folk artists from England. We listened to various kinds of English music and started putting them into this progressive rock sound that we discovered on *2112* and tried to expand that more and more. And synthesizers were starting to come along, and the next album, *Hemispheres*, was bringing those tones in more and more. And we were also listening to more jazz and listening to more complex time signatures. So you've got a hunger to keep pulling more influences into your music. That's your role as a progressive musician, to do that and to keep pushing it . . . running the risk that you're going to make mistakes and that not everything is going to be likable. That just comes with the territory. But yeah, those next few records were very exciting for us. So many new sounds to absorb."

There's a subtle fusion jazz feel to parts of *A Farewell to Kings* as well, especially on "Xanadu" and even "Cinderella Man" and the title track.

"We were listening to Weather Report a little bit and sure, those things were always there," Geddy continues. "And we never drifted so far from rock, but progressive rock, per se, was kind of disappearing at that time. I can't remember what Yes were like. I think Genesis were evolving . . . Peter Gabriel had left so Genesis were becoming more of an intricate pop band. We were finding less and less to feed on, so we started diversifying what we listened to quite a lot — some jazz, some reggae, some whatever. Just keeping our ear to the ground. We're always waiting for some new music to fire us up. And when it wasn't music by other people, it was new instruments, like synthesizers, or maybe we could use acoustics more in context with the rock stuff. Like on 'Fly by Night,' we had an acoustic track, and there's always one soft track, and it was like, 'Well, maybe there's room for acoustics within the context of something heavier, something more aggressive.' So we started mixing all that up."

Though, frankly, despite the list of influences, beyond prog, there's not much outside influence to be found in *A Farewell to Kings*. There most definitely are additions to the range of sounds, however, some from new instruments, some from new recording techniques. There is also a better marriage, a better synthesis, of acoustic (or synths, or percussion) happening in amongst the typical rock instrumentation. Across *2112*, the switch is either on or off, like Led Zeppelin, but here there are switches all over the place.

"These were special days for us because we were transitioning and we could feel it," continues Geddy. "Touring Europe, the world was expanding for us and that was a very, very, exciting time. Working in these studios we've always dreamed of working in in England and to have all these people wanting to see us and play the Hammersmith Odeon, that was a really heady time for us, really a great moment in our career. And so that was a buildup to *Moving Pictures*. Confidence is so important in what you do. And when you're young, you're confident without any good reason to be, and when you're a little bit older, you need reasons, I think. And your reasons are experience and success and knowledge, things that you don't really have when you're young. But you've got cockiness on your side. So that whole English period for us was tremendous and really fascinating and educational, and it built up to coming back home to record *Moving Pictures* because that was the first album that we did in Canada in quite some time."

But we're getting ahead of ourselves. *A Farewell to Kings* was the first of three albums recorded in the U.K. This album was made at Rockfield, in Wales, and mixed at Advision — the plan at first was to use George Martin's Air Studios, but it was unavailable. Naturally Rockfield was used by Welsh power trio Budgie, but it had also been home to albums by Van der Graaf Generator's Peter Hammill, Hawkwind, Black Sabbath and Queen.

"It's the first time we had spent any real time overseas," recalls Liam Birt. "This was an old farm that had been owned by the Royce family, half of Rolls-Royce. It was an interesting cast of characters who spent way too much time out in the farmland, away from civilization. There was Otto, the engineer, a German gentlemen who only came out at night, wore the same sweater, I think, for the full three months we were there. It was fun; it almost had a boys club vibe to it. I found some Polaroids the other day of Neil out in this open courtyard. It was basically a series of buildings that were all interconnected. One was the accommodations, another wing was the guest-house, another was a big, giant echo chamber. I can't remember what the fourth structure was. And Neil is in this wide-open courtyard. I took some photos of him; he's out there with a bunch of microphones around him, he's got a hoodie on and a jacket, freezing to death. I'm sure it was the middle of summer, but that's Wales.

"They'd go in without having material written for some of these albums, and they'd spend the first month or two writing in Wales. Very depressing. I mean, I love Wales and everything, don't get me wrong, but it was just way too long for them to be away from home. And it would go on for months. They'd write for a month and then record for a couple of months. We'd probably already toured for a month or more and it was just a painful period for everybody. I wasn't there for *Hemispheres*, but I heard stories after the fact as to what was happening, how people were on the verge of cracking up over there, and I think some of the crew may actually have gone to the dark side at some point.

"But *A Farewell to Kings* was fun; it was something different," continues Birt. "They had broken out of a mold, and they were trying something new. It was different because you were in the countryside. You'd wake up every morning and cows would be staring in your window. It was just totally foreign to us. But with some of us, Neil and myself both having English heritage, British heritage, it was a lot of fun, and we wanted to enjoy it and experience it all. And it was obviously the home of a lot of the artists that had initially attracted them and got them into music. And bands that they looked up to — this is probably what they lived through. Thinking of the people that had recorded there before was all very exciting."

"It really wasn't until *Kings* that we had dedicated writing time," says Alex wistfully. "And the interesting thing is we were writing on an acoustic guitar, Geddy and I. I think all that stuff was written on an acoustic guitar — although they were rock songs — with no kind of recording situation until we could get a boombox later and kind of throw our ideas onto that."

"All those songs were recorded at Rockfield in Wales, and recording there was an experience," continues Geddy, who had tantalizingly hinted before the release of the album that Rush would be pursuing a direction somewhat akin to Yes meets Led Zeppelin. "It was the first time we had worked away from home at a residential studio. Here we are in Wales, and the sun never shines in Wales, for weeks. And we started utilizing the opportunity of being in a residential studio to do different experiments.

"The acoustic for *A Farewell to Kings* was recorded outdoors, and all of the woodblock and percussion sounds that Neil used were recorded outdoors at the same time. You can hear them echoing off the other buildings and you can hear the birds tweeting. I think we would do it early in the morning. We would experiment with all kinds of wacky things [note: this mysterious tweeting has also been cited by the band, presumably in jest, as recordings of Neil's *pet* birds]. They had a big echo room there, an acoustic room. It was a really interesting immersion course into country life in Britain, being at the farm, having this whole attitude of having people come in to cook these hearty British meals for us, and just getting to learn a different culture by working there with these wacky, interesting characters of Rockfield."

The sessions for the new album took place in July of '77, right after the band's first U.K. tour. Says Alex, "Everything else before that had been done in Toronto. We did the short tour, the first time for us in England, then came home, then went back. It was so exciting to go to the country where we really felt our musical roots were, with those progressive bands, and even further back to those bands from the '60s; it's kind of the heart of modern rock music." Three weeks were spent at Rockfield with a little over a week ensconced at Advision in West London, where

Terry was impressed to see an automated console. Brown was relieved that when they left England, the entirety of the album was recorded and mixed.

"Monmouth was quite an experience because it's basically a farm," continues Lifeson. "We were surrounded by sheep and farm smells and that sort of thing. And back in those days, we used to work the stupid hours where it would gradually get later and later and you'd get up later and later. So eventually we were getting up at five o'clock in the afternoon and having breakfast and then in the studio until seven or eight the next morning. But it was really a great experience.

"You know, even the lighting is different. They use different kinds of gas bulbs in all their lighting, so there's a different look to everything there. You feel like you're somewhere quite different. At least that was my impression back then. And of course, the architecture and the countryside . . . then we went to London to mix at Advision. And again, that was such a treat staying in London for three weeks to mix. So we were going out to the pubs, hitting all the great Indian restaurants in the area. And musically we were . . . going to a new level. We still had some of the longer songs like 'Cygnus X-1' and 'Xanadu,' but we were getting a little more melodic and a little more dynamic. There's 'Closer to the Heart' and 'Farewell to Kings,' both with the use of the acoustics. Six songs . . ." says an amused Alex, probably looking at the back cover for the first time in a long time.

"We heard things and we felt things needed to be somewhere in the tune," muses Terry. "Different colors should appear in the tune. It was pretty much a group effort."

Brown was also freed up from his usual engineering duties this time out, assisted by Rockfield engineer Pat Moran, who sadly succumbed to Pick's disease in 2011. The mix was handled by Terry with Declan O'Doherty and Ken Thomas, Advision assistant soon to be a producer in his own right, working with the likes of Sigur Rós.

"Not having to worry about the engineering did make it easier for me to concentrate on the production," says Terry, "and plus, it was a demanding record. I needed to have plenty of time to concentrate on exactly what was going on. So it was the perfect time for me not to be doing the engineering and concentrating on the production. But I didn't see it at that time as being a major changeup for me. There was a little period that I went through, because then I got back to engineering again, as well as producing. But it meant I didn't have to be in two places at once. I could be out in the courtyard making sure everything was going the way it should out there, with a pair of headphones, as opposed to being in the control room sitting at the console. So it did make a difference, no doubt about that."

The erudite, rarefied mood of *A Farewell to Kings* is set by its album art, both outside and in. On the cover, Ian Thomas Band guitarist Josh Onderisin is pictured, dressed like a petulant prince in front of a demolished building down the highway in Buffalo, New York (although the sky was shot in Toronto), evoking the similarly enigmatic cover art of Led Zeppelin's untitled fourth album. Hugh Syme had been the keyboardist in Ian's band and thought the tall and thin Onderisin would be good for the role. He applied makeup to his mouth, shoulder and knee joints to make him look like a puppet. And if he is puppeted, by whom? Perhaps ultimately it is the Solar Federation, given the reprise of *2112*'s five-pointed star, shown here with Starman on the inner sleeve. The text on the front was rendered using the font Uncial, picked for its medieval look. Moving to the back cover, the puppet narrative is further enforced through illustration, in the thematic black and red of the last record. Inside the gate, the band looks impossibly British and aristocratic as does the presentation of the credits and Peart's words of wisdom. Here, we are worlds away from the band as portrayed on the back cover of the debut album.

Once past the pricey packaging, the listener is ushered behind the velvet curtain by the title track, a spirited, hard-enough rocker rife with twists and turns, as well as the expected flourishes at the end of many if not every bar. The opening renaissance-style acoustic guitar was recorded outside and augmented with chimes and a fairy-dusting of synth. The scene is set.

In the *A Farewell to Kings* tour program, Neil wrote, "We found the seclusion and the mellow atmosphere at Rockfield very conducive to work, and we made good use of the varied facilities, including a huge acoustic room and the unique opportunity to record outdoors. The birds of Rockfield can be heard out on the Elizabethan-jazz flavored introduction to the title cut. This song is one of our favorites on the album, as it seems to encapsulate everything that we want Rush to represent."

Peart examines power from above, masters and proverbial puppet strings in a timeless fashion that matches the traditional English feel of the music and the classy graphics and pastoral photography across the project. In fact, his words read like something straight off an old scroll. Amusingly, the last four words are "closer to the heart."

"Xanadu" is next, and at eleven minutes, it is the longest song on the album, representing a shift away from the side-longs. As Iron Maiden later did with "Rime of the Ancient Mariner," Neil takes inspiration from Samuel Taylor Coleridge, in this case, the poet's unfinished and fantastical drug reverie "Kubla Khan."

"My original thought was *Citizen Kane*," explained Neil, in conversation at the time with the *Georgia Straight*'s Tom Harrison. "I really wanted to do something aligned with *Citizen Kane*, so I had this title written around that angle. Then I came across that poem and those four lines just etched like a burning image in my head. It hit me so strongly that all of a sudden the whole scope of the theme changed. It just made me freeze inside; it's so frightening. I'm not into poetry and never have been, but I just happened to see that one, 'Kubla Khan,' and I wanted to read it because of the *Citizen Kane* connection. It just grabbed me; it was so powerful."

"The birds can be heard once again on the introduction to the second piece," wrote Neil in the tour program, "which is a fantasy exercise entitled 'Xanadu.' Anyone who saw the band on the last part of our most recent American tour, or on the British tour, will perhaps remember this one as having been featured in our show during this time. On the album, it forms an eleven-minute tour de force and is certainly the most complex and multi-textured piece we have ever attempted. It also contains one of Alex's most emotive and lyrical guitar solos, as well as a very dramatic vocal from Geddy."

Much more than "Tears," in this one, synthesizers are integral, gamely part of the all-hands-on-deck spider-fingered prog rockiness of the song. And our attention is drawn to them, for strangely half the song is essentially instrumental intro or, given the action-packed movements, an instrumental proper, followed by a more conventional song. Although, the musical switchbacks, including changes in tempo and challenging rhythm, continue.

"We had keyboards because the keyboards were introduced at Rockfield," notes Terry. "So that was the first time. And I remember them being very problematic, needing to be rebuilt two or three times so we could actually use them. But yeah, there are a lot more keys and textures on that record. Different types of tunes too. It wasn't a sci-fi record. Again, I wasn't involved in the writing process, prior to going in. The first time I was exposed to those tunes was at rehearsals and then in the studio. And so for me, a lot of it was very spontaneous because I was dealing with it and building this record as we went along."

There are synths throughout "Xanadu," but what happens at the six-minute mark really represents the coming of keyboards to Rush, Geddy tearing off a short lick that passes for a fleeting Rick Wakeman–like synth solo.

Credit Max Webster's eccentric key wizard Terry Watkinson with helping Geddy along in the early stages. "I would say I was one of the pioneers on synthesizers," says Watkinson. "At that time, there were just a few different kinds. I got an Arp Odyssey and had a lot of fun with it and worked it into the music. And that was good. I developed ways of playing kind of solo guitar or interacting with a guitar. Yeah, strangely, not that many rock bands are guitar, bass, keyboards and drums." On the road, Watkinson taught Geddy a few things playing-wise and answered his questions about gear, and seeing how Max Webster used Watkinson proved to be instructive.

Back to "Xanadu," amongst the bird tweeting, Neil got to create a forest effect with his growing percussion array, the idyllic calm soon pierced by church bells and then the band crashing in. "Yes, all the percussive things added really nice colors," says Terry Brown, "and we hadn't really explored those before either. So that was really a lot of fun and not that difficult to do. It's a question of using them properly, in the right places. I think we did. The Moog pedals were great because it would add thunderous low end to tracks when we needed them. That was a really nice addition to the palette."

The band wasn't just reproducing the imagery of the outdoors, as mentioned, at times they were literally recording outdoors.

"We were doing this medieval piece, and I thought, 'Well, if it was medieval, it would be outside,'" continues Terry. "So it was a simple idea. We thought it would give us a different vibe if we were out in daylight, outside recording. It's going to sound different for a start, isn't it? That's a given. But it would just make the feel different, and it would probably add to the vibe of what we were doing. So that's why we were outside. We also did some fancy recording outside, using the courtyard as a delay line in order to record the odd guitar. We used it pretty much to its fullest. We did the wood blocks in the echo room; Rockfield had a really amazing echo room, and it was full of glass plates that you could adjust, and it was the most reverberant room I think I'd ever been in.

"We'd introduced electronic keyboards on *2112*, but when we got to Rockfield and did *A Farewell to Kings*, we added more keyboards and new keyboards, more modern keyboards, so they were staying on top of it then. And the keyboards were very simplistic then. I remember we did string lines with one note, but it was a color that was more than enough, plus I didn't want to overdo the keyboards at that stage. The band was a three-piece band, and I didn't want to get into too many keyboards and take away from the fact that it was a three-piece and should remain a three-piece. I felt pretty strongly that it should stay that way. But needless to say, we colored the sound with a lot of different keyboards, and bass pedals, which was adding some more strength to the low end. And then the keyboards developed every time they went into the studio. They were always the latest keyboards — thank Ged for staying on top of that. The keyboards were always state of the art. Whatever was current, Geddy had."

In that sentiment, the seed was sown for a future creative disagreement with Terry, as the keys really began to take a central roll in 1982's *Signals* album. "Yes, I was concerned about not overdoing the keys, already at *A Farewell to Kings*. In the same way, I don't like putting a lot of harmony vocals on. It just didn't work for me. I think Geddy sounds fantastic as a lead singer, and lots of background vocals don't work for me. Lots of keyboards don't work for me, not in the idea of Rush. I like the three-piece; that was important to me.

"The live thing was not my concern," continues Terry, addressing the usual reason a band doesn't want to pile up too many tracks in the studio. "It had nothing to do with it. As far as that went, that was their problem. If we wanted to put more keyboards on, we would figure a way of doing it live, running tapes or triggering samples. There are many, many ways of doing it. Even back then, there was a choice. It was not a question that they couldn't play it, because yes, we could play it. Even if we hired a keyboard player. I mean, that wasn't out of the realm of possibility. Somebody could be a side-man, as it were. So that wasn't a choice. The choice was it didn't work for me harmonically, and it lost the aggressiveness of the band if the keyboards became too predominate. That was my theory."

It's a good point, and very much illustrated within "Xanadu." Despite the fact that this was the most three-way integrated and progressive composition by Rush thus far, additionally textured by prominent synthesizers, it's still driven by a power trio. And beyond that, we are starting to see Neil come to the fore as the gas in the engine, the combustible component. His fills across "Xanadu" are legion. Bass is bass — Geddy can only elicit so much attention with those four strings, but quite significantly, Alex is becoming more textural, less riffy and picking more single strings. Contrast both "A Farewell to Kings" and "Xanadu" to the likes of "Working Man," "Anthem" and "The Temples of Syrinx," and you get to see why Rush is becoming an oddball, a case of a band where the drummer is the hero, not the guitarist.

But Terry's onto something there. Think about Rush's prime influences in Cream, the Jimi Hendrix Experience, The Who and Led Zeppelin, even Blue Cheer: these were all at their core power trios. And on *A Farewell to Kings*, the band is paying an even richer sort of tribute to those bands. Neil is, crudely speaking, the Keith Moon of the band. While they are universes away in terms of discipline, they match up in their level of prominence.

But Alex, already comparable to Pete Townshend, is also picking up an essence of Entwistle here. In other words, as Neil makes more pure music with his rhythms — he is the Beatles of drummers — Alex takes on more of a color, shade and texture role, joined in that spirit by a busy bassist. Essentially, no one is holding the fort, but as often as not, a rigid, written, hooky, accessible, eminently air-drummable fill is the core of the music, as is conventional bass (less all the time) and dependable stacked power chords (also less all the time). And so as Terry suggests, the magic indeed is in those three firing off each other, but at this point it's moving away from power trio music and into this new, energetic, bubbly, buoyant sound. This is the crux of why we can call *A Farewell to Kings* a new chapter — Rush previous to this had an angle, mixing prog with metal. Now they had a sound all their own.

And so I'm not sure I buy Neil's and Geddy's claim that they found their identity on *2112*. Maybe that's true from a literary and packaging standpoint, but bands sometimes let these sentiments be clouded by that first gold record, the number of tickets that got sold on the ensuing tour and the fact that they could eat for the first time.

"Xanadu" heralded the rise of double-neck guitars and basses within Rush, resulting in those iconic live shots fans love. "Well, I always thought it was cool that Jimmy Page had one," says Alex. "I was such Jimmy Page fan. I thought maybe I would like to have one and I thought that we could really utilize it. There were some songs that had twelve-string in them, so it became necessary to have one; with 'Xanadu,' the twelve-string played such an important role. And Geddy got a double-neck.

And then in probably eighty percent of the pictures I've seen of me, it's with that fucking guitar. And you use it for two songs. It's the same thing with Jimmy Page; most of the pictures you see of him are with his double-neck. It's unusual and people like it."

Geddy agrees. "The double-neck was all 'Xanadu,' the reason we started using double-necks," but then corrects himself. "Actually, it might have been 'A Passage to Bangkok' before that, because I played rhythm guitar in the middle section while Alex soloed, and I used bass pedals to supply the bottom end. So I think that's when I first got a double-neck. But 'Xanadu' is the song that we really both utilized them in, just so I could go back and play a couple of guitar bits. Because I used to play rhythm guitar in the middle section of 'Xanadu' as well." Of note, Geddy's double-neck was heralded at the time as the very first double-neck Rickenbacker, constructed in LA specifically for Rush. He is correct about playing double-neck on "A Passage to Bangkok," but it wasn't exactly "before" "Xanadu," as the first time they played the *2112* selection live was on the *A Farewell to Kings* tour. Neil bulked up onstage as well, speaking in the press of "keyboard percussion" and a "whole array of tubular bells and chimes."

Side two of the original vinyl of *A Farewell to Kings* kicks off with "Closer to the Heart," which is perhaps tied with "Tom Sawyer" and "The Spirit of Radio" in popularity in the pantheon of the band's signature pieces. Deceptively a ballad, and fondly consumed by ducat-relinquishing crowds in that sublime spirit, the song contains sneaky dollops of fast sections and progressive bits. When it was later performed live, the band added a reggae-tinged crowd participation piece and then rode it high for the close in similar manner to "The Big Money." Neil has said that lyrically the song offers solutions to the concerns raised within the title track, and indeed, the lyrics of the two songs link up seamlessly. Additionally, "Closer to the Heart," with its chimes, is quite evocative of a Christmas carol, a fitting circum-stance, in that its hit status was most intense during the yule season of '77.

Music by Lee and Lifeson, "Closer to the Heart" finds Neil sharing the lyric credit with a buddy of his from Seattle named Peter Talbot. The track, which Geddy says is "as close as we ever came to a pop song," was issued as a single backed with "Madrigal." Although it grew in stature over time, back then "Closer to the Heart" only got to #76 in the Billboard charts, although in Canada, it managed #45 and in the U.K., #36. On March 28, 2010, it was inducted into the Canadian Songwriters Hall of Fame, along with four other Rush classics. Alex is known to tout the song's energy and positivity, going so far as to call "Closer to the Heart" "the ultimate Rush song."

Notes Alex, "The interesting thing is that Ged always liked playing guitar, and he played guitar like he played bass, you know, basically with one finger. And he always knew a bunch of chords, but he always played a lot of lines. It always was a part of his musical being. When we wrote 'Closer to the Heart,' that opening line that's so iconic about that song, he wrote on an acoustic guitar himself. And because of where he came from as a bass player, he always had a really interesting way of playing the acoustic. You know, picking with this one finger and playing in a certain way that I would never think of playing. I always found it interesting. Whenever he wrote a part on the guitar, to learn the part myself, I had to play it the way he would play it, because I wouldn't play it that way.

"In fact, most of those early records, we wrote on acoustic guitar together. He didn't play bass. We wrote 'em on acous-tic guitar into a little recorder of some type, a cassette player or whatever. And then the next stage would be learning it as a band on our individual instruments. But it always started with two acoustic guitars together. So it's interesting. He would play bass lines on the four bottom strings. But every once in a while, he would play a more open melody and it would become an integral part of the song."

"Cinderella Man" contrasts acoustic and electric guitars quite dynamically in a manner consciously addressed in the Rupert Hine years with songs like "Roll the Bones" and "Presto." It's a track very much in-line with this new Rush sound, the idea of a more buoyant and almost percolating, punctuating prog metal sound. Together with this mélange, Alex sounds more distorted and carnal on the soloing than he does on the riffs, although his solo section is also obscured by wah-wah and lots of panning between channels. All told, however, given the vigorous acoustic strumming and the algebraic rhythms, there's a thespian Jethro Tull vibe to the song. "Cinderella Man" served as an encore track on the tour.

Wrote Neil, "'Cinderella Man' is a strong story written by Geddy with some help from Alex, and it concerns some of his feelings engendered by the film *Mr. Deeds Goes to Town*. This one features a very unusual (for us) middle instrumental section that might even be called (shudder) funky!"

"Madrigal" is the album's true ballad and is the only track on the record that would never be played live. Wrote Neil, "We mellow out for a moment on a light little ballad entitled 'Madrigal.' A love song nicely touched with haunting synthesizer melody, and the drums recorded in the echo room. Geddy turns in a nice vocal on this one too."

Synth is again prominent, although simple, deftly massaged in between the acoustic guitar, bass and vocal (the song, brief as it is, is half over before drums arrive, and even then, they're mixed way back and drenched in echo).

"It's so melodic," chuckles Alex. "I recall the parts and how

Geddy wrote around the melody. Again, it was a vocal melody, and it was a softer vocal that he did on it. It's a much softer ballady kind of song. The guitar parts were written to emulate strings, so there's the volume pedal stuff with lots of reverb. In fact, I recorded guitars in the echo chamber. I actually went in there with my guitar and recorded in there with an amp. That's a great example of that more melodic approach, simpler, more rooted bass playing Geddy does. But at the same time, you can hear he's going up on the neck and playing lots of melodies. It's got a little bit of Jaco Pastorius chorusing on it, flanging. Yeah, a little sweeter, more intimate."

Space tale "Cygnus X-1" closes the album with rhythmic aplomb. This one might be viewed as the evil stepchild of "Xanadu." It is virtually the same length, but it seems to fly by quicker, due to its "Necromancer"-like malevolence and aggression, as well as its thornier rhythmic and melodic sense. On tour, the song had its own themed film, as well as extra technological considerations with respect to instrumentation.

Also like "Xanadu," besides the nightmarish, effects-drenched spoken section at the beginning (performed by Terry and not Neil), the lyrics proper don't start until halfway through.

One of Ian Grandy's favorite memories of Wales was when he got to contribute an effect to this very track. "We were in the studio and we had our effects rack there, and I was their sound engineer. And so they're playing that, he's recording that. And I had an Eventide Clockworks echo machine that you could run and get an echo going back and forth from side to side; it was kind of freaky. And we added that and some harmonizer to it. And they all kind of looked at me like, wow. Even Terry Brown is telling me, 'I got one of those for the record we're going to do next, but it wouldn't do what yours was doing.' And so he asked me if he could borrow it."

Comments Neil, "A quick change of setting and atmosphere, and we find ourselves in the farthest reaches of outer space, in the middle of the black hole of 'Cygnus X-1.' This is the first part of an epic story which is to be continued and concluded on our next album. The music was almost entirely created right in the studio, and it was a very satisfying accomplishment for us all. It has to be one of the most powerful things we have done. If it doesn't give you goose bumps, you're not playing it loud enough!"

Speaking with Tom Harrison, Neil adds to the story, explaining, "There's varying theories on Cygnus X-1. My favorite one is that it's a crack in our dimension, our universe, our plane, and it leads to something different. I read a *Scientific American* article dealing with the same thing but from another point of view. It's black globules forming dust and gas and particles that are eventually going to become a star. Science fiction is just an opening to your imagination. I think that's science fiction at its best; it throws your imagination wide open. There's no limit."

Oddly, Neil says he wasn't much of a science fiction fan growing up, only getting into it after finding a bunch of stuff to read in a closet in the place he was renting pre-Rush, when he was trying to make it in London. And his lyrics here are only vaguely science fiction, more like astronomy mixed with ancient mythology. He also points out that his use of the name Rocinante is a reference to Don Quixote's horse and the truck in John Steinbeck's *Travels with Charley*.

First inspired by a *Time* article, Neil writes of a voyage into a black hole, a time warp or both. The soundtrack to this trip of all trips is disorienting, rhythmically befuddling and often atonal. Geddy's vocals also underscore the sense of claustrophobia. He's using a variety of microphones and he's singing full-throated, even maniacally at the chaotic close, where the music behind him is a form of hyper-doom, rife and rifled through with the devil's tritone.

"Cygnus X-1" ends with what amounts to a threat, at least in print, with the printed lyrics stating, "To be continued." Rush made good with that threat through the next record's "Cygnus X-1 Book II Hemispheres," although the links are tenuous, and common parlance just has the song referred to as "Hemispheres," helping to diminish any continuity.

Years later, long removed from constructing songs like "Cygnus X-1," Geddy can still see the appeal. "Sure, there's always a portion of fan base that wants to be a player, and they are more intrigued by conceptual music because it's a little more complicated and harder. It's just like when I was fourteen, the guys who played fast were who I wanted to emulate because I couldn't do that. I think for a young musician or a young kid who imagines himself being a musician, that appeal still exists, and they're not going to find that everywhere. They're going to find it in Tool; they're going to find it in Rush. And even if you're not finding it in those bands in their present-day versions, they're going to find it in their past versions.

"And the other thing is empty calories. There's a lot of empty calories on the radio, so there's going to be a need for people, always, to listen to something interesting or something challenging, if you're that kind of person. Whether you want to call it thinking man's rock, or whatever preposterous term you want to give it, there's always the past and this music that has that in abundance — young fans, when they can't find that on the radio, they'll turn to that. It's fun, it's interesting, it's hard. The same reasons we did songs forty years ago — fun, interesting, hard. Gotta be all those elements. It's a hallmark of what I call progressive music, and that doesn't just apply to rock music — that's any music. If you're someone that needs more from their music than just a catchy melody, you're going to go looking for it and you're going to find it in classical or in jazz or in progressive rock music. Those are three legitimate places to go look for that. Whether you're a listener or whether you're a player, the same thing applies."

And as "Cygnus X-1" demonstrates, prog rock "allows for the big concept, right? The big idea. Pop music generally is about a smaller idea. That might be offensive to people that write pop music. I don't mean it in that regard. I don't mean small in terms of importance. But more songs about love and heartbreak and relationships and all that stuff. And yet a lot of bands want to tackle some big idea, some flight of fancy. And for some reason our genre — if I'm still even considered part of that genre — can handle it. We can handle it. We can create a soundscape for that. Big ideas, big concepts — the music becomes a vehicle to wrestle with those ideas. And maybe that's the part that critics view as pretentious, the whole idea of the big idea. Same thing exists in films, these big films versus small, touching films. But that's why that genre exists — for those musicians to deal with that kind of idea."

A Farewell to Kings was well received in a world briefly caught up in the bluster of punk rock. But it's a myth, a rock journalist narrative as it were, that punk rock took over at this time. As loud and boorish as the Pistols, the Clash, the Damned and the Dead Boys were in 1977, prog was doing just fine, with Yes scoring a hit with *Going for the One*, with Genesis easily going gold on their way to platinum in '78 and with Tull back on their feet with *Songs from the Wood*. In the U.K., where the battle was most heated, *A Farewell to Kings* rose to #22 in the charts, while the U.S. responded almost in kind with a #33 placement.

"Criticism? I've very few to make, actually," wrote Geoff Barton of *Sounds*, concluding a very long and glowing review. "I do find 'Cygnus X-1' rather piecemeal at the moment, but I've confidence that it'll grow on me given time. The only thing that does concern me, something I've never really paid much attention to before, is the fact that Geddy Lee's voice may represent a stumbling block in Rush's bid for world domination. Let me explain. Playing *A Farewell to Kings* in the office, a number of staffers were quite impressed by Rush's new, more complex musical direction but confessed that the reason they didn't particularly like the band was because of Lee's voice — 'pixie' or 'elf-like,' they complained. Me, I've always found his shrill vocal style essential, part and parcel to the Rush scheme of things, but nonetheless it may serve the band well to take notice. Truth to tell, ol' Geddy does seem to go a little overboard on the wailing during 'Book Three' of 'Cygnus X-1.' See what you think. But this is a snail quibble, paling into insignificance against the album's overall magnificence. For, just like Rush's British tour, *A Farewell to Kings* is a triumph. A total, out-and-out, honest-to-God, five star-studded, complete, utter, unmitigated triumph. Really."

"It just seemed to be a very natural progression," reflects Terry, offering some final words on the record. "But when you are so close to something, it's hard to stand back and be super-objective. To me, it seemed to make sense. If you're going to have an audience that is going to follow you and grow with you, then the band has to grow musically. If it stays on one level, you're going to lose your original audience. You might have new audiences, but I think the longevity suffers. Rush has always been a little progressive. It may not be overly progressive, certainly not to their detriment. But I think they were progressive enough that they've managed to weave it into a very commercial sound."

The tour for *A Farewell to Kings* was particularly grueling — so much so that the band dubbed it the Drive 'til You Die Tour. Commencing in August of '77, the band executed a particularly detailed western Canadian swing, which kicked off five solid months throughout all of America. A sixth solid month, February of '78, was spent playing to twice as much of the U.K. than they had half a year previous. A mid-March tour of the southern States was next, followed by Ontario and eastern Canada in early April, again with Max Webster in tow. On March 29, the band won their first Juno Award for Group of the Year, beating out April Wine, Bachman–Turner Overdrive, the Stampeders and Trooper.

The band had a month off starting the second week of April, which was followed by Middle America dates starting in May. April was kept open for the arrival of Neil and Jackie's new baby, Selena, who came on schedule on April 22. These latter dates were essentially considered part of the *Archives* tour, *Archives* being Rush's version of Kiss's *Originals*, each a repackaging of the first three albums, a reintroduction to the band's early works. The lack of promotional support for *Caress of Steel*, as it turned out, was still rankling the band years later, with Geddy on the press trail in '78 saying that one of the prime purposes of *Archives* was to give *Caress of Steel*, a record the boys still believed in, a second life. Geddy also quipped, with a reference to his former face-painted tour mates and their *Originals* album, that fans won't be asked to join anything and that they should not expect Rush Army stickers upon the purchase of *Archives*.

The so-called *Archives* tour, May 10 to May 28 of 1978, found the tables turning. Uriah Heep, on their heels due to firing lead vocalist David Byron, were now supporting Rush — if you recall, Rush got their start in the States supporting Heep.

"I don't think there was any bad feeling or anything like that," recalls Heep guitarist Mick Box. "It was all just good vibes. I was very pleased for them. They had the success and were getting great album sales and stuff, and they *should* be headlining — you had to say, 'Okay, cool.' We'd do the same sort of thing. We broke Kiss right across America, and the next time, we were opening up for Kiss. It's not to say that the next time it couldn't be reversed; that's the way the business goes. And power to you — if you are headlining, that's wonderful. Because when we're onstage, we own that stage for that time we're on, and then it's all over. It doesn't matter who's on first or last. And that's the way our mentality is. So there's no animosity, no bad feelings, just, 'Well done and long may it last.' They obviously reached a lot of people very quickly. Some of that was through our audience. They might've converted our audience and built upon that. If anyone makes it in this business, tip your hat, because it doesn't come easy. They paid their dues."

Contrasting Kiss and Rush, Mick says, "The funny thing with Kiss was that there were a lot of explosions. It was really funny, because we had a few explosions in our show at the time, very little, just sort of like the end of the show, bang . . . a bit of confetti or something. And I remember Kiss saying, 'Do you mind if we use a few explosions? We only use them at the end.' 'Do what you want to do.' We wished we hadn't said that. Every third bar, bang bang bang! It was like a fireworks display onstage. Duck! Of course we came out, and it made our show look very bland. But that's the way it goes.

"But Rush never really needed that, did they? Some do, some don't. Kiss was very theatrical, with the clothes and everything. But I think, similar with Heep, with Rush the image was all about the music. They didn't have to dress up, put your hair up, put your makeup on, wear funny clothes — the music was the image. And that stands the test of time as well. That's why they've continued to be successful. Their music was always first. And I think that's the best way to be. Heep's the same way. Another band we broke, Foreigner . . . similar to the Rush thing. They didn't have the whiz-bangs either, just good songs, played them well, straight to the heart, playing to a rock audience — happy days. So Rush never needed an image. The music was always it.

And I think that speaks volumes for them, that their confidence was strong enough for it to happen. They didn't have to follow anything that was happening. They didn't have to do the hair spray or the eyeliner. They just let their music do it all, and that's the best way — believe me."

But not everybody was buying what Rush was selling. Alex says that at the time, shows in western Canada were somewhat rare. "Well, we played Vancouver almost every Canadian tour. But for *Farewell*, we started in Winnipeg and veered west and played all those places that we could play. Other than those couple of tours, we never went back to places like Saskatoon, Regina and the smaller Canadian cities, because there was no interest in seeing us. We were playing to nine hundred people, eleven hundred people. That's why we stopped playing Winnipeg; it was the same thing. There was never a crowd there for us. And you know, as things go on, it gets expensive to do a big show. And if you don't have the interest, it's hard to justify going there. It's hard because for the few thousand fans that are there who do really want to see you, it's a little unfair to them. But it just doesn't make sense."

When Neil was asked why Rush didn't get to western Canada much, he says, "No, I think western Canada didn't get to us very much. Oh, it's true. We go to Vancouver and we play to six thousand people, and we go across the border to Seattle, not any bigger of a city, and we play to twenty thousand! And the level of their enthusiasm too . . . it's not just numeric. No, we get a certain amount of grief from all over Canada."

As mentioned, support for the Drive 'til You Die Tour came from dependable hometown friends Max Webster, as well as AC/DC, April Wine, Blue Öyster Cult (another reversal of bills), Cheap Trick, City Boy, Hush, Lynx, Tom Petty and the Heartbreakers, Crawler, the Pat Travers Band, Head East, the Babys and UFO. Over in the U.K., support came from Tyla Gang.

"Yes, they were funny," begins Alex, cajoled into dredging up the memory of legendary pint-swillers UFO — in particular an encounter with them on September 16, 1977. "We did a show with them and I remember it was in Spokane. It's amazing that I remember these places. And I just remember looking over and they were all standing there in these robes. They'd just got these granny robes and they had the big fluffy slippers, and they were really taking the piss out of us." If you recall, Rush for a short time wore "Chinese housecoats," as Alex calls them, exhibiting between them a rare period of wardrobe synchronicity.

"If I had said take them off, they would've worn them longer," laughs Ray when asked about the housecoats, offering what might be a joke or a glimpse into the actual band-manager dynamic. "No, I would've made comments, if something looks good or whatever. But no, this is their thing. It is very much how they saw themselves and see themselves to this day. I don't think they've ever had a designer or a wardrobe person or anything, none of that. I didn't think any of that ever really mattered. Rush was a band that was a good ninety percent male audience, and nobody was coming to look like them. They were coming in their Rush shirts, so it was like this club they joined, a secret society, in the early days. If you look at the merchandising sales on Rush, it could compete with bands that had handsome guys that you wanted to be just like, and yet Rush would outsell them. It was that club. So they were cool with the people who loved them. And to other people, they were generally unaware of them. But they were not fashion trendsetters. And I think to their credit, it never got in the way of the music. I could cite acts that it did get in the way of, and they paid a price for it. Maybe there's some initial success because of it, but later on it can come back to bite you."

"Man, those dates we did with UFO . . . ugh, I don't know how we survived them," continues Alex. "Just the level of drinking! Every night with them was a riot, but it was just heavy, heavy drinking. Those guys would start drinking . . . they'd show up for sound check, but they never did a sound check. They'd show up for sound check so they could start drinking because they knew the booze was at the gig and it was free. We'd always see them before we went on. They would go back to their dressing room, change and always come up to our dressing room before we went on. And they were tanked by that time. But they were the kind of fun drunks. Pete Way especially; he was just so hilarious the whole time."

Neil claims never to have assumed the drum throne under the influence, but sick as a dog, yes. "I remember being onstage in Houston one night with a bucket beside me to throw up in between songs, just hoping I could get through the song and just at least, you know, throw up in the dark. I mean, there's no question of not doing it. There are twelve thousand people out there. It's the only job in the world that you can't call in sick on that I can think of. Really, think about it. People do, but for us, for all of us, if there's any chance at all that we can pull it off, we do it. And we very rarely cancel the show. None on the last two tours that I can think of [here, he's speaking of *Test for Echo* and *Vapor Trails*], and maybe one tour, where Geddy's voice would just be gone completely. Maybe one show a tour, we would postpone. But there's one thing about getting older. You do get more consistent health-wise, or we have."

"We opened up for them in '76 and '77 about a half dozen times," recalls Cheap Trick drummer Bun E. Carlos. "They went from a three-piece band, with like Cream-type gear. We did maybe six or eight gigs in the year with them, and every time we'd do another year with them, they'd have something different.

Neil would have some chimes up on the drum set or some other new toys. One gig, they had a couple of acoustic guitars on stands so they could just walk up and play them, while they had their electrics still on. They started to get a lot more proggy and stuff like that and people were saying, well, let's see what happens with Rush. It's all or nothing here. People are saying they're gonna fall flat on their face. That was the word I was hearing in the business from people. We were in the business by then."

As far as interaction with the guys went, Bun says, "They didn't really have much to say to us for a couple of gigs, and then one day — I think it was the Palladium in New York after a sound check, and it was our first sound check we ever got with them — one of the roadies came down with two or three joints and went, 'The guys in the band got these for you, and they said if you want to stop up and say hello . . .' And after that, they were pretty friendly and stuff. But for the first few gigs, they weren't. The first gig we did with them was here in Rockford. They didn't give us an inch of sound or an inch of stage or anything like that, because we were local heroes. But they turned out to be nice guys."

Asked what Neil Peart brought to Bun's profession, drumming, he says, "Way more than most drummers could handle. He was kind of an uber-drummer. He did the most complicated stuff. And even back then, he was a lot more basic than he turned out to be. He really got wings on his drumming style a few years after that, I think, where suddenly everything was all planned and choreographed to the note. He had more than just bass drum, two tom-toms, two floor toms and a few little percussion things. Suddenly all that got doubled; it really got complicated. He was with Ludwig for a while in the '80s while I was with Ludwig, and they said it was like trying to deal with God or something, trying to deal with him. They'd wait two hours after a gig just to say hello and some roadie would come out and go,

'Neil doesn't feel like seeing anybody tonight.' And they'd say, 'We've been here since seven o'clock.' You know, it didn't always end well because he was Neil."

As alluded to, the *A Farewell to Kings* tour was particularly grinding. "Yes, we felt like we were just dying out there on the road," recalls Geddy, hence the grim nickname for the tour. "It was incredibly difficult and very frustrating. Because at one point, I think we did seventeen or eighteen one-nighters in a row and each with a minimum of a two-hundred-mile drive after the gig. So we would just gig and drive, gig and drive, gig and drive, and we were just insane by the end of it. We would do anything to keep ourselves awake. We've all talked about certain things that change you. That tour changed us. Making *Hemispheres* changed us. *Grace Under Pressure* changed us. Those were records that were so difficult to make, and that tour was so difficult to do, that they took a piece out of you. You weren't the same person at the end of those experiences that you were at the beginning. Not all bad, but some bad, you know?"

And who dealt with it best? "Well, Pratt was always very in control," says Geddy. "He's probably the most in-control person. Because he would disappear into his books; he was always very disciplined. He knew when he had too much to drink or when he had done too much of this or that; he knew when it was time to go to bed. And he was very reliable like that. In that sense, he was a good role model because he knew his limits.

"Alex never knew his limits. And I was kind of a conservative guy, so I would never get that out of control. But it would happen. And that lifestyle lends itself to that. Because you don't know what side is up after a while. After six months of touring like that, you're just running on fumes. It's all about the gig, getting to the gig, being in shape for the gig. I would have to say because our gigs are so hard to play, and the playing was so important to us, it kept us in-line. We allowed ourselves some indulgences, but we knew the worst thing that could happen was to blow the gig; to not play well, to not be able to sing well.

"And I really had a lot of trouble on that tour staying healthy. I would get colds a lot in those days and be singing through colds. I mean, we would rarely cancel gigs. It just wasn't done. I think our saving grace has always been the fact that we really embarrass easily, and we don't want to go out there and embarrass ourselves in front of a crowd of people. Playing is so important to us that it's really kept us straight, or as straight as we need to be. I would say that was an overriding, very helpful thing, our sort of professional instincts."

"It was called Drive 'til You Die because that's all we were doing," affirms Neil, adding his impression of this particularly tough slog and comparing those days with more recent years. "We were still driving ourselves in the camper van and we would do all these one-nighters in a row across the Southwest, driving three, four hundred miles ourselves, taking shifts, and then play a headline set night after night. Oh yeah, we were in an awful state; it was soul-destroying.

"But even now, I'm constantly short of sleep, just because of the way I've done it the last couple times . . . motorcycling all the time; I want to get up early and get out there. But when your day peaks at eleven o'clock at night, the time doesn't work out. So I would be backstage in my warm-up room with an alarm clock and just, 'Okay, twenty minutes,' and sleep for twenty minutes, literally. It's a question of adaptation. If you can't deal with lack of sleep and irregular hours and diet and all that stuff, you won't survive. But right back to the earliest days, we would be going without enough sleep and too much traveling and bad food and all of that stuff."

Back on the ledger books, however, things were humming along, so much so that the band, somewhat ironically, got themselves some wheels to die for. Alex hooked up with a Jag, while Neil opted for a Mercedes, Geddy a Porsche. It wasn't necessarily an extravagant indulgence, as halfway through the tour, *A Farewell to Kings, All the World's a Stage* and *2112* each received their gold record designations in the States (many golds and platinums in Canada were a given), the band finally reaping the benefit of all that deadly driving.

Recalls Neil's dad, Glen, "We were in St. Catharines when the three boys all got their first cars. Neil got a Mercedes 450-SL, and it was a beautiful car. Then he came around to the dealership immediately and we had to go for a ride in this car. And there was no question that the three of them had got cars of their own desire. And no question, that was a highlight when he came home with that car. And then I think the next one maybe was a Ferrari, when he came around with the red Ferrari.

"Maple Leaf Gardens was a lot of fun. First of all, the fact that they were headlining Maple Leaf Gardens, but then afterwards to see all the media there. And they were clamoring to get to Neil and Alex and Geddy and wanted to talk with them. In the meantime, the three boys had decided that they were going to devote this night to their fathers; they had had enough of being in the spotlight. And up in the Hot Stove Lounge in Maple Leaf Gardens, they had banners made up with our three names on them, and they made sure that the photographers were following us around and taking pictures of us. So of course, they were having a ball, putting us on, putting all the onus on us, and we were having a good time as well.

"But the way it usually happened at most of the concerts we'd been to is that there would be this great flurry of media and the two other boys would try to handle most of it because Neil didn't want too much to do with it. But after it had all died down, and even at Maple Leaf Gardens that night, it ended up with the three boys sort of back in the corner with their families and letting all this hoopla go on by itself, and they were just spending a bit of quiet time with us."

Recalls Vic, "I went out one day and leased a Jag XJS, a 911 Porsche Targa and a 450-SL for the band. I mean, what does that tell you? That they're making too much money? They liked their little luxuries. They liked to fly first class, and they didn't at first. They flew in the back of the plane like everybody else — we all did. And later they flew the Concorde. Just before I left, they were starting to make demands. They had a right to."

"Yeah, we leased those cars," confirms Lifeson. "In '77, we couldn't afford it; I was still living in an apartment at Bayview and the 401. But the band paid for it. And I remember we were allowing ourselves one phone call a week home, on a Sunday, after midnight, for twenty minutes, and the band would pay. Otherwise it was all writing letters to each other. My wife and I still have all the letters we wrote to each other. 'Send it to the Holiday Inn in Harrisburg, Pennsylvania . . .'"

chapter 8

Hemispheres

"The big shift between supply and demand."

By the summer of 1978, Rush had achieved all the notions, emotions and tour bus motions experienced by proper rock stars, but as anyone in the business will tell you, it's a long way to the top if you want to rock 'n' roll. The band was now a headline act, in control of their own destiny — a functioning organism perceived by the world as established and establishment. The money wasn't there yet — the band was reportedly $325,000 in debt prior to making *2112* — but nobody needed to know that. To the public, Rush were those guys in the gatefold of *A Farewell to Kings*, gathering at one of their castles for a quick photo shoot before the fox hunt.

As we've learned, the reality was quite different, but no one had time to think about that. After nearly driving 'til they died on the *A Farewell to Kings* tour, it was time to make another album. Though given their success and the size of their backlist, it probably wasn't of dire necessity — this is a time when management might tell you to continue touring, selling further that catalogue of records nicely going gold and platinum. But Geddy, Alex and Neil were restless creatives, and they were eager to get back to generating new Rush material, less because they were bursting to break into song and more because the method of making the last record was inspiring. The guys wanted to relive the sense of being rock stars, to again feel like they were part of rock history, as they did working at Rockfield and at Advision.

But, loyal to their credo of moving forward in some way from record to record, the guys shifted more of the writing overseas.

"With *Hemispheres*, we did some preliminary writing in Toronto and rehearsed a few ideas when we had the opportunity," begins Alex. "We were still touring a lot, and there really wasn't a lot of free time. And we decided to write the record when we were in England. We rented a farmhouse just down the road from the studio and parked ourselves there for three weeks. And we felt we would write and move into the studio and start recording and continue the process. Looking back, it was a crazy idea because that meant that this project would've been about six months long, unending, with no time off.

"And when I say no time, I mean no time — not even a day. And that's kind of what happened. We started working for that three-week period, and that's all we did for three weeks. You start off with good intentions and slowly the clock . . . you worked an hour later this one night, and then two hours later the next night. And we basically finished late morning, like eleven o'clock or something on a Monday morning, and all the gear got loaded out and we went to the mixing studio, and we showered and basically went down to the studio and started working. So the whole thing was like that."

The time-creep the band experienced turned the sessions into an unholy rock 'n' roll night shift, with the guys sleeping during the day, having breakfast at seven at night and working until noon the following day. "We worked later and later at night and slept later and later into the day," says Geddy, "until our clocks got completely reversed and we were up all night, sleeping all day. Not good for your head. And then we started running out of time. It was taking so long to make the record. Everything was going slowly. And the newness . . . we had already recorded before in Wales, so it wasn't new anymore. The novelty of being in a residential studio in the country had worn off and we were starting to feel cabin fever."

Adds Ian, "All I know is in the rehearsals and at the studio, they worked hard; they really did. And we didn't even call it . . . we took the expression for the end of the day as 'the interval.' Because you can't say it's nighttime because it's five o'clock in the freaking morning. It's 'the interval' now, until noon. They worked hard."

It was as if the guys were chasing a high but then found out that they were at the point where the drug no longer worked. Says Terry, "*A Farewell to Kings* went really smoothly and it was a very successful record. And so in our infinite wisdom, we felt we could do the same thing for *Hemispheres*. We went back to Rockfield and sort of adopted the same time frame. We felt we were capable of that."

"But we were feeling a bit like we were on a treadmill," says Geddy. "When we wrote *Hemispheres*, it was a very intense record, a very hard record to play. It was one of those things where we sketched it out . . . we went to Wales to write it, and we really had very little written. So we moved into this farmhouse and we did nothing but write every day. We put this album together bit by bit.

"It was a fascinating process. That's the first time we were away from home writing on the clock, so to speak, because we didn't have the luxury of being in our own backyard. And this record developed as dark and complex, and the concept was quite weighty. And yet I kept having this feeling that we were just following the blueprint of *2112*, but in a much more complex way. So in a sense, it felt formulaic to me, and ultimately, even though I like the music we ended up with a lot, I didn't want to keep repeating that idea of taking a concept and having these instrumental introductions. It just felt like it was becoming repetitious from a conceptual point of view. I guess that's what it boils down to."

The writing and rehearsal sessions took place at the part of the Rockfield complex called the Old Mill House, which was about a mile and a half away from the studio. Sporting high ceilings and seven bedrooms and essentially a riverside hotel, it became a studio itself in 1989. In 2001, it was sold. Ian figures the guys were there for a week or ten days, "jamming away for eight hours a day," while he went fishing to stay out of the way.

Transitioning to the studio, amidst the long hours of back-breaking work, the guys received the odd visitor. "We had just finished supper and maybe had some wine and a communal smoke like we usually did," recalls Ian Grandy. "There was a knock on the door and Neil went over and opened the door and I just kinda thought, 'Who's this bum?' So scruffy and decrepit-looking. And he just kind of had his head down and he mumbled something to Neil. Neil went over to his stash and broke off a couple of grams of black hash and gave it to him and this guy shuffled off. And we were like, hmm, kind of a little different for Neil to do that. And it was Ozzy Osbourne."

Aside from Oz, Ian's most distinct memory from this time is of sleep. "I was sleeping from three in the morning until three in the afternoon because, first of all, Terry really didn't want you in the studio. He thought we were a distraction, though we knew a lot better than to distract anybody. I remember one time he asked me if I liked the fourteenth take or the thirty-first take after thirty-five times, and it was just a blur. I just tried to stay out of their way. There was a World Cup on. I watched every game, every minute. And I fed the horses apples. We played a lot of ping-pong, actually; all of us got pretty good at ping-pong.

"There wasn't a lot else to do. We would go into the pub and break for a couple hours to have some beer, but it was nose to the grindstone for them. As a sound engineer — I wasn't the drum roadie like I had been — I was just kind of listening. And I'll tell you, the songs were ingrained in your mind. I knew every note, every change. And by the time we were mixing it live, like in arenas, I had it down, because it was ingrained. That was the advantage of going to the studio — you knew the songs intimately. As opposed to *Permanent Waves*, where I wasn't there for the recording because I had a brand-new baby. I remember right before the first show, Geddy goes, 'You know that note in the song?' I'm going, 'Geddy, I wasn't at the studio. I wasn't at rehearsals. I had to beg Ray Danniels for a copy of the tape, and I listened to it four times, so no, don't talk to me about notes yet.' But *Hemispheres*, yes, I knew every note."

But in terms of real work, says Grandy, "You would go around with Neil at the beginning of the day, you look at his drum kit and he might ask you to change a head. Whatever, you're there. I was never a guitar roadie; they had Skip Gildersleeve, Geddy's bass tech, there for that. So basically, I swear to God, I slept twelve hours a day. Because you're away from your wife and there's literally nothing you can do. You went in there and you heard the song thirty-one times before. It was in your brain and you couldn't get it out. I can still listen to tapes and go, 'There's the setting for the harmonizer, there's the setting for . . .'

"You've got to understand, both of those — we did tours in

England and then went to the studio. So you were gone, I was gone, they were gone, I'm guessing all of May, June and July. If you're married . . . it's not good for it, that's for sure. But I guess they wanted to get away. *Caress of Steel* was recorded five kilometers from where I live."

"*Hemispheres* — and I'm sure the other guys will agree — is the one that just about killed us," explains Neil. "Again, on tour, on tour, on tour, and then we stopped. And I think we had two weeks preproduction — that was our new luxury for *Hemispheres*. So experimental and so pure. We loved it. You know, that's the bottom line in all those cases. Yes, I can look back and of course I can hear the flaws and what we could have done differently. You know, there are mistakes we made along the way of making it. That's a great title from Dave Eggers's *A Heartbreaking Work of Staggering Genius*; on the back of it there's a little explanation called, "Mistakes we knew we were making.""

With respect to the urge to push so hard, Neil figures, "Part of it was circumstantial. We had just started to achieve some success, in late '76, '77. So we had only been in demand for about a year. Your career is a matter of supply and demand. At first there is a whole lot of supply and not so much demand. And if that demand grows, suddenly they are saying, 'Look, I know you are doing five shows in a row, but can you do a matinee on this day? And you are supposed to have a day off, but can you do St. Louis on that day?'

"And then you feel arrogant saying no. What right do I have to say no to any of this? It's a dream come true. Of course. But it became so grindingly soul-destroying after a while. You're giving so much. And often I say now, it's true, after a tour is tough. Your performance doesn't suffer — you do. You pay an enormous price for that. And we had been on such a high of creative output, in the middle of touring and everything with making *A Farewell to*

Kings and going off to England. Very rich, rewarding experience for us, with a lot of experimentation and work at the time, sort of thinking, 'Yes, we can do an English tour. Yeah!' And then we'd go straight into the studio and make an album. 'Yeah, we can do that!' Again, it wasn't wrong; it was just a circumstantial. So that was the time of the big shift between supply and demand. Sometimes there was more demand than there was supply of us three guys. And so we went in there with all the same motivations that carried us through *A Farewell to Kings*, of wanting to explore. But it was all done on the fly."

Hemispheres was issued on October 29, 1978, after the guys had already hit the road again, logging a dozen dates close to home before reaching Alberta on the big day. For packaging, the band opted for something similar to its last album, a gatefold with additional printed inner sleeve. On home soil, the record was issued on red vinyl. Hugh Syme's cover art depicted the brain/heart balance of the title track theme, passion versus reason, naked creative man (marking continuity from *2112*) reaching out to a bowler-hatted man (modeled by Bob King, who had earlier posed for *2112*'s "Starman") of convention and reason. Both are standing on a big brain. Hugh had actually got permission from the family of a deceased man to photograph his brain, but ultimately he found that unsettling and went with a model of a brain.

The album was recorded at a cost of more than $100,000, the most the band had spent on a record, and fortunately, it sounds like it. "I would've been aware of it," says Ray, concerning the cost. "I would've been concerned about how long it was taking and how much money it was taking to make the record. Every record was taking longer than the previous one. It had definitely become a pattern. They had become perfectionists. My concern would've been on the financial side. I was always wanting to get it out there. It's interesting, the manager's perspective is 'Give me the record so I can get the tour happening,' and get the cycle going. Geddy has always said he's never delivered a record. He's only ever had records taken away from him. So we're opposites when it comes to that."

In any event, *Hemispheres* was the most high-fidelity album of the band's career to that point — it comes across instantly as "Cygnus X-1 Book II Hemispheres" reverse fades into full splendor.

Explains Neil on why he did this, "I was reading a book at the time, I think, called *Powers of Mind*, and one of the chapters was about the divisions of the hemispheres of the brain, and I thought it was fascinating, and another fun vehicle for the mythological expression, which intrigued me at the time. So that's what I was interested in. And I remember thinking of it while touring. I remember sitting on cases, outlining the scheme of 'Hemispheres' for them. And when we got to Rockfield, we had two weeks in the Mill House to write and then start recording. But the creative well, like any other aquifer, needs to refill, and that was really a problem for that time — there just wasn't time to fill up again. So we kept giving and giving and giving, whether in performance or writing songs, and getting ever more depleted. That was the soul-destroying part."

Powers of Mind is a 1975 book by Adam Smith. Both Ayn Rand and Friedrich Nietzsche, most notably in *Human, All Too Human* and *Birth of Tragedy*, have addressed this left brain/right brain duality using the allegory of these Greek gods.

Presented in six parts (with the titling inconsistent even across the printed pieces of the original packaging), "Hemispheres" begins with "Prelude," which is assigned four minutes and twenty-nine seconds and features two minutes of intro, followed by a second intro of almost exactly a minute. Throughout, the band throws a number of heavy metal shapes, the heaviness of the riffing underscored by the much fuller sound Alex gets here compared to *A Farewell to Kings* and *Caress of Steel* in addressing similar material. Once Geddy's vocal begins, the band is onto a new, still quite rocking bit of architecture as Neil informs us that the gods imbued man with an equal amount of love and reason, and that struggle between the two was the inevitable result.

Really, the band shot themselves in the foot calling something like this "Prelude," because not only does it have vocals and sensible parts (many of them), it starts quickly and it ends like a proper song, one final chord that fades, followed by a few seconds of silence. Next is "Apollo: Bringer of Wisdom," dark and dreamy but still full volume, repeating two of the musical themes from "Prelude" — now the idea of these tracks being self-contained and separate songs has broken down. We are in for an eighteen-minute progressive rock feast.

The story is of course a continuation of "Cygnus X-1" from *A Farewell to Kings*. When that record came out, Geddy had cautioned that sure, it was to be continued, but not necessarily on the next record. Turned out it was, but like everything on *Hemispheres*, it was concocted under pressure. Neil had it only half down when the band arrived in England, having started it three weeks previous. As mentioned, links to the original story are tenuous — there's a significant contrast between old gods here and shooting through the universe sci-fi style on the original "Cygnus X-1." Also, Cygnus X-1 is a character in this ancient tale, and on the original, it's an element of cosmic geography.

Part three, "Dionysus: Bringer of Love" uses the same musical motifs as its predecessor, with Neil presenting the same sense of lyrical geometry: the god speaks, explains its nature, and then in the second part, we see the effect of each's personality on a society. "Armageddon: The Battle of Heart and Mind" retains the theme thus far, being pretty guitar-charged and dark although still prog, rife with time signature hiccups. Here we see love and reason divided, tearing people asunder, only to be saved by Cygnus arriving upon his Rocinante, another tie-in with the original tale.

"Cygnus: Bringer of Balance" begins with the album's first dispersal of energy, for a moody almost-narrated bit. This is followed by triumphant hard rock over which Cygnus fixes things and is rewarded with godship as the newly instated God of Balance.

Finally, after seventeen minutes of dramatic and dynamic Rush rock, "The Sphere: A Kind of Dream" takes us out on a hopeful note, Geddy singing plaintively over spare, simple acoustic guitar and a bit of synth for textural effect. And yet even here, the chord changes strike a balance of somber and malevolent. It's not as happy and resolved as some of the band's other conclusions.

"It's the purest sense of fun," answers Neil when asked what makes the band want to do music this complicated. "Wouldn't it be fun to do that? Or if you learned to play something, 'Guys, check this out and see if you can do something that goes with this.' And so they were little challenges, and it must be a shared nature among us, to get excited about a challenge. Yes, we could go overboard: 'No, that's too hard. I want to be able to play that for the next three years.' But there's another factor in the occasion too. We knew by then we were going to play the songs night after night after night, so making them difficult and challenging made them satisfying. There was no tedium in the live rendition of that stuff. So that was partly a factor. But really, it was much simpler — it's just exciting. That's what all of us shared. Let's do this thing together."

"To many fans, that's their favorite Rush record and certainly in some ways it's the most prog rock of all the Rush records, but it really burnt us out," says Geddy, who has reservations about the success of "Hemispheres." "But that whole being a slave to one concept for twenty minutes became almost formulaic in a strange way. People associate it with the other thing, but it was becoming a formula for us. Now you got your overture, now you got your . . . it was redundant to do it again. And we felt at the time it was very successful in terms of writing this side-long piece of music, so it just didn't feel appropriate to do it anymore. Moving forward, it felt like, okay, let's try something else, let's try the kind of concept album where it's a 'small c' concept, where you've got threads linking all the songs, you've got a spirit that links the songs, you're not smashing someone over the head with it. Let them find it. Add some mystery to your lyrics, add some mystery to the concept, but let them find the different levels of the music, if they care to. So that was a big turning point. That's what *Moving Pictures* was, the first of the 'small c' concept records.

"But the whole concept of 'Hemispheres' on side one, you know, we really were trying to be kind of purist about it, play the whole thing, the bed tracks, as one performance, and then do our overdubs. But there are so many time changes and subtleties and so many complex things going on in that song, we just couldn't do it as one song. And we became very particular about the sound of it. The sound we were chasing, I'm not sure we knew what it was until we heard it."

"Circumstances" opens side two of the original vinyl, and the record's theme of the progressive power trio continues with this one, which hits hard instantly, Alex riffing while the rhythm section punctuates with force. Lyrically, Neil is couching the big issue of fate versus randomness (not free will) in a universal short tale of a boy alone. That boy is, in fact, Neil recounting his demoralizing pilgrimage to London in seek of his rock 'n' roll dream.

Next is "The Trees," which was issued, backed with "Circumstances," as the album's single — and wholly appropriately, I might add, for after a renaissance music intro very similar to that of "A Farewell to Kings," it roars to life and rocks accessibly, despite the band utilizing 4/4, 6/8 and 5/4 time signatures. Many say that a new era of Rush starts with "The Spirit of Radio," but I think that spirit starts right here. Like "The Spirit of Radio" and "YYZ," "The Trees" is deceptively proggy in the aggregate, yet all the parts are hummable and even easy to assimilate by music novices.

Neil has always been pretty dismissive of the lyrics, calling it "doggerel" and "a very simple statement." As he told Geoff Barton, "The song's about a forest full of maple and oak trees. The maples begin to get uptight because the oaks are growing too big and tall and are taking all the sunlight away from them. So they form a union and endeavor to get the oaks chopped back down to a reasonable size."

Peart told the *NME*'s John Hamblett that it isn't about organized labor, curiously, given that's exactly what the last verse is about. "I can assure you that wasn't the intention. Initially that song came about as a cartoon. I sat down after a gig somewhere and it came to me all of a sudden, this very vivid visual cartoon. It was the fastest song I ever wrote; I wrote it in about five minutes, actually. I suppose it's basically about the crazy way people act. This false ideal of equality they try and create. I simply believe that certain people are better at doing certain things than other people. Some people are naturally talented — they have a gift or whatever — and some people aren't. This doesn't mean that these people are greater human beings, by virtue of that talent; it merely means they are more talented."

"Hemispheres" and "The Trees," like select songs on *Fly by Night* and *2112*, resulted in Neil getting dragged into political discussions in interviews, especially in the U.K. His frustration was palpable when this happened, and it usually didn't end well.

Hemispheres closes with another composition that could have easily been added to that list of improbably accessible math rock songs from Rush, even more challenging in its likability because it's got no vocals. "La Villa Strangiato," subtitled "An Exercise in Self-Indulgence," is chock-full of classic air drumming moments as well as a wacky nod to an old jazz standard, Raymond Scott's 1937 recording "Powerhouse" — although really, the inspiration came from that music's many uses in cartoons. Says Ian, "As soon as I heard it, I went, 'That's a *Popeye* cartoon.' I think that came from Alex goofing around with his boys on a Saturday morning. And they settled with the estate for whoever wrote it. But that song, wow, at least they didn't have to sing it. But they worked hard at it. I like that song; I think it's an awesome song. And live, we could do so many things with echo and other effects."

"La Villa Strangiato" also contains what Alex considers his most notable and beloved guitar solo, an exercise in tension-building, effects and all-around tasty playing. What shouldn't be forgotten, as its nearly ten minutes develop and resolve, is "La Villa Strangiato" winds up maintaining this record's spirited hard rock joie de vivre. What has passed has been most definitely a progressive metal album in every sense of the term.

"It's really peculiar, really off-the-wall and totally unlike anything we've ever done before," remarked Alex, speaking back in 1978 with Geoff Barton. "It's a — would you believe — musical recreation of some of my nightmares!" "Yes, seriously," added Neil. "Alex has some of the most bizarre bad dreams, especially when we're away touring on the road. Sometimes, when we're all supposed to be fast asleep in our hotel rooms, he'll wake up either Geddy or me with a phone call in the middle of the night and start telling us all about these terrible dreams he's been having.

When you're barely conscious, some of the stories he comes up with can be quite mind-blowing."

Geddy says that the band had challenged themselves to try to do the song in one take. "It's like an eleven-minute song, and after trying for days and days and days, we finally had to admit defeat and we did it in three parts that were glued together. It wasn't that we couldn't play it, but we were all perfectionists, and we didn't want to go back and redo parts. Like nowadays, you do a track, you go back and you fix this part and you fix that part, and recording is so different now. As a matter of fact, a lot of bands are going back to that. There's something good about the way we used to do it. But it was all supposed to be off the floor, and you keep the rhythm track, and you keep the bass track and it becomes the thing. So it was really hard. It was really ambitious, considering our level of musicianship at that time. We were always playing up to ourselves, you know, stretching. Of course, the experience turns you into a better musician, and then going out and playing those songs live. Now if we were to play 'Strangiato,' we could do it in one take without nearly the pain. But we're more seasoned now than we were then. So yeah, looking back, it was a ridiculous thing to attempt, but that's who we were and who we wanted to be, our reach exceeded our grasp, so to speak."

"It was too long to do in one take," adds Terry, "because it wouldn't go on a piece of tape. So we had to do it in sections, and then we would get the section and find a convenient place where we could actually pause and . . . we'd stop and then we'd go back and we'd start recording again and do the next eight or ten minutes. And then we put it all together. It's a long piece and obviously they can play it, but you have to remember that we were developing a lot of the nuances and parts and details at the time we were recording. Now, in hindsight, they can go back and listen to it and it's imbedded now; they know every nuance and note. But at the time, we were developing. To develop the whole piece in one go, certainly for me, was a challenge that I wasn't really up for. I needed to make sure that we had this section right, then do this section, then put the three sections together.

"But it needed to be listened to as one piece. It wasn't three songs. It was out of convenience that I said, 'Let's just tackle this section, and then we'll find a convenient edit point, and then we'll do the second section. And then when we put it all together, it will sound exactly as if it was played all as one piece.' But it needed to be approached with detail, and the detail was a little overwhelming. So, I certainly didn't feel comfortable doing it in one piece. You don't just throw up a few microphones and run it off and say, 'Thanks guys, go home.' There's so much detail in that tune, and detail requires time. It did take a long time, but it's a stunning track and well worth all the effort. The whole experience of that album was tough on everybody, emotionally, there's no question. We were away from home for a long period of time, so it was a bit rough. But hey, we're big guys, we can handle it. We got there."

No need to name all the parts to this song, for it gets a little superfluous — one wonders if Rush was making fun of themselves and their past (and present, as in three songs earlier!) penchant for doing this. The section based on "Powerhouse" is called "Monsters!" and the authors lived just down the street from "Danforth and Pape" (the title of part seven) for thirty years, and a more nondescript intersection you will never find. Of note, Rush didn't exactly "settle" with respect to the inspiration of "Powerhouse." Any ability to sue had passed the statute of limitations, but Rush generously offered a one-time "penance" payment, and all parties went away happy. Additionally, Rush was not required to credit Scott in future issues of the song.

If the writing and recording of the songs that comprised *Hemispheres* were both scrambles, leaving Rockfield didn't mean the band's troubles were over.

"So we kept the same time frame to record and do vocals," explains Terry, meaning the process was the same as for *A Farewell to Kings.* "Well, on the last night of the month at Rockfield, we did our first vocal, and it was not good. It was okay, but it wasn't what had been expected . . . what we were used to. Ged wasn't comfortable. So we got in the car the following morning and headed to Advision for the mix session, which turned into vocal sessions. Spent two weeks doing vocals.

"And the whole record was just a semitone too high for Geddy, which made him uncomfortable. He wasn't thrilled about it. He had to work extra hard to get the vocals. And how we missed it, we don't know. It was just one of those things that came up and bit us on the last day, when we started doing vocals. Up until that point, we were totally comfortable. All the time we were laying tracks, Ged was just sort of going over vocals, thinking about how to do his vocals, and it never occurred to him and it never occurred to me, and we blindly went forward and got these fabulous tracks, and then spent these two weeks, which was mixing time, doing vocals. And it was a rough two weeks; it was rough on everybody. It turned out great in the end, but because we had to put in mixing time, we came home and then we went back and we mixed."

So the vocals were recorded at Advision, engineered by Declan O'Doherty. At Rockfield, Pat Moran was back again engineering, leaving Terry to produce, sharing official credit with the band. For the mix, they had to go to Trident Studios in Soho, London, with Terry getting the credit "with invaluable assistance" from John Brand. "It was pretty ambitious," adds Brown, "and it needed a little more time than we had allocated in order to play it the way it needed to be played. I mean, we got the tapes that we wanted to do, but we didn't have time for vocals. It's hard to see that in front, and we didn't see that coming."

There was another issue, says Terry. "I'm pretty sure this was in the middle of *Hemispheres* when we were mixing, although I may be wrong — the multi-track ate one of the masters. And we were very fortunate. This is one of those weird stories. We were in the middle of mixing. We had already done four or five days, and we were right in the middle of a tune and the machine just started making this horrible noise. I hit the stop button and turned around and the machine had just crunched the track. So I had to take it all apart, put it on the floor and sort of iron it out by hand. And when I got it back on the machine and pressed play, after we'd ascertained the machine was actually okay — it was just one of those quirks of fate — when it ran through the machine, the only undamaged tracks were the ones right in the center of the two inches of tape. And it was an acoustic guitar piece, so it ran all the way through because all the other eighteen or twenty-two tracks were off. Never heard a sound and you'd never know. We managed to finish the tune. We never re-recorded. I can't imagine re-recording a Rush album. I mean, they are so intense and so complex that to re-record it, I think we'd probably just throw it all in the can and start on something else."

Adds Geddy, on his memories of the final days making *Hemispheres*, "By the time we got to Advision, we hadn't recorded any vocals yet. So the whole time that was supposed to be mixing time, I was doing vocals. We had written the album and we hadn't even considered . . . like I kind of sketched out how the vocals would go, but I hadn't sung them out at any rehearsal or anything because we were writing it as we went. But by the time it was all recorded, it was a difficult key for me to sing in. It was really high. I was like, 'Holy shit, what the hell did I do to myself?' So the vocal sessions were very tense. We were now months away from home, and I don't think the sun shone more than two days the whole time we were in Wales.

"Very frustrating, and the vocal sessions were tough, really tough. It was just a ballbuster to record. And I remember having huge blowouts doing the vocals with Terry, just because I was so frustrated, just having to get out of the studio and go for a walk on the streets and cool out. Everything to do with that album was like pulling teeth. It was turning into the never-ending album, a real test of your patience and determination. When we finally got all the vocals down and then started mixing it at Advision, we couldn't get the mix; everything sounded wrong. And that's when we moved studios again to Trident Studios, where it all came together; it was just the right room for it. But every stage of that record, there were unforeseen problems, also worsened by the fact that we were months away from home in England. Our families were becoming just a rumor."

"I think we all felt like we were at the end of that whole idea of doing an album, or a least a whole side of an album, based on a single concept," adds Alex, "as diverse as those bits and pieces were . . . You know, rock opera or whatever you want to call it. But really, the most difficult part came with mixing. We got into Advision in London, where we mixed the previous record, and we really enjoyed working there, and I think we got good results with *A Farewell to Kings*. But it was just not happening. Terry wasn't happy; it wasn't sounding right. We're struggling, and we had recording left do there because we basically ran out of time. And then finally, after a few very frustrating weeks there, Terry said, 'That's it, that's it, I can't do it anymore. I have to take a break, I've got to get out of here, and we have to think about going somewhere else.'

"And we came home for a week, and we'd already spent months there, away from home, working all the time, and we took no days off. So we took that week off, came home, sort of got recharged. I can't say that we really felt recharged because it was weighing heavily on us. Then we went back to London and we moved studios to Trident and everything started coming together. We really felt much better, and we could get a sense of where we were going. But it was really the record that made us think about changing direction, looking for another place to go. And that's exactly what happened."

"Mixing was a nightmare on that," says Neil, seconding Alex's view that mixing at Advision in such a short amount of time just wasn't happening. "The studio we had excellent success with on the previous record was not working, and it was so mysterious — why? The studio was wonderful for mixing last time. Why isn't this working? So we went off to another studio and started again. We had been away from home for months-on-end touring, so it's taking a huge toll on us internally — relationships, friendships — but it didn't cause friction among us, because we still had this common drive. But oh, it hurts. It put the hurt on us."

For all of these reasons combined, encapsulated in the famous comment that "*Hemispheres* was the album that broke the camel's back," the band had it in their minds that things were going to change next time they made an album, if they could ever see mustering the energy to make another.

"It was becoming a stereotype and we weren't comfortable with that," says Geddy, looking back on *Hemispheres*. "We all agreed about that. It wasn't one of us saying I don't want to do that. And it's not that we had anything against the ten-minute songs, but in a way, it seemed easy to do. Easier to do than writing a concise, or relatively concise, five- or six-minute song that still had that kind of interest."

"We said that we're not making this kind of record again," seconds Neil. "We knew that was the end of that era of the epics. And fine. You know, we had to learn so much by doing that, that when we started learning to compress, we had all of that sense of arrangement skills and instrumental skills among the three of us that had been growing and growing by playing, and by playing together every night and exploring when we were experimenting. There was all that we were learning about each other's playing and how to interlock together. All those things were being absorbed into us as a band as well as individual musicians. So that was another remarkable era of growth and change. But it still surprises me now that we knew that much in '78. 'Okay, we're done with this and we're moving on.' Music was changing so much then as well, which was wonderful in the late '70s because we were young enough to adapt to it.

"Like *Power Windows* and *Hold Your Fire*, *Farewell* and *Hemispheres* are very much of a period. They represent a period to themselves. It was *A Farewell to Kings* where we started with a lot of the textural experimentation and we took it to its apogee with *Hemispheres*. Then we decided tacitly — or no, vocally — that we wouldn't do that anymore. That *Hemispheres* was the end, that we didn't want to do side-long pieces, the overblown arranging, anymore. We agreed at the time, even then, that we were done with that and we of course moved on come *Permanent Waves*; more in an evolutionary way, but it was more than that."

The tour itinerary was once again exhaustive, Rush setting out in October of 1978 on a nine-month trek (deemed dauntingly enough Tour of the Hemispheres) that saw the band play extensively in central Canada and fairly thoroughly in western Canada as well as every crease and corner of America. In March, the band received the Juno Award for Group of the Year (for the second year in a row), and two months earlier, they were named Canada's official Ambassadors of Music.

The band had become an undisputed headline act by this point. "Obviously we were very happy that we were in that position," muses Liam, keeper of sanity on the road, "where we weren't constantly under someone else's thumb and we could actually put forward the show that we thought represented us. It gave us the ability, instead of having a forty-five-minute set, to play for an hour and a half, to actually be in control of a show. And hopefully for their audience to be able to appreciate the length of the set, which has always been a challenge with this band. Hence the reason for the past few years where they've opted to go without an opening act. That gave them a longer time frame to whittle down the multitude of songs that they have to choose from, which is probably one of the toughest things prior to every tour, actually coming up with a set list.

"We were probably in four or five semis at that juncture," continues Liam, "and we had a fairly substantial lighting system. Plus the PA system kept growing. There was never much onstage. They were never a prop band as such. That came up much later in life, and it was always with a good sense of humor. But the band ventured into purchasing their own buses, and at one point, they owned three buses. Turned out to be a mistake because unless you want to be in the bus business, you really shouldn't buy your own buses. But it was an interesting experiment that worked for a while.

"But yeah, the production grew. They realized that they weren't obviously very active onstage. It's hard when, especially if you're Geddy, you're singing, playing bass guitar and synthesizers and Neil, you're trapped behind a drum kit. Plus Alex is augmenting on synthesizers and playing guitar and singing. And they had been to see a Supertramp show. I believe it was in Milwaukee, and it was the first show that I can recall where we had seen someone using film as an atmospheric and a way of creating space and a sense of movement onstage. And they were so impressed with it, they decided to try incorporating film into the backdrop for them, to give the audience something more to look at, to tie in to the music. It worked out extremely well over the years, and it became a large, key part of the show since that point."

Charting the evolution of the band's transport over the years, Liam explains that "in the early days we were just using an Econoline van, a Ford product that was completely packed to the gills with everything: our small PA system, small lighting system and all the band's gear. The band themselves would travel with their own vehicles or occasionally have a friend drive them. A few years down the road from there, once we started touring in the U.S. with Neil, we moved into what I believe was a twenty-foot truck with a tailgate and a sleeper cab. There were three or four of us on the crew at that point, so we'd take turns sleeping in the sleeper. Somebody would sleep on the floor, and out of the two remaining people, one person would drive and the other would try to nod off as little as possible. At that point, the band had the Funcraft as it was known — that was actually its official name.

"A couple of years after that, they moved into the Barth, which was a full-blown RV unit, similar to a bus but not quite. The crew at that point were given the Funcraft as a secondary vehicle to move around in, along with the truck. And then a couple of years beyond that, we moved into buses and used semis with professional drivers because we were putting in very long hours and having to drive between cities on top of that. It was pretty dangerous, and I'm surprised we actually got away with it for so many years. In the end, the last tour, we were at seven semis and five buses, including Neil's bus. And that seemed to be a good level for us. We could put on a very nice production without spending excessively, and fans seemed to be quite happy with it."

In late April of 1979, Rush did their largest European tour yet, split roughly between the U.K. and the mainland. The European tour was accompanied by the unauthorized release of a Dutch-pressed single LP compilation called *Rush through Time*. This coincided with a rare festival date for Rush, where on June 4, 1979, they played Holland's Pinkpop Festival, alongside The Police, Elvis Costello, Peter Tosh and Dire Straits. This followed three canceled dates because Alex had broken his finger, but in an extreme case of "the show must go on," he did the festival gig without compromise to his performance.

Recalls Vic Wilson, "We had to cancel a date in Paris because Alex smashed his fingers on the headboard. They drove the Mercedes Benz and wedged it under the sign on the autobahn. Did they tell you that? Wedged 'er under there. Threw the keys to Howard and said, 'Get me another car.' They were driving instead of going on a bus at that time. To me, that's dangerous, when you don't have control of each one of them."

Across the entirety of the *Hemispheres* tour, acts called upon in various cities to warm up Rush's crowd included Ambrosia, April Wine, Blackfoot, Blondie, the Boyzz, Cheap Trick, Falcon Eddy, Golden Earring, Good Rats, Granmax, Head East, Kickin', Madcats, Max Webster (for the European jaunt), Molly Hatchet, the Pat Travers Band, Sad Café, Starz, Stillwater, Toto, UFO, Wild Horses and Wireless, who were part of the Anthem Records stable.

Every track from the album was presented live, although "Circumstances" got dropped late in the tour. "Hemispheres" lived on in mercifully shortened form. "The Trees" had the longest shelf life, with "La Villa Strangiato" continuing well, given its pliability for freedoms, abbreviation and segue-ability.

On tour, Alex hit the books. "The first thing that I applied myself to was getting my pilot's license, in 1979. I took my training at Buttonville Airport, but we were on tour so much. So I took all my books with me and did all my studying, and when I came home for those few days off, I'd go to the airport and get a couple of hours in. It took me a year to get my license that way. But it was the first time I really applied myself to something outside of the band that required a lot of work. And I was really proud of the fact."

Alex explains why the band had always played only scattered European shows around numerous, regular shows for the U.K. and Germany. "Well, we went back and did a couple of shows in Sweden. We played Stockholm and Gothenburg a few tours later. But yes, Britain was always the main thing, and in Germany there were so many American and Canadian troops stationed there — even British troops — that you could play a place like Frankfurt and do good business, and have a good crowd of ten thousand, eleven thousand people.

"That's not so much the case now. Even the last time we were there in '92, I think, those military bases, a lot of them are closed down, so you're playing more to a German audience, which is really what you want, but there's not that many of them. So it was because there was such a broader audience in those places. And we played Paris as well, later. We tried to play there a few times before, but something always came up. We've usually done a gig in Rotterdam but that's like playing in England. Everybody speaks perfect English in Holland. They're sort of in between, I guess, the Germans and the Brits. But I think we were just much more popular in Britain than we were anywhere else on the continent."

Rush left their formative decade — the action-packed and at times manic and desperate 1970s — burnt-out and yet hopeful.

The famous narrative is that *Hemispheres* was the record that nearly drove the guys out of their minds. But as they stared down the '80s, the band's enthusiasm for modern music, their love of learning and their energy toward staying engaged would hold them in good stead. The '80s would begin with a bang, just after New Year's, in fact, with a joyous and compact hit single opening wide an album, *Permanent Waves*, that otherwise was more of an evolution than a revolution. On its own, "The Spirit of Radio" would prove to be a landmark, but as a microcosm of the band's evolution, it might have been more important in terms of lighting the way toward "Red Barchetta," "YYZ," "Limelight" and "Tom Sawyer." Because of that packed side of radio wonders, Rush left the '70s as a struggling yet headlining act to become what is unarguably an institution of well-regarded, everlasting, establishment rock royalty.

Discography

elow is a U.S. discography featuring Rush's 1970s releases; it lists U.S. chart placements, U.S. certifications and when we get to singles, official U.S. singles only (save for the all-important independent debut). I've provided the greatest level of detail for the studio albums and less for live albums and compilations. Side 1 and Side 2 designations are provided for everything here, given that all of these albums were issued in the age of vinyl.

A: Studio Albums

Rush
(Mercury SRM-1-1011, July 1, 1974)
PEAK U.S. CHART POSITION: #105
U.S. RIAA CERTIFICATION: Gold

PRODUCED BY: Rush

SIDE 1:   1. Finding My Way 5:03; 2. Need Some Love 2:16; 3. Take a Friend 4:27; 4. Here Again 7:30

SIDE 2:   1. What You're Doing 4:19; 2. In the Mood 3:36; 3. Before and After 5:33; 4. Working Man 7:07

NOTES: Original lineup: Geddy Lee, Alex Lifeson, John Rutsey. Issued in Canada first, as an indie, March 1, 1974: Moon Records (MN-100). The original Moon issue features a red logo on the cover, which was changed to pink for the U.S. issue and subsequent Canadian issues. The U.S. issue includes additional thanks to Donna Halper of WMMS. The original eight-track issue also uses the red logo.

Fly by Night

(Mercury SRM-1-1023, February 15, 1975)

PEAK U.S. CHART POSITION: #113

U.S. RIAA CERTIFICATION: Gold

PRODUCED BY: Rush and Terry Brown

SIDE 1:   1. Anthem 4:10; 2. Best I Can 3:24; 3. Beneath, Between & Behind 3:00; 4. By-Tor & the Snow Dog — I. At the Tobes of Hades, II. Across the Styx, III. Of the Battle, IV. Epilogue 8:57

SIDE 2:   1. Fly by Night 3:20; 2. Making Memories 2:56; 3. Rivendell 5:00; 4. In the End 6:51

NOTES: Drummer John Rutsey is replaced by Neil Peart.

Caress of Steel

(Mercury SRM-1-1046, September 24, 1975)

PEAK U.S. CHART POSITION: #148

U.S. RIAA CERTIFICATION: Gold

PRODUCED BY: Rush and Terry Brown

SIDE 1: 1. Bastille Day 4:36; 2. I Think I'm Going Bald 3:35; 3. Lakeside Park 4:07; 4. The Necromancer — I. Into Darkness 4:20; II. Under the Shadow 4:25; III. Return of the Prince 3:51

SIDE 2: 1. The Fountain of Lamneth — I. In the Valley 4:17; II. Didacts and Narpets 1:00; III. No One at the Bridge 4:15; IV. Panacea 3:12; V. Bacchus Plateau 3:12; VI. The Fountain 3:48

NOTES: U.S. cassette issue features different track sequence.

2112

(Mercury SRM-1-1079, April 1, 1976)

PEAK U.S. CHART POSITION: #61

U.S. RIAA CERTIFICATION: 3 x Platinum

PRODUCED BY: Rush and Terry Brown

SIDE 1: 1. 2112 — I. Overture 4:32; II. The Temples of Syrinx 2:13; III. Discovery 3:30; IV. Presentation 3:40; V. Oracle: The Dream 2:00; VI. Soliloquy 2:23; VII. Grand Finale 2:18 Total: 20:36

SIDE 2: 1. A Passage to Bangkok 3:30; 2. The Twilight Zone 3:14; 3. Lessons 3:48; 4. Tears 3:29; 5. Something for Nothing 3:56

NOTES: Reissued December 16, 2016, as deluxe fortieth anniversary edition.

A Farewell to Kings

(Mercury SRM-1-1184, September 1, 1977)

PEAK U.S. CHART POSITION: #33

U.S. RIAA CERTIFICATION: Platinum

PRODUCED BY: Rush and Terry Brown

SIDE 1: 1. A Farewell to Kings 5:49; 2. Xanadu 11:05

SIDE 2: 1. Closer to the Heart 2:52; 2. Cinderella Man 4:19; 3. Madrigal 2:33; 4. Cygnus X-1 Book 1 The Voyage 10:21

NOTES: Only Rush album issued on vinyl in Russia; with a different cover. Reissued December 1, 2017, as deluxe fortieth anniversary edition.

Hemispheres
(Mercury SRM-1-3743, October 29, 1978)
PEAK U.S. CHART POSITION: #47
U.S. RIAA CERTIFICATION: Platinum
PRODUCED BY: Rush and Terry Brown
SIDE 1: 1. Cygnus X-1 Book II Hemispheres — I. Prelude 4:30; II. Apollo Bringer of Wisdom 2:30; III. Dionysus Bringer of Love 4:36; IV. Armageddon the Battle of Heart and Mind 2:52; V. Cygnus Bringer of Balance 5:00; VI. The Sphere a Kind of Dream 1:09

SIDE 2: 1. Circumstances 3:41; 2. The Trees 4:46; 3. La Villa Strangiato — I. Buenos Nochas, Mein Froinds!; II. To Sleep, Perchance to Dream . . . ; III. Strangiato Theme; IV. A Lerxst in Wonderland; V. Monsters!; VI. The Ghost of the Aragon; VII. Danforth and Pape; VIII. The Waltz of the Shreves; IX. Never Turn Your Back on a Monster!; X. Monsters! (Reprise); XI. Strangiato Theme (Reprise); XII. A Farewell to Things 9:35

NOTES: Reissued November 16, 2018, as deluxe fortieth anniversary edition.

B: Live Albums

All the World's a Stage
(Mercury SRM-2-7508, September 29, 1976)
PEAK U.S. CHART POSITION: #40
U.S. RIAA CERTIFICATION: Platinum
SIDE 1: 1. Bastille Day 4:48; 2. Anthem 4:48; 3. Fly by Night;
    In the Mood 4:50; 4. Something for Nothing 3:50
SIDE 2: 1. Lakeside Park 4:45; 2. *2112* 15.45
SIDE 3: 1. By-Tor & the Snow Dog 11:24; 2. In the End 7:50
SIDE 4: 1. Working Man; Finding My Way 13:45; 2. What You're
    Doing 5:44
NOTES: "What You're Doing" was omitted from the CD reissue.

C: Offical Compilation

Archives
(Mercury SRM-3-9200, April, 1978)
PEAK U.S. CHART POSITION: #121
U.S. RIAA CERTIFICATION: Platinum
NOTES: *Archives* is a straightforward repackaging of the first three
    Rush albums. The U.S. issue featured a gray cover; the
    Canadian issues had gray and black covers. The foremost
    non-U.S. compilation is called *Rush through Time*, an
    eleven-track package covering the debut through *Moving
    Pictures*, issued in the Netherlands.

D: Selected Singles

When it comes to singles, this is perhaps where it most bears reminding that this is a U.S. discography. Having said that, we're starting with a Canadian issue. Because, frankly, the singles story for Rush is pretty dull, given the complete lack of non-LP (studio) tracks from the lads. So yeah, the debut single — two non-LP tracks, but Canadian — is a major discography item, and then after that, it gets pretty workmanlike. A further note, I've included all commercial U.S. releases but only select promos, as some of the promos are slight variations upon each other, or slight variations on the official release (beginning with same catalogue number). PS denotes picture sleeve.

7" Vinyl Singles
Not Fade Away / You Can't Fight It (Moon, MN-001)
Finding My Way / Finding My Way (DJ-407) promo
Finding My Way (edit) / Need Some Love (73623)
In the Mood / In the Mood (DJ-417) promo
In the Mood / What You're Doing (73647)
Fly by Night / Anthem (73681)
Lakeside Park / Bastille Day (73737)
The Twilight Zone / Lessons (73803)
Fly by Night — In the Mood (live) / Something for Nothing (live) (73873)
The Temples of Syrinx / Making Memories (73912)
Closer to the Heart / Madrigal (73958)
Fly by Night / Fly by Night (DJ 553) promo; promoting the *Archives* album
Fly by Night / Anthem (73990); promoting the *Archives* album
The Trees / The Trees (74051) promo
The Trees / Circumstances (74051)

12" Vinyl Singles, EPs, LPs (all promo)
Mercury In-Store Play Special (MK-8) PS
Everything Your Listeners Ever Wanted to Hear by Rush . . . But You Were Afraid to Play (MK-32) PS
The Trees / Prelude, Circumstances (MK-75) PS

Credits

INTERVIEWS WITH THE AUTHOR

Pete Agnew, Terry Brown, Bun E. Carlos, Dennis DeYoung, Pye Dubois, Tony Geranios, Scott Gorham, Ian Grandy, Paul Kersey, Geddy Lee, Alex Lifeson, Gary McCracken, Kim Mitchell, Neil Peart, Mark Reale, Mike Tilka, Howard Ungerleider

INTERVIEWS WITH SAM DUNN AND SCOT MCFADYEN

Liam Birt, Terry Brown, Mick Box, Cliff Burnstein, Ray Danniels, Donna Halper, Geddy Lee, Alex Lifeson, Kim Mitchell, Betty Peart, Glen Peart, Neil Peart, Gene Simmons, Howard Ungerleider, Mary Weinrib, Vic Wilson, Milla Živojinović

Barton, Geoff. "*A Farewell to Kings* Record Review." *Sounds*, September 1977.

Barton, Geoff. "This Man Has Nightmares." *Sounds*, September 30, 1978.

Hamblett, John. "Rock Against Right-Wing Rock Being Called Fascist." *New Musical Express*, May 5, 1979.

Harrison, Tom. "Canada's Most Successful (and Least Recognized) Rock Band." *The Georgia Straight*, September 8–15, 1977.

Johnson, Rick. "Rush: Pebbles & Bam-Bam in Alphaville." *Creem*, March 1976.

Nooger, Dan. "Rush Goes into Future Shock: 'Music Will Not Exist in *2112*.'" *Circus*, April 27, 1976.

Peart, Neil. "Rush: World Tour 77–78 Exclusive Concert Edition: A Condensed Rush Primer." Tour program, 1977.

Rush. "Live at Massey Hall: June 11–13, 1976 — Rush 2112. The Story of '2112.'" Tour flyer, June 1976.

Smith, Robin. "Power Pop?" *Record Mirror*, March 4, 1978.

About the Author

At approximately 7,900 (with over 7,000 appearing in his books), Martin Popoff has unofficially written more record reviews than anybody in the history of music, writing across all genres. Additionally, Martin has penned eighty-five books on hard rock, heavy metal, classic rock and record-collecting. He was editor in chief of the now retired *Brave Words & Bloody Knuckles*, Canada's foremost metal publication, for fourteen years and has also contributed to *Revolver, Guitar World, Goldmine, Record Collector*, bravewords.com, lollipop.com and hardradio.com, with many record label band bios and liner notes to his credit as well. Additionally, Martin has been a regular contractor to Banger Films and worked for two years as researcher on the award-winning documentary *Rush: Beyond the Lighted Stage*, on the writing and research team for the eleven-episode *Metal Evolution* and on the ten-episode *Rock Icons*, both for VH1 Classic. Additionally, Martin is the writer of the original metal genre chart used in

Metal: A Headbanger's Journey and throughout the *Metal Evolution* episodes. Martin currently resides in Toronto and can be reached through martinp@inforamp.net or martinpopoff.com.

Martin Popoff – A Complete Bibliography

Driven: Rush in the '90s and "In the End" (2021)

The Fortune: On the Rocks with Angel (2020)

Van Halen: A Visual Biography (2020)

Limelight: Rush in the '80s (2020)

Thin Lizzy: A Visual Biography (2020)

Empire of the Clouds: Iron Maiden in the 2000s (2020)

Blue Öyster Cult: A Visual Biography (2020)

Anthem: Rush in the '70s (2020)

Denim and Leather: Saxon's First Ten Years (2020)

Black Funeral: Into the Coven with Mercyful Fate (2020)

Satisfaction: 10 Albums That Changed My Life (2019)

Holy Smoke: Iron Maiden in the '90s (2019)

Sensitive to Light: The Rainbow Story (2019)

Where Eagles Dare: Iron Maiden in the '80s (2019)

Aces High: The Top 250 Heavy Metal Songs of the '80s (2019)

Lettin' Go: UFO in the Eighties and Nineties (2019)

Judas Priest: Turbo 'til Now (2019)

Born Again! Black Sabbath in the Eighties and Nineties (2019)

Riff Raff: The Top 250 Heavy Metal Songs of the '70s (2018)

Unchained: A Van Halen User Manual (2018)

Queen: Album by Album (2018)

Iron Maiden: Album by Album (2018)

Welcome to My Nightmare: 50 Years of Alice Cooper (2018)

Sabotage! Black Sabbath in the Seventies (2018)

Judas Priest: Decade of Domination (2018)

Popoff Archive — 6: American Power Metal (2018)

Popoff Archive — 5: European Power Metal (2018)

The Sun Goes Down: Thin Lizzy 1977–83 (2018)

The Clash: All the Albums, All the Songs (2018)

Led Zeppelin: All the Albums, All the Songs (2017)

AC/DC: Album by Album (2017)

Lights Out: Surviving the '70s with UFO (2017)

Tornado of Souls: Thrash's Titanic Clash (2017)

Caught in a Mosh: The Golden Era of Thrash (2017)

Rush: Album by Album (2017)

Beer Drinkers and Hell Raisers: The Rise of Motörhead (2017)

Metal Collector: Gathered Tales from Headbangers (2017)

Hit the Lights: The Birth of Thrash (2017)

Popoff Archive — 4: Classic Rock (2017)

Popoff Archive — 3: Hair Metal (2017)

From Dublin to Jailbreak: Thin Lizzy 1969–76 (2016)

Popoff Archive — 2: Progressive Rock (2016)

Popoff Archive — 1: Doom Metal (2016)

Rock the Nation: Montrose, Gamma and Ronnie Redefined (2016)

Punk Tees: The Punk Revolution in 125 T-Shirts (2016)

Metal Heart: Aiming High with Accept (2016)

Ramones at 40 (2016)

Time and a Word: The Yes Story (2016)

Kickstart My Heart: A Mötley Crüe Day-by-Day (2015)

This Means War: The Sunset Years of the NWOBHM (2015)

Wheels of Steel: The Explosive Early Years of the NWOBHM (2015)

Swords and Tequila: Riot's Classic First Decade (2015)

Who Invented Heavy Metal? (2015)

Sail Away: Whitesnake's Fantastic Voyage (2015)

Live Magnetic Air: The Unlikely Saga of the Superlative Max Webster (2014)

Steal Away the Night: An Ozzy Osbourne Day-by-Day (2014)

The Big Book of Hair Metal (2014)

Sweating Bullets: The Deth and Rebirth of Megadeth (2014)

Smokin' Valves: A Headbanger's Guide to 900 NWOBHM Records (2014)

The Art of Metal (co-edit with Malcolm Dome; 2013)

2 Minutes to Midnight: An Iron Maiden Day-by-Day (2013)

Metallica: The Complete Illustrated History (2013); update and reissue (2016)

Rush: The Illustrated History (2013); update and reissue (2016)

Ye Olde Metal: 1979 (2013)

Scorpions: Top of the Bill (2013); updated and reissued as *Wind of Change: The Scorpions Story* (2016)

Epic Ted Nugent (2012); updated and reissued as *Motor City Madhouse: Going Gonzo with Ted Nugent* (2017)

Fade to Black: Hard Rock Cover Art of the Vinyl Age (2012)

It's Getting Dangerous: Thin Lizzy 81–12 (2012)

We Will Be Strong: Thin Lizzy 76–81 (2012)

Fighting My Way Back: Thin Lizzy 69-76 (2011)

The Deep Purple Royal Family: Chain of Events '80–'11 (2011); reissued as *The Deep Purple Family Year by Year Volume Two (1980–2011)* (2018)

The Deep Purple Royal Family: Chain of Events Through '79 (2011); reissued as *The Deep Purple Family Year by Year (to 1979)* (2016)

Black Sabbath FAQ (2011)

The Collector's Guide to Heavy Metal: Volume 4: The '00s (2011; co-authored with David Perri)

Goldmine Standard Catalog of American Records 1948–1991, 7th Edition (2010)

Goldmine Record Album Price Guide, 6th Edition (2009)

Goldmine 45 RPM Price Guide, 7th Edition (2009)

A Castle Full of Rascals: Deep Purple '83–'09 (2009)
Worlds Away: Voivod and the Art of Michel Langevin (2009)
Ye Olde Metal: 1978 (2009)
Gettin' Tighter: Deep Purple '68–'76 (2008)
All Access: The Art of the Backstage Pass (2008)
Ye Olde Metal: 1977 (2008)
Ye Olde Metal: 1976 (2008)
Judas Priest: Heavy Metal Painkillers (2007)
Ye Olde Metal: 1973 to 1975 (2007)
The Collector's Guide to Heavy Metal: Volume 3: The Nineties (2007)
Ye Olde Metal: 1968 to 1972 (2007)
Run for Cover: The Art of Derek Riggs (2006)
Black Sabbath: Doom Let Loose (2006)
Dio: Light Beyond the Black (2006)
The Collector's Guide to Heavy Metal: Volume 2: The Eighties (2005)
Rainbow: English Castle Magic (2005)
UFO: Shoot Out the Lights (2005)
The New Wave of British Heavy Metal Singles (2005)
Blue Öyster Cult: Secrets Revealed! (2004); update and reissue (2009);
      updated and reissued as *Agents of Fortune: The Blue Öyster Cult Story*
      (2016)
Contents Under Pressure: 30 Years of Rush at Home & Away (2004)
The Top 500 Heavy Metal Albums of All Time (2004)
The Collector's Guide to Heavy Metal: Volume 1: The Seventies (2003)
The Top 500 Heavy Metal Songs of All Time (2003)
Southern Rock Review (2001)
Heavy Metal: 20th Century Rock and Roll (2000)
The Goldmine Price Guide to Heavy Metal Records (2000)
The Collector's Guide to Heavy Metal (1997)
Riff Kills Man! 25 Years of Recorded Hard Rock & Heavy Metal (1993)

See martinpopoff.com for complete details
and ordering information.